THE UNITED STATES BOOK

Written by Rebecca Siegel
Illustrated by Ellen Weinstein

EL PUNTO BAKERY

LITTLE EGYPT Deli

THAKALI KITCHEN NEPALESE CUISINE TIBETAN

東方 EASTERN CHINESE FOOD TO TAKE OUT

W
WELBECK
EDITIONS

For the librarians - R.S.

*To the Native American/Indigenous
people of the United States - E.W.*

With special thanks to the
following consultants:

Taelson Larrow of the Ho'omau Foundation,
Chief George Spring Buffalo of the Pocasset Tribe
of the Pokanoket Nation and Benjamin Fillipp

Published in 2024 by Welbeck Editions, an imprint of
Welbeck Children's Limited, part of Hachette Children's Group,
Carmelite House, 50 Victoria Embankment, London EC4Y 0DZ.
www.welbeckpublishing.com
www.hachette.co.uk

Text © 2024 Rebecca Siegel
Illustrations © 2024 Ellen Weinstein
Design and layout © Hachette Children's Books 2024

A CIP catalogue record for this book is available from the British Library and The Library of Congress.

ISBN: 978 1 80338 114 5

Printed in China

10 9 8 7 6 5 4 3 2 1

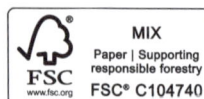

FSC
MIX
Paper | Supporting
responsible forestry
www.fsc.org   FSC® C104740

CONTENTS

WHERE IN THE UNITED STATES WOULD YOU LIKE TO GO TODAY?

INTRODUCTION

THE UNITED STATES OF AMERICA HAS BEEN CALLED MANY THINGS:
THE LAND OF OPPORTUNITY, THE LAND OF THE FREE,
AND THE GREATEST COUNTRY ON EARTH.

FAST FACTS

Date Established: **1776**

Population: **334 million**

Capital: **Washington, D.C.**

National Animal: **Bald eagle**

National Motto: **In God We Trust**

It's the mother of baseball and the father of spaceflight. It's home to entertainment hubs like Hollywood, Nashville, and Broadway, and to the tech giants of Silicon Valley. America gave the world Chicago-style hotdogs, New York-style bagels, and all things Tex-Mex. Under the Stars and Stripes lies a vast nation filled with vibrant cultures and traditions. But what is America, exactly?

People used to talk about America as a melting pot. They thought of it as a place where unique people from diverse places came together in a lovely sort of soup. It was a country where differences melted away. Today, we've thrown that old pot out the door. Americans don't want their unique traits to dissolve. They want to embrace differences. Instead of a pot of simmering soup, many Americans now compare their country to a big bowl of salad. Each of the ingredients stands out on its own—juicy tomato, crunchy lettuce, spicy onion—but taken together they form a delicious dish.

The poet Walt Whitman once wrote that America was
"not merely a nation but a teeming nation of nations."

A country as big and diverse as America is impossible to sum up in a single book. There are simply too many beautiful parks and forests, too many outstanding monuments and achievements to ever cover. However, this book will give you a brief taste of the crisp, gorgeous American salad. You'll learn about American history and its present day. You'll read about the states, territories, and commonwealths, as well as attractions, cultures, landmarks, and neighbors. And even after all of that, you'll still have so much more to learn about this country.

WHAT'S IN A NAME?

In the late 1400s and early 1500s, an Italian-born explorer named Amerigo Vespucci made at least two trips to what is now called South America. This was around the time Christopher Columbus made his famous journeys, as well. Vespucci believed that the lands he'd seen on his voyages were a "new world." When a German mapmaker drew a map of the lands Vespucci had seen, he labeled them America in his honor.

UNCLE SAM

The United States is often referred to as Uncle Sam. This is a friendly character who encourages Americans. Uncle Sam was probably inspired by a real man named Samuel Wilson. He was a meat packer who helped supply barrels of meat to American soldiers during the war of 1812. After he prepared each barrel, Wilson stamped them with the letters US. These stood for United States. But grateful soldiers said they stood for Uncle Sam's.

Newspaper cartoonists helped make Uncle Sam into the character he is today. Over time, his appearance changed. He grew a white beard and looked older and more friendly.

LADY LIBERTY

Uncle Sam isn't the only embodiment of the United States. The Statue of Liberty has come to symbolize the country, too. This 305-foot (93-meter) sculpture stands on Liberty Island, in New York Harbor. She is positioned to welcome ships to New York City, but many think of her welcoming people to the entire country.

Pacific Ocean

Canada

CASCADE RANGE

BLUE MOUNTAINS

ROCKY MOUNTAINS

MISSOURI RIVER

COAST RANGES

SIERRA NEVADA

GREAT BASIN

GREAT PLAINS

COLORADO RIVER

ARKANSAS RIVER

BRAZOS RIVER

RIO GRANDE

Mexico

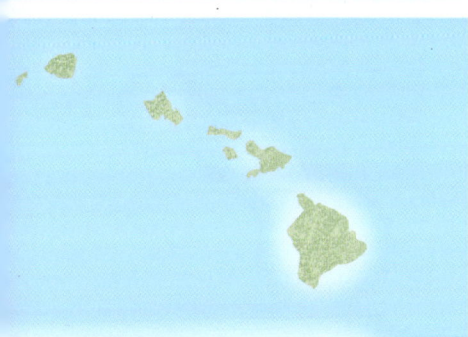

Russia

BROOKES RANGE

ALASKA RANGE

Canada

MISSISSIPPI RIVER

1

3

2

5

4

OHIO RIVER

APPALACHIAN MOUNTAINS

MISSISSIPPI RIVER

TENNESSEE RIVER

1 Lake Superior
2 Lake Michigan
3 Lake Huron
4 Lake Erie
5 Lake Ontario

COASTAL PLAINS

Atlantic Ocean

Gulf of Mexico

THE UNITED STATES

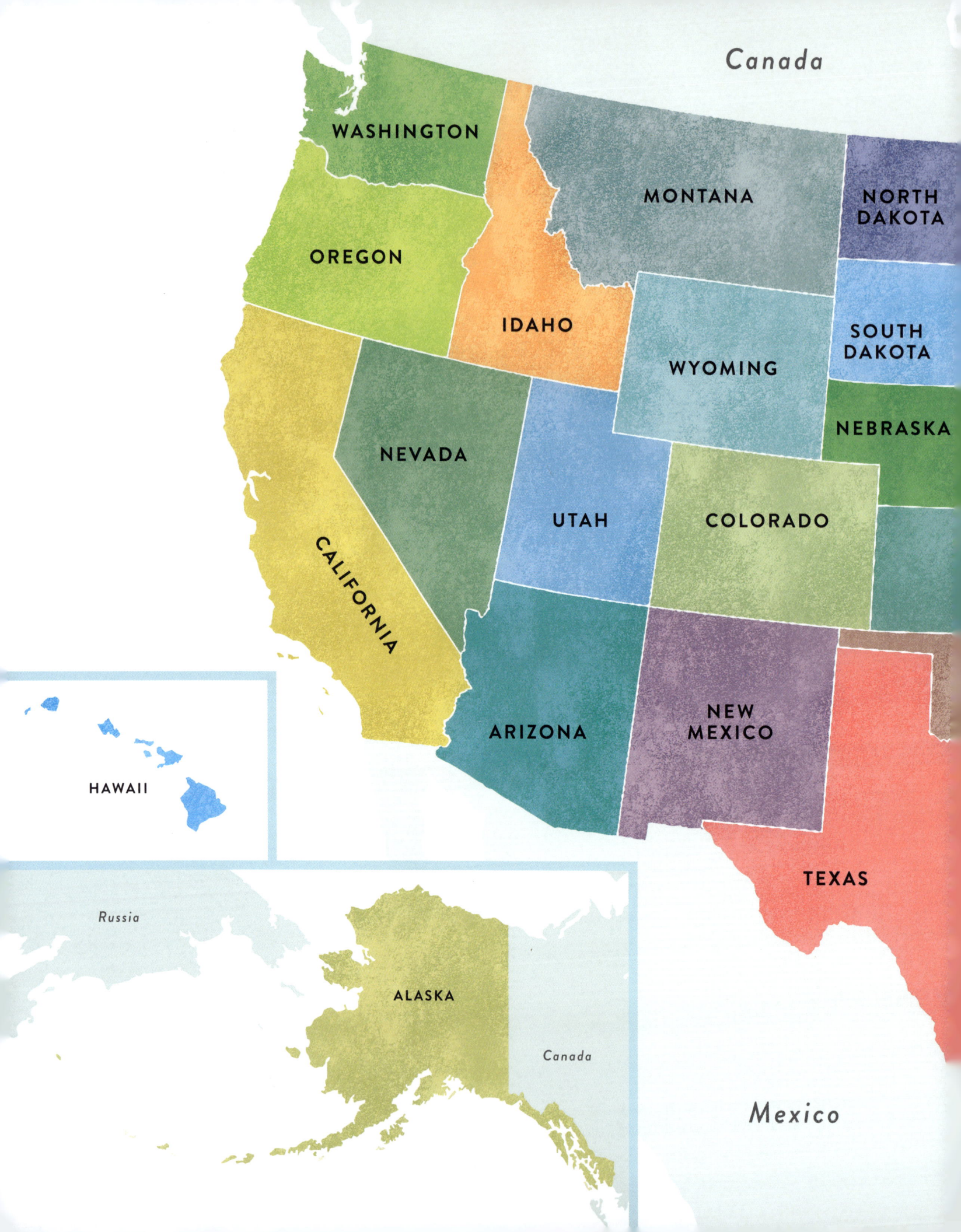

Canada

WASHINGTON

MONTANA

NORTH
DAKOTA

OREGON

IDAHO

SOUTH
DAKOTA

WYOMING

NEBRASKA

NEVADA

UTAH

COLORADO

CALIFORNIA

ARIZONA

NEW
MEXICO

HAWAII

TEXAS

Russia

ALASKA

Canada

Mexico

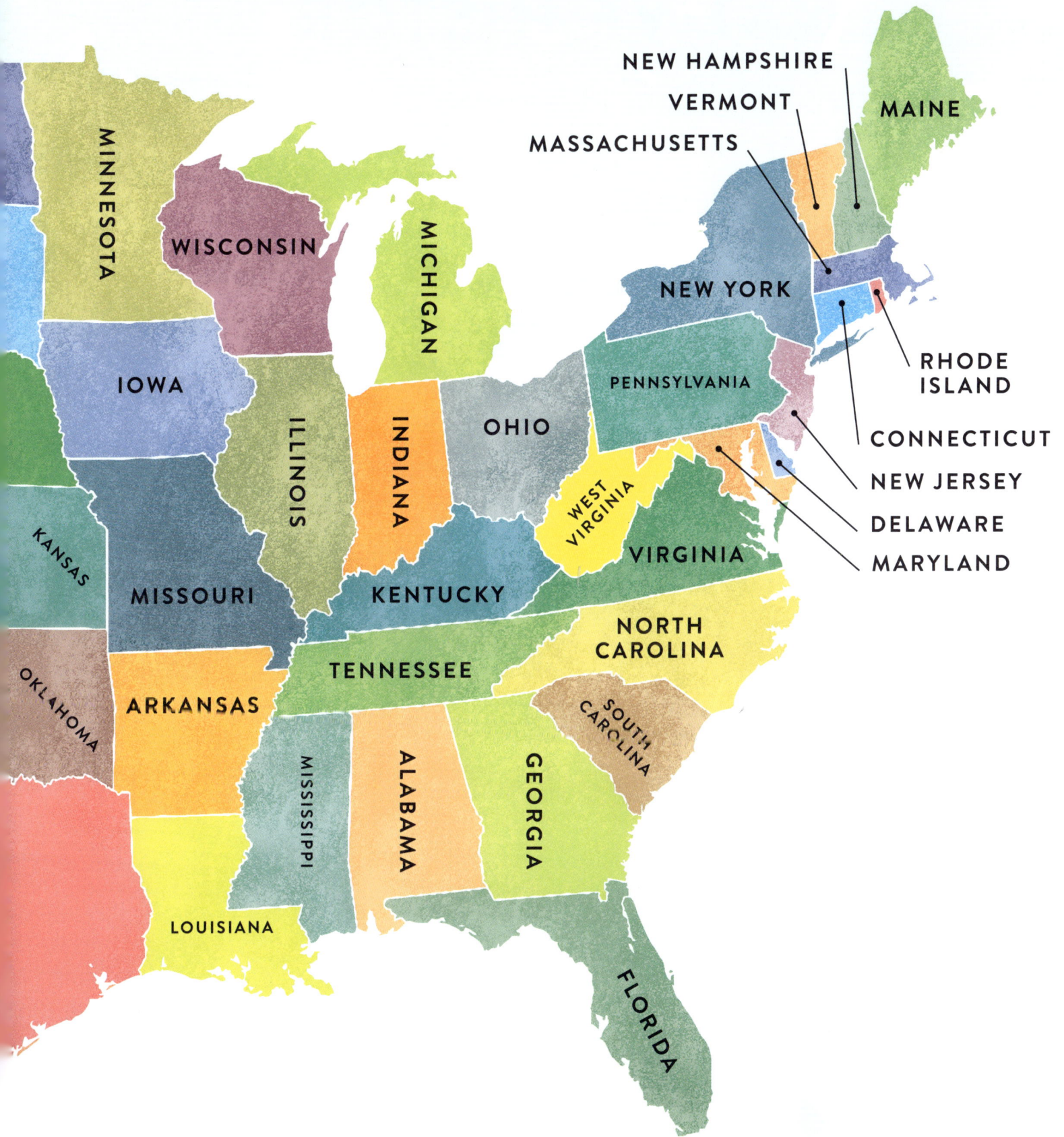

NEW HAMPSHIRE
VERMONT
MASSACHUSETTS

MAINE

MINNESOTA

WISCONSIN

MICHIGAN

NEW YORK

IOWA

ILLINOIS

INDIANA

OHIO

PENNSYLVANIA

RHODE ISLAND

CONNECTICUT

NEW JERSEY

DELAWARE

MARYLAND

KANSAS

MISSOURI

KENTUCKY

WEST VIRGINIA

VIRGINIA

OKLAHOMA

ARKANSAS

TENNESSEE

NORTH CAROLINA

SOUTH CAROLINA

MISSISSIPPI

ALABAMA

GEORGIA

LOUISIANA

FLORIDA

THE 50 STATES

NATIVE HISTORY

RICH AND DIVERSE

People have lived in the area now known as the United States for as many as 30,000 years. The first men and women were travelers who came to the area from Asia along the Bering Strait Land Bridge. Over the thousands of years that followed, their ancestors spread across the land. Tribes formed, and people learned to hunt, farm, and govern. They traded, traveled, made war, and made peace. At the same time, they made art, sang songs, and built fantastic structures.

BUSTLING CITIES

Many Native people lived in busy villages, such as Cahokia. This was a sprawling settlement in modern-day Illinois that had a population of about 20,000. Cahokia had residential areas and river access. At its center were huge earthen mounds used for ceremonies or for housing the elite. Its heyday was about 1250 CE. At that time, Cahokia was larger than many European cities, including London.

By the time European explorers reached North America in the 15th century, there may have been 10 million Native people living there.

GREAT HOUSES

In what is now New Mexico, the Chacoan people built dozens of jaw-dropping Great Houses. These were large, public structures that were probably used as hubs for trading, ceremonies, or other important activities. The largest of these was Pueblo Bonito. It had 600 rooms inside and was four to five stories tall.

WHAT'S IN A NAME?

Is it Native American, American Indian, First Nation person, Indigenous American, or Aboriginal American? There are many titles for the people who lived in the United States before European settlers and who continue to live there today. While each Native person is different, many prefer to be identified by their tribe's name. Rather than Native American, they may ask to be called by their tribal name, such as Navajo or Diné. The best way to handle this is to politely ask a person what they prefer to be called.

Tribes from across the nation have distinct cultures. There is no one "Native" identity.

ANCIENT EVIDENCE

Native American petroglyphs, or rock carvings, are found in 27 states and two American territories. Some feature simple shapes or lines. Others show complex images, maps, or patterns. Minnesota's Jeffers Petroglyphs are a collection of 8,000 carvings. They show people, animals, spirits, and other subjects. The earliest of these carvings are likely 9,000 years old. That means the artists carving them shared the Earth with woolly mammoths.

HOMES

Native people built different types of homes depending on their climate and culture. Here are some examples:

Tipis: These cone-shaped dwellings are made from leather and long wooden poles. They were commonly used in the Great Plains.

Grass Houses: People built this type of home in the Southern Plains using a wooden frame and prairie grass.

Wigwams or Wetus: These dome-shaped homes are made from wooden frames that are wrapped in tree bark or woven mats. They were often found in the Northeast.

Earthen Houses: These homes were found in many parts of America. Earthen houses were holes dug into the earth, then covered with mounded roofs over the top.

Adobe Houses or Pueblos: These were built by the Pueblo Indians in the Southwest, and are made from sun-dried bricks called adobe.

THE COLONIES

EARLY EXPLORERS

European people first arrived in North America around the year 1000 CE. However, it was not until the 1500s that they began to have a big impact on the area and its people. This was when Spanish, French, Dutch, and English people came to the New World. Having colonies there gave European countries trading opportunities, exotic goods, and the chance to spread Christianity. While the Dutch, French, and Spanish colonies ultimately did not remain in North America, the English did.

THE MYSTERY OF ROANOKE

In 1587, a boatload of 115 English settlers arrived on Roanoke Island, on the coast of present-day North Carolina. They began setting up a colony. Months later, the colony's governor, John White, left for England to get supplies. He was unable to return for three years. When he finally made it back to Roanoke, the settlement was empty. What happened to the colonists remains a mystery today.

JAMES TOWNE

In 1607, a group of English people set up the first permanent English settlement in America in an area called Virginia. They named it James Towne after King James I. Jamestown's English residents struggled to survive. One of the colonists, John Smith, met a Powhatan girl named Pocahontas. They became friendly. Pocahontas helped Smith and other colonists by giving them food and delivering messages from Native people.

John Smith later wrote that Pocahontas was "the instrument to pursurve this colonie from death, famine, and utter confusion."

THE MAYFLOWER

In the 1600s, religion in England was heavily regulated. A group of Protestants who wanted to practice their faith freely decided to establish a permanent settlement in the New World. Together with a group of merchants, tradespeople, and others interested in starting a new life, they boarded a small boat called the *Mayflower* and set sail. It took two months to cross the Atlantic. After the long, difficult journey, the passengers spotted Cape Cod on November 9, 1620. They set up a colony in a place they called New Plymouth in today's Massachusetts.

In 1619, a ship carrying 20 kidnapped Black Africans arrived in Jamestown. They were the first of about 400,000 kidnapped African people to be sold into slavery in America. 10 million additional Black African people were kidnapped and sold into slavery elsewhere.

ENGLISH COLONIES

Over the following century, the English established 13 permanent colonies.

ENGLISH RULE

The 13 colonies were under English rule. This meant that the colonists were subject to English laws. They also shipped goods such as sugar, tobacco, and lumber to England. In return, England supplied the colonies with manufactured items such as tools and cloth.

Claimed by New York and New Hampshire

Maine (part of Massachusetts)

New Hampshire

Massachusetts

Rhode Island

Connecticut

New York

New Jersey

Pennsylvania

Delaware

Maryland

Virginia

North Carolina

South Carolina

Georgia

THE BIRTH OF A NATION

Great Britain began imposing expensive taxes on the colonies in the 1760s. Colonists were required to pay taxes on sugar, paper, and other goods that were brought to America. This made many colonists angry. They thought that if they were being taxed, they should be represented in British Parliament. They were not. Many said "taxation without representation" was unfair.

BOSTON TEA PARTY

Seeing how angry the colonists were, Britain removed many colonial taxes. However, a tax on tea remained. Colonists smuggled tea in from Dutch companies and drank that instead. Still, British rulers insisted that colonists buy and drink the taxed tea. On December 16, 1773, a group of Bostonian colonists dressed as Mohawk Indians and snuck onto three ships in the harbor that were delivering the taxed tea. The colonists dumped the ships' tea overboard. This event was later called the Boston Tea Party. It was one of the first big acts of rebellion against the British. Following the Boston Tea Party, the British enforced punishments and more rules on the colonies.

DID YOU KNOW?

More than 100 colonists participated in the Boston Tea Party.

It took about three hours for the colonists to dump 342 chests of tea.

The tea weighed about 92,000 pounds (46 tons).

The value of the tea destroyed would equal about $1.7 million today.

George Washington did not approve of the Boston Tea Party.

Many smaller "tea parties" followed this one in other colonial cities.

WAR BEGINS

Tensions between the colonists and the British rose. On April 19, 1775, fights broke out between British troops and colonists in the battles of Lexington and Concord. These were the first clashes of what would become the Revolutionary War.

The British fought because they wanted the American colonies to remain part of the British Empire. The colonies provided goods as well as money from trade and taxes. On the other side, the colonists fought because they were tired of British rule. They wanted to become an independent nation.

GEORGE WASHINGTON

In 1775, the colonies officially created their own armed forces, called the Continental Army. George Washington was the commander-in-chief. The Continental Army was small, but Washington was a great leader. He led his troops against the British army in clash after clash.

DECLARATION OF INDEPENDENCE

On July 4, 1776, a group called the Second Continental Congress voted to adopt a document called the Declaration of Independence. This very important paper announced that the colonies were separating from Great Britain, and that they were becoming an independent nation. On August 2, members of the Continental Congress signed an official copy of the document. The president of the Continental Congress, John Hancock, wrote his name in especially large print.

VICTORY

The years that followed were filled with battles. The French officially joined the fight in 1778 by partnering with the colonies. In October 1781, Washington's army defeated the British at the Battle of Yorktown. The war finally ended in 1783, when Great Britain recognized American independence.

One important line from the Declaration of Independence reads, "We hold these truths to be self-evident, that all men are created equal, that they are endowed by their Creator with certain unalienable Rights, that among these are Life, Liberty, and the pursuit of Happiness."

A GROWING AND CHANGING COUNTRY

Following the Revolutionary War, the population of the United States grew quickly. Families had many children. Immigrants came to the new country to escape overcrowding, famine, and poor work conditions elsewhere, especially in Europe. Soon, the East Coast began to seem crowded. Americans started spreading west.

LOUISIANA PURCHASE

In 1803, President Thomas Jefferson led the United States to buy a huge territory from the French in the Louisiana Purchase. The deal, which cost $15 million, gave the United States 827,000 square miles (2.14 million square kilometers) of land to the west of the Mississippi River.

The Louisiana Purchase nearly doubled the country's size.

LEWIS AND CLARK

President Jefferson asked Meriwether Lewis and William Clark to make a survey of the country's new land. They agreed, and set off in 1804. Over the course of their two-year journey, the pair met more than 50 Native groups, recorded hundreds of new types of animals and plants, and made it all the way to the Pacific Ocean. A Shoshone woman named Sacagawea helped them during much of their journey.

OREGON TRAIL

In the mid-1800s, the country continued to press westward. Many moved west along a 2,000-mi (5,179-km) pathway called the Oregon Trail. It started in Independence, Missouri, and snaked all the way to Oregon. Taking the Oregon Trail was very difficult and dangerous. Roughly 400,000 people made the trek between the 1840s and 1880s. About 20,000 of them died along the way from sickness, hunger, thirst, or injuries. Those hearty enough to survive the trip were greeted with beautiful landscapes out west, and the challenging prospect of forging new lives as settlers.

60,000 PEOPLE

America was expanding. A set of rules was created to determine how new states in the west could form. One of the requirements was that the population of the new state had to be at least 60,000. In 1848, California had only about 7,000 non-Native residents. This was not nearly enough for it to become a state. The discovery of gold changed that. In one year, the population jumped to well over 60,000 and California became a state in 1850.

CIVIL WAR

Slavery was practiced in the English colonies starting in 1619, and continued in many states after America became a country. Over time, the northern states developed economies that depended on manufacturing and industry. They did not use many slaves. In the south, large-scale farms were very important to the economy. These relied on slave labor. In 1860, Abraham Lincoln became president. He wanted to abolish, or end, slavery. In response, seven southern states seceded, or left, the United States. Four more states soon followed. These became the Confederate States of America. The states in the North became known as the Union.

In 1861 the Confederate States and the Union began fighting in the Civil War. The Confederate States were led by Jefferson Davis. The Union was led by President Lincoln. After four years of war, on April 9, 1865, the Union defeated the Confederates. Five days later, Lincoln was assassinated by John Wilkes Booth, a man who supported slavery. That December, the 13th Amendment ended slavery in America. All of the ex-Confederate states returned to the Union by 1870, once again reuniting the country.

THE ALASKAN PURCHASE

In the mid-1700s, Russians came to the area now called Alaska. They wanted the land for fur hunting and trading. Over time, though, the Russians struggled on the land. It was far from their home, cold, and a difficult place to live.

In 1867, Russia found a solution to their problem. They sold their Alaska territory to the United States for two cents an acre. This increased the size of the United States by 586,000 sq mi (1.52 million sq km).

TRIBAL TERRITORIES AND RESETTLEMENT

As the United States grew, its citizens often came into conflict with the Native people already living on the land. American settlers wanted the land the Native people were living on.

At first, the US government treated each tribe as its own self-governing nation. They negotiated treaties and land deals. Over time, this became difficult as America was growing so quickly and there were so many different tribes living across the land. Some settlers wanted to "civilize" the Native people by teaching them to speak English and converting them to Christianity. Others moved the Native people off their land through treaties or by force. This resulted in many violent clashes between the groups. Some Native people fled westward, but many stayed on their land.

In response, the government reserved special areas of land for the Native people. The idea was that if the Native people could be moved to their own land, then there would be less fighting. However, not all of the Native people wanted to move. And even when they did, settlers continued to come onto their new land.

RESERVATIONS

Over time, more and more Native people were forced onto lands called Indian reservations. These are officially recognized tribal lands that are ruled by Native governments. Today, there are about 326 Indian reservations located throughout the country. Here are some of the biggest:

Navajo Nation: 173,000 people

Pine Ridge Reservation: 19,000 people

Fort Apache Reservation: 13,000 people

Gila River Indian Reservation: 11,000 people

Osage Reservation: 10,000 people

TRAIL OF TEARS

In 1830, President Andrew Jackson signed the Indian Removal Act. This was a law that forced Native people off their land and into an area in what is now Oklahoma. Eight years later, about 100,000 people from the Choctaw, Creek, Cherokee, Chickasaw, and Seminole tribes were made to walk to their new land. It was a long and difficult journey. About 15,000 Native people died during the walk, which became known as the Trail of Tears.

THE UNCONQUERED PEOPLE

When the US government tried to force the Seminole people off their land in Florida, most of them went. But not all. About 200 to 300 of them remained hidden in Florida's thick swamps. These Seminoles stayed in the remote and wild territory for decades, slowly growing in number. They began to call themselves the "unconquered people."

Today, there are about 2,000 Seminole people in Florida living in six reservations.

SIOUX AND THE BLACK HILLS

In 1868, the US government signed a treaty with the Sioux people. It gave the Sioux ownership of an area called the Black Hills, which they believed was sacred. In 1876, gold was discovered in the Black Hills. White gold miners rushed to the area. The government tried to buy back the land for $6 million. The Sioux people refused the offer. This led to a bloody conflict called the Black Hills War. In 1877, Congress passed an act that took back the Black Hills.

In 1980, the Supreme Court decided that the Sioux people should be paid for their loss. It said that they should be given $105 million. The Sioux refused to take the money because the land was never for sale in the first place. Today, the payment offered to them equals about $1.3 billion. But still, the Sioux reject the deal. They do not want the money. They want the land.

People living on Indian reservations are some of the poorest in America. One of the reasons for this is that the federal government owns and manages much of the land on Indian reservations. This stops Native people from buying or selling their land, which could help them earn generational wealth.

ALABAMA

The name Alabama probably comes from an Indian tribe of the Creek Confederacy called the Alibamons, or the Alabamas. A river was named after the tribe. Over time, the area of land around the river also took the name. The Spanish, British, and French colonists all put a different spin on the word. Some said *Albama*, while others said *Alebamon*, or *Allibamou*. Eventually, the modern spelling and pronunciation were adopted.

FAST FACTS

Admitted to the Union:
December 14, 1819

State Number: **22**

Population: **5 million**

Capital: **Montgomery**

Nickname: **The Heart of Dixie**

State Mammal: **Black bear**

HISTORY

Alabama might have been established as a state in 1819, but people lived there long before that. Humans first came to the area more than 10,000 years ago. They lived in many different parts of the state. One such place was Russell Cave. This large stone cave had a small stream running through it. People living inside the cave could enjoy shelter from the weather and a source of fresh water. It made such an attractive living place that it was occupied for thousands of years. Archaeologists have found tools and other artifacts from different groups of early people in the layers of soil inside the cave.

One of Alabama's most iconic dishes is fried catfish served with coleslaw and fries.

ROCKET CITY

Huntsville, Alabama is also known as Rocket City. This is because the rockets that first took humans to the moon were developed there. Huntsville is also the location of the US Space and Rocket Center, the largest space museum in the world.

One of Huntsville's most exciting attractions is Space Camp. Space-loving campers go there to learn about spaceflight, experience mission simulations, and have fun.

Space Camp graduates include at least five astronauts who have flown in space.

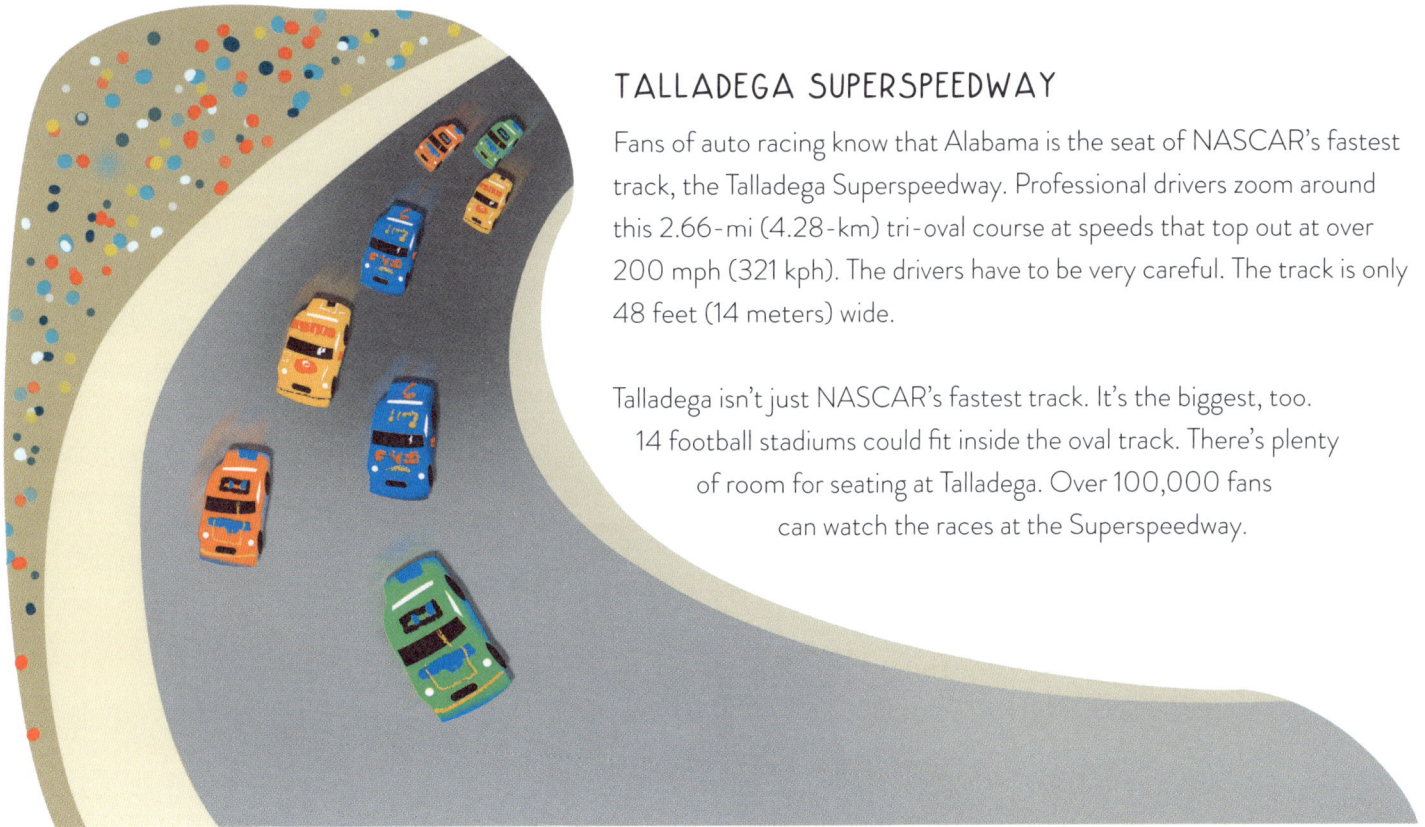

TALLADEGA SUPERSPEEDWAY

Fans of auto racing know that Alabama is the seat of NASCAR's fastest track, the Talladega Superspeedway. Professional drivers zoom around this 2.66-mi (4.28-km) tri-oval course at speeds that top out at over 200 mph (321 kph). The drivers have to be very careful. The track is only 48 feet (14 meters) wide.

Talladega isn't just NASCAR's fastest track. It's the biggest, too. 14 football stadiums could fit inside the oval track. There's plenty of room for seating at Talladega. Over 100,000 fans can watch the races at the Superspeedway.

HIGHS AND LOWS

Alabama has low valleys, high mountains, sandy beaches, and flat plains. The Tennessee River runs through the northern part of the state. To the south and east of the river is the Appalachian Ridge and Valley region. A hilly area called the Piedmont Upland in the central eastern part of Alabama holds the state's highest peak: Cheaha Mountain. It is 2,407 ft (733 m) tall. The Alabama River flows from central Alabama to the Southwest and is 315 mi (506 km) long.

WEATHER

Alabama enjoys a temperate climate. In the summer, temperatures average 79 °Fahrenheit (26 °Celsius). In the winter, temperatures dip to the high 40s °F (7.2–9.4 °C). Tropical storms, including hurricanes, sometimes hit the southern part of the state. In 2005, Hurricane Katrina destroyed coastal areas of Alabama.

ALASKA

The word Alaska comes from the Aleut word, *alaxsxaq*. This means "the mainland." Alaska is also often called *Alyeska*, an Aleut word for the "great land."

FAST FACTS

Admitted to the Union:
January 3, 1959

State Number: **49**

Population: **732,000**

Capital: **Juneau**

Nickname: **The Last Frontier**

State Land Animal: **Moose**

A LONG HISTORY

About 17,000 years ago, some early people traveled from Asia to Alaska on boats. Later, others traveled along the Bering Land Bridge, an area of land that has long since disappeared.

NATIVE PEOPLE

Alaska is home to many Native cultures and histories. There are 228 federally recognized tribes in Alaska. The most populous are the Inupiat, Yup'ik, Tlingit-Haida, Athabascan, and Aleut.

Many Alaskan Native groups are known for their art. The Inupiat Eskimos, who live near the Bering Sea and Arctic Ocean, are famous for carved walrus tusks. In Southeastern Alaska, the Tlingit, Haidas, and Tsimshians make towering totem poles.

Today, about 20.7 percent of Alaska's population is Native.

DOG SLEDDING

Each winter, dog sledding teams compete in races across Alaska. The most famous race is called the Iditarod. Teams race from Anchorage to Nome, a distance of nearly 1,000 mi (1,600 km). Winning teams often finish in eight days or less.

GREAT HEIGHTS

17 out of 20 of the United States' tallest mountain peaks are in Alaska. The top three are Denali at 20,310 ft (6,190 m), Mount Saint Elias at 18,009 ft (5,489 m), and Mount Foraker at 17,400 ft (5,303 m). While most people are content to simply look at the beautiful mountains, some adventurous folks climb them.

Climbing such high peaks can be extremely dangerous. In 2019, 1,226 people tried to climb Denali. Only 726 of them made it to the top. Most of the climbers simply got too tired, cold, or worn down to reach the summit, but 18 were seriously sick or injured.

VERY COLD

Alaska is known for its frigid winters. But sometimes, even Alaskans are surprised by how cold it can get. In 1971, temperatures at Prospect Creek Camp dropped to a record-breaking -80 °F (-62 °C).

BIGGEST STATE

Alaska is the country's biggest state, by far. If you placed it on top of the lower 48 states, it would stretch from California's western coast all the way to Georgia. Alaska has 6,640 mi (10,690 km) of shoreline. This is more than half of the United States' total shorelines combined.

Getting around the giant state isn't always easy. About 60 percent of Alaska's roads aren't paved. Sometimes, the only way to get from one place to another is by plane or boat. When Alaskans need to get from one body of water to another, they take sea planes. These are aircraft that can take off from and land on water. The state has 102 seaplane bases.

On average, only 1.2 people live on each square mile of Alaskan land.

THE AMERICAN FLAG

The Stars and Stripes might seem like they've been around forever, but they haven't.
Early American flags look nothing like the modern banner.

COLONIAL FLAGS

LIBERTY AND UNION

LIBERTY

The Taunton Flag was flown in 1774 in Taunton, Massachusetts as a symbol of resistance to British rule. Later, it was flown elsewhere in the colonies.

The Moultrie Flag was flown in 1776 during the Battle of Sullivan's Island, which the colonists won.

In 1776, George Washington raised a new flag. It had an early version of the British flag in its upper left corner, and 13 red and white stripes. This would be called the Grand Union.

BETSY ROSS

Betsy Ross is at the center of a popular American legend. As the story goes, in 1776, she was working as a seamstress when a group of men walked into her shop. It was George Washington and other colonial leaders. They asked her to make a flag with 13 stripes and 13 six-sided stars. Ross agreed, but suggested five-sided stars instead. She went to work and produced a beautiful flag with red and white stripes, and a ring of white stars on a blue box in the upper left corner.

While a lovely tale, this is probably untrue. It is more likely that a man named Francis Hopkinson designed the flag. In 1780, he billed the Continental Congress for his work, which included "the flag of the United States of America." His fee, which the Continental Congress never paid, was a little unusual: a quarter-cask of wine.

MANY VERSIONS

The American flag was officially adopted on June 14, 1777. The first version of the flag had just 13 stars, each representing one of the first 13 colonies. As a state or states joined the Union, the flag design also changed, with additional stars being added. In total, there have been 27 versions of the American flag, with the last appearing in 1960 after Hawaii became a state.

SYMBOLS

The American flag is very symbolic. Each of its components has special meaning. The 13 red and white stripes represent the 13 colonies, and the 50 stars represent the 50 states. The colors are important, too. The red stands for valor, or bravery. The white is meant to represent innocence or purity. And the blue is for perseverance, vigilance, and justice.

FLYING HIGH

In July of 1969, an American flag was flown in an extreme location: the Moon! Apollo 11 astronauts, Neil Armstrong and Buzz Aldrin, brought the flag with them when they became the first humans to walk on the Moon. Because there is no air on the Moon, scientists at NASA knew the flag would not "fly" like it would on Earth. To allow the flag to be fully visible, they sent the astronauts with a special flagpole that included a horizontal rod to support the top edge of the flag.

Five additional Apollo missions left American flags on the Moon.

ARIZONA

Historians aren't sure how Arizona got its name. Some think it was a Native name for a place. Others think it comes from a Basque word for "The Good Oak Tree." Still others think it might come from the Aztec work *arizuma*, which means "silver-bearing."

LANDSCAPE

Most people think that Arizona is one big desert. In fact, only about one half of the state is made up of desert. The rest is grassland, woodland, or forests. The Grand Canyon snakes across the northwestern part of the state, drawing nearly 6 million tourists each year. (Turn to page 112 to learn more about the Grand Canyon.) The painted desert in the northeast includes rock formations in vivid reds, yellows, purples, and pinks.

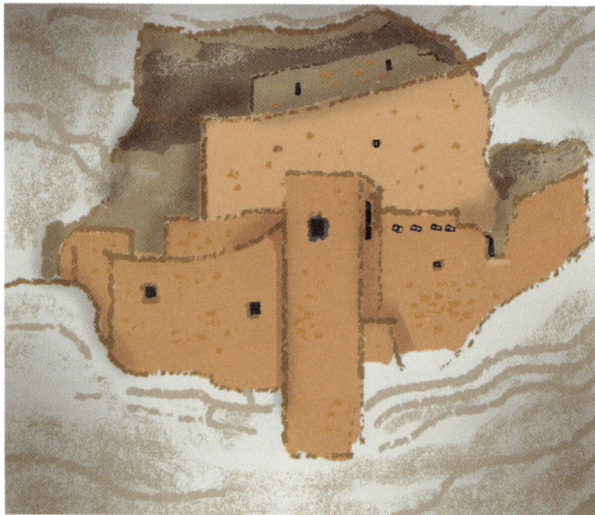

(Turn to page 112 to learn more about the Grand Canyon.)

FAST FACTS

Admitted to the Union:
February 14, 1912

State Number: **48**

Population: **7.3 million**

Capital: **Phoenix**

Nickname:
The Grand Canyon State

State Mammal: **Ringtail cat**

EARLY PEOPLE

Some of the country's most amazing cliff dwellings are in Arizona. These are stone structures that were built right into cliffs, caves, or mountainsides in around 1200 CE. Early people such as the Anasazi and Sinagua lived, worshipped, and stored their goods in these stone buildings. One of the most fascinating is called Montezuma's Castle. This five-story building, perched about 100 ft (30 m) into the air, was likely inhabited by about 50 people.

NATIVE AMERICAN TRIBES

Arizona is home to 22 federally recognized tribes. Its biggest tribe is the Navajo, or Diné. Many Navajo live on a reservation called the Navajo Nation, a huge swath of land located at the junction of Arizona, New Mexico, and Utah. The Navajo Nation is the biggest Indian reservation in the United States. It is about the same size as West Virginia. The Navajo welcome tourists to visit their reservation and learn about their culture through fairs, hikes, museum visits, and art shows.

Arizona produces more copper than any other state.

MINING

Arizona is rich with many precious metals, such as silver, gold, and copper. In fact, the bronze star on the state's flag is meant to symbolize copper.

PETRIFIED

Many precious stones are found in Arizona, including turquoise, garnet, and peridot. Petrified wood is another Arizona beauty. This type of fossil is made when the organic material of a tree is replaced by minerals. The result is a colorful, sparkling fossil. Arizona's Petrified Forest National Park is littered with these ancient treasures. But beware: collecting petrified wood there is against the rules. It is also said to be bad luck, or even cursed. People who steal from the Petrified Forest report having bad things happen to them, such as divorce or illness. Some people mail their stolen petrified wood back to the park, along with apology letters. A few of these are on display in a museum there.

GHOST TOWNS

Arizona has more than 200 ghost towns. These are small settlements, villages, or even cities that were abandoned long ago. Many were founded around silver, gold, or copper mines. When the mines stopped producing, people moved on, and left the town behind. Today, these crumbling towns are popular with tourists.

WEATHER

Arizona is known for its scorching summer temperatures. In 2023, Pheonix had 54 days at 110 °F (43.3 °C) or above.

THE HOOVER DAM

Controlling the flow of the Colorado River is no small task. Luckily, the massive Hoover Dam is up for the challenge. This 726-ft (221-m) structure also produces power, agricultural irrigation, and domestic water.

ARKANSAS

Like many other states, Arkansas gets its name from an Indian tribe. A group of people called the Quapaws lived in the area. A nearby group of Algonquin-speaking people called them the *akansea*. Over time, the way people said the word changed. Some people called the area *Acansa*, *Les Akansas*, and *Arkansaw*. Two US Senators argued about the pronunciation of the word. One said "AR-can-SAW," while the other said "Ar-KANZIS." In 1881, the state's General Assembly passed a resolution clearing it up. From then on, the state was officially given its modern pronunciation: AR-can-SAW.

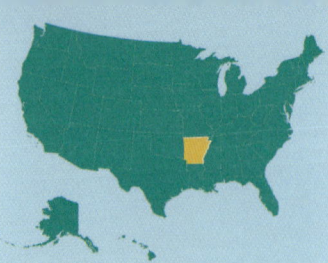

AR-can-SAW

ar-KANZIS

FAST FACTS

Admitted to the Union:
June 15, 1836

State Number: **25**

Population: **3 million**

Capital: **Little Rock**

Nickname: **The Natural State**

State Mammal:
White-tailed deer

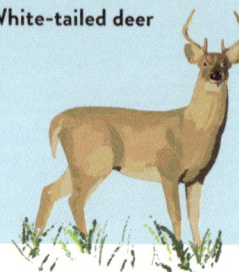

HOT SPRINGS

Arkansas has many hot springs. These form deep in the ground, when water touches very hot rock and then rises to the surface. There are 47 hot springs in Arkansas' Hot Springs National Park. While a quick dip in the steaming natural pools might sound tempting, don't try it. The water is an average of 143 °F (61 °C)—far too hot for a person to enjoy. Luckily, there are many naturally heated bath houses that allow visitors to enjoy a slightly cooler soak.

MOUNDS

People have lived in the area of Arkansas since about 11,000 BCE. In around 650 CE, a group of early residents now called the Plum Bayou left a lasting impression on the land by building massive earthen mounds.

These mounds were probably involved in ceremonies or burials. Today, visitors come to Toltec Mounds Archaeological State Park to visit the mounds and learn about the people who built them.

LITTLE ROCK NINE

In 1954, the Supreme Court ruled in *Brown V. Board of Education* that segregation in public schools was unconstitutional. Three years later, nine African American students enrolled at the previously all-white Central High School in Little Rock, Arkansas. This made many people very angry. They wanted segregation in schools to continue. The state's governor, Orval Faubus, even called in the state's National Guard to stop the students from entering the school. Weeks of angry protests followed. The students were threatened and harassed. Finally, President Eisenhower sent National Guard and Army soldiers to protect the nine students, and they were able to attend school. This was an important event in the struggle for civil rights in America.

THE OZARKS

Much of northern Arkansas is dominated by a region of plateaus called the Ozarks. The Ozarks contain the state's highest peak, Magazine Mountain, which is 2,753 ft (839 m) high. The Ozarks are filled with places to hike, swim, climb, mountain bike, and camp.

WEATHER

Arkansas has mild weather during the spring and fall. Its winters are often cold and wet, and its summers get very hot. The highest temperature ever recorded in Arkansas was 120 °F (48.9 °C) in Ozark in August, 1936.

NATIONAL PARKS

America has more than 400 national parks. These are scenic areas, historic sites, and monuments that have been set aside for the public to use and enjoy. The national parks are protected and preserved. They cannot be changed by housing, agriculture, or other human activities.

YELLOWSTONE

Yellowstone National Park covers an incredible 3,472 sq mi (8,992 sq km) of land in Wyoming, Montana, and Idaho. That means it's bigger than Rhode Island and Delaware combined.

Yellowstone includes mountains, forests, waterfalls, and lakes. But it is most famous for its more than 10,000 hydrothermal features. These are landforms such as geysers, mudpots, hot springs, and fumaroles. Heat from below the Earth's surface rises as boiling water or billowing steam to cause spectacular effects. Old Faithful, the most famous of Yellowstone's 500 geysers, was named for its regular eruptions. Visitors can watch the cone geyser erupt roughly every 90 minutes, shooting thousands of gallons of water over 100 ft (30 m) into the air.

ARCHES NATIONAL PARK

Tall spires, winding canyons, and mind-boggling balanced rocks are just some of the geological features found in Utah's Arches National Park. The most striking features found in this red-rocked park are its more than 2,000 rainbow-shaped arches. Some arches are small, with openings of just 3 ft (1 m). Others are enormous. Landscape Arch spans a distance of 306 ft (93 m) in width. Double Arch is the park's tallest, soaring 112 ft (34 m) into the air.

The park's most famous feature is Delicate Arch. Sometimes called "Cowboy's Chaps" or "Old Maid's Bloomers," it almost looks like a person's lower body stretching into the sky.

MAMMOTH CAVE NATIONAL PARK

Most national parks call attention to wonders above the ground. Kentucky's Mammoth Cave National Park does the opposite, inviting visitors into a maze of underground beauty. The park contains about 400 mi (643 km) of explored caves, and an estimated 600 mi (965 km) more that haven't been mapped.

BIGGEST AND SMALLEST

Alaska's Wrangell-St. Elias National Park is the country's biggest national park. It covers over 20,000 sq mi (53,000 sq km), which means that six Yellowstones could fit inside. It includes a wide range of landscapes, from glaciers to volcanoes, as well as the second tallest mountain peak in America, Mt. Saint Elias.

In contrast, the Thaddeus Kosciuszko National Memorial is America's smallest national park. This Philadelphia home is a tribute to Kosciuszko, a Polish freedom fighter and helper in the American Revolutionary war. The house makes up the entire park, which makes it the only national park you can entirely tour in just a few minutes.

ALL KINDS OF ATTRACTIONS

Many national parks protect natural areas, such as mountain ranges, glaciers, or vast lakes. Others center around human-made attractions. In St. Louis, Missouri, the Gateway Arch National Park highlights a towering 630-ft (192-m) steel arch. In South Dakota's Black Hills, Mount Rushmore National Memorial invites visitors to see the faces of Presidents George Washington, Thomas Jefferson, Theodore Roosevelt, and Abraham Lincoln carved into the face of the mountain. Even the Statue of Liberty National Monument is part of the National Park System.

JUNIOR RANGERS

National parks are cared for by park rangers. Kids can become junior park rangers. All they have to do is complete a set of activities at a national park, and answer a ranger's questions. Then they are sworn in and get their very own badge.

The National Park Service was created in 1916.

NATIONAL FORESTS

From the Arctic reaches of Alaska to the tropical rainforests of Puerto Rico, America's national forests include some of the country's most beautiful sights. These are areas of land reserved for public use, such as hiking, fishing, and camping.

WHAT'S THE DIFFERENCE?

People often confuse national parks and national forests. The biggest difference between the two has to do with preservation. The lands inside national parks are strictly protected. People cannot hunt, cut down timber, or farm there. Inside national forests, these activities may be allowed.

TONGASS NATIONAL FOREST

Covering about 26,000 sq mi (68,000 sq km) of land in southeast Alaska, Tongass National Forest is the largest national forest in America. Animals such as wolves, bears, and beavers roam its land, while orcas and humpback whales swim its icy waters. Visitors to Tongass can view some of its spectacular glaciers and icefields.

Tongass is home to more than just wildlife. About 70,000 people live throughout the land, including in Juneau, the state's capital.

BY THE NUMBERS

There are 294,000 sq mi (761,000 sq km) of national forest land in the United States.

There are 155 national forests.

More than 3,000 species of wildlife live inside the National Forest System.

"Conservation means the greatest good to the greatest number for the longest time."
– Gifford Pinchot, the first National Forest Service Chief, 1910.

COCONINO: OUT OF THIS WORLD

Arizona's Coconino National Forest is made up of many types of landscapes across its 2,900 sq mi (7,500 sq km). In addition to pine forests, deserts, red rocks, and tundra, it also includes something that's out of this world: the practice grounds for America's moon missions. NASA's astronauts rehearsed for their moon landings in what is now known as the Cinder Hills OHV Area. There, geologists blasted holes into the rocky earth to simulate the craters on the Moon. Then, Apollo astronauts practiced walking, driving, and observing their surroundings, pretending they were on the Moon the whole time.

SUPERIOR NATIONAL FOREST

The Superior National Forest covers 6,100 sq mi (16,000 sq km) of forested land. However beautiful, the land isn't what this forest is known for. It's the 695 sq mi (1,800 sq km) of pristine water that makes this forest so spectacular.

Inside the Superior National Forest is the Boundary Waters Canoe Area Wilderness. This includes a 100-mi (160-km) stretch of lakes and forests that hug the boundary between Minnesota and Ontario, Canada. The Boundary Waters contain more than 1,000 bodies of water that are connected by short land trails called "portages." People travel the Boundary Waters by canoeing, "portaging," and then canoeing again.

In 1968, canoers Verien Kruger and Clint Waddell set a record for traveling the Border Route, a 216-mi (348-km) canoe and portage trek through the Boundary Waters. They completed the journey in 80 hours and 40 minutes. In 2019, that record was shattered by Matthew Peterson and Peter Wagner, who finished in 69 hours and 25 minutes.

NOT JUST FORESTS

The National Forest System includes more than just forests. It also includes 20 national grasslands, and one national tallgrass prairie.

CALIFORNIA

The name California likely comes from the Spanish novel, *Las Sergas de Esplandian*, which was published in 1510. The novel featured a character named Queen Califia who ruled a place called California. When Spanish explorers came to the area in 1542, they may have named the land after this fictional place.

49ERS

In 1848 gold was discovered at Sutter's Mill, in northern California. In 1849, more than 60,000 people arrived in the area hoping to strike gold, too. They became known as 49ers. Some 49ers did manage to find gold. But the people who flourished in the greatest numbers were those who formed businesses to support the miners. These were merchants who sold goods such as tools and clothes.

In 1946, the San Francisco 49ers became an NFL team. Their original logo paid tribute to the gold miners of the past. It showed a miner wearing a flannel shirt and boots, firing a pair of pistols.

HOT AND COLD

While California might have a reputation for always being sunny and pleasant, the state does have its fair share of weather extremes. Cities such as Bakersfield, Fresno, and the state's capital, Sacramento, regularly experience temperatures of over 90 °F (32 °C) during the summer. When these hot temperatures combine with droughts, wildfires can ignite. These fires rage across dry hillsides, forests, and neighborhoods alike.

FAST FACTS

Admitted to the Union:
September 9, 1850

State Number: **31**

Population: **39.2 million**

Capital: **Sacramento**

Nickname: **The Golden State**

State Animal:
California grizzly bear

In the first four years of the California Gold Rush, $207 million worth of gold was discovered. Today, that equals about $7.4 billion.

In contrast, San Francisco is quite cold and gray during the summer. A classic joke sums it up: "The coldest winter I ever spent was a summer in San Francisco."

LAND AND AGRICULTURE

California has a wide range of landscapes, from the Sierra Nevada mountains, to sandy beaches, to baking deserts, and to the fertile farmland in the Central Valley. About one-fourth of California's land is used for farming. The state produces over 400 types of farm goods, providing a third of the country's vegetables and two-thirds of its fruit and nuts.

A DIVERSE STATE

California is a very diverse state, with people from many different backgrounds.

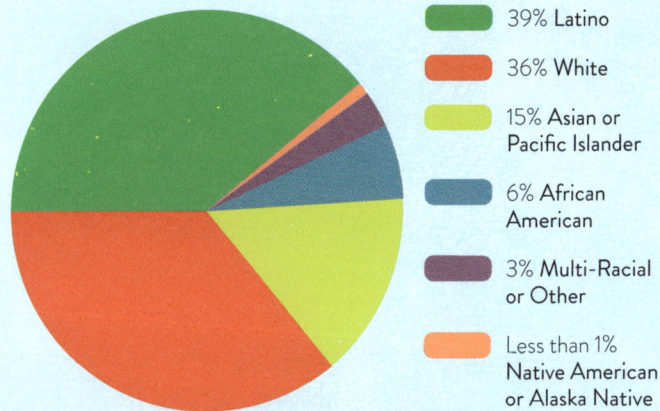

- 39% Latino
- 36% White
- 15% Asian or Pacific Islander
- 6% African American
- 3% Multi-Racial or Other
- Less than 1% Native American or Alaska Native

California is the country's most populated state. In fact, about one in every eight Americans lives in California. From 1900 to 2000, the state's population jumped from under 2 million to 34 million. Experts guess that 45 million people will live there by 2050.

THEME PARKS

Some of the country's best theme parks are found in California. Here are just a few.

Disneyland
Built in 1955, this sprawling park was Walt Disney's first theme park.

Santa Cruz Beach Boardwalk Amusement Park
Often called the world's best seaside amusement park, this gem in Santa Cruz has it all: food, games, and thrilling rollercoasters.

Universal Studios Hollywood
This park is a hit among movie fans and thrill seekers alike. Magic lovers especially enjoy the Wizarding World of Harry Potter.

Legoland
Fans of the classic toy love visiting Legoland, where they can go on rides, build, and play all day.

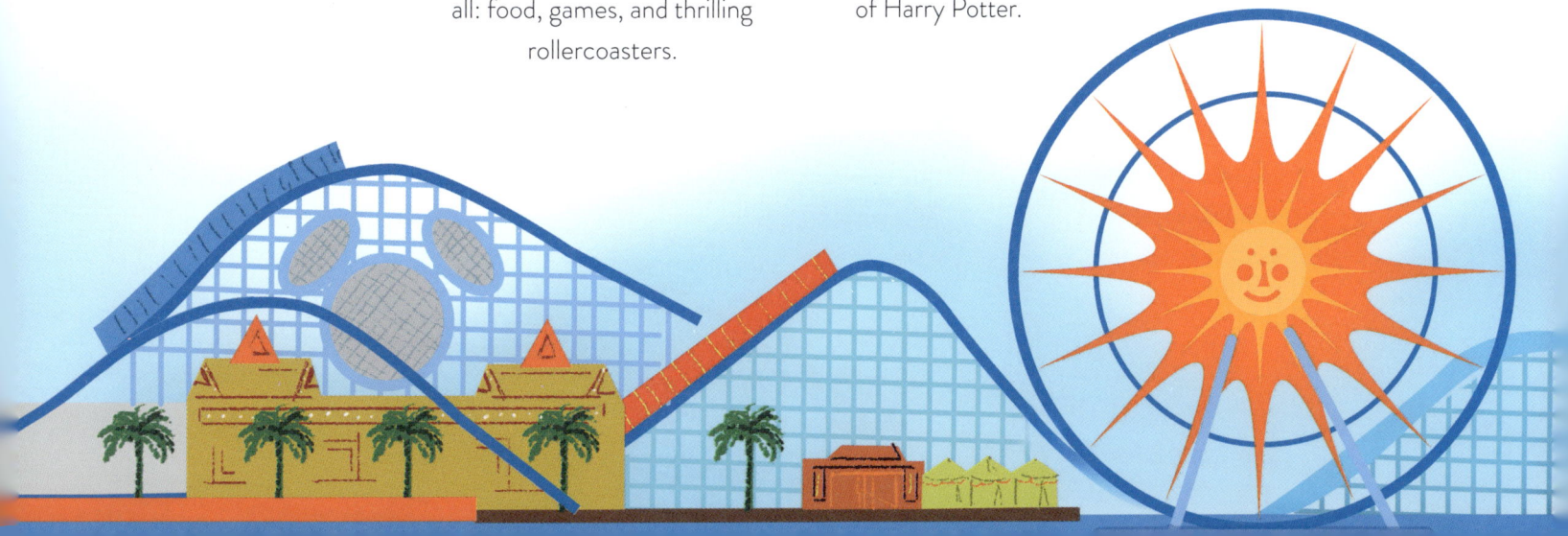

HOLLYWOOD

Strictly speaking, the name Hollywood refers to a geographic area in Los Angeles, California. But for the last 100 years, Hollywood has had another meaning entirely: *show business.*

HISTORY

The first film made entirely in Hollywood was 1910's *In Old California*, which was 17 minutes long. After that, Hollywood soon grew into a bustling hot spot. Movie studios and actors alike flocked there, cranking out hundreds of silent, black and white films a year. In 1927, the first film with sound, "a talkie," was released. The 1930s brought more exciting changes, with major films appearing in color. Hollywood evolved even more with the advent of television. Shows like *Dragnet* and *Father Knows Best* captured the hearts of American viewers, and kept Hollywood stars busy. In the decades that followed, the Hollywood film industry remained a leader in movies, television, and all things celebrity.

In 1923, the town's famous Hollywood sign was built. The first version of the sign said "Hollywoodland" and was a real estate advertisement.

TINSELTOWN

Hollywood—and the film industry within it—is often called Tinseltown. This nickname comes from the glittering, glitzy movie stars who work there.

One of the first cartoons broadcast on television came out of Hollywood in 1939. It was a Disney creation called "Donald's Cousin Gus."

WALK OF FAME

One of Hollywood's most famous attractions is its Walk of Fame, an 18-block stretch of paved sidewalk along Hollywood Boulevard and Vine Street. Set into the pathway are about 2,700 red and gold stars. Each star honors a performer in one of five categories: Movies, television, radio, music, or live performance. Some celebrities have multiple stars in the different categories, and one, Gene Autry, has five!

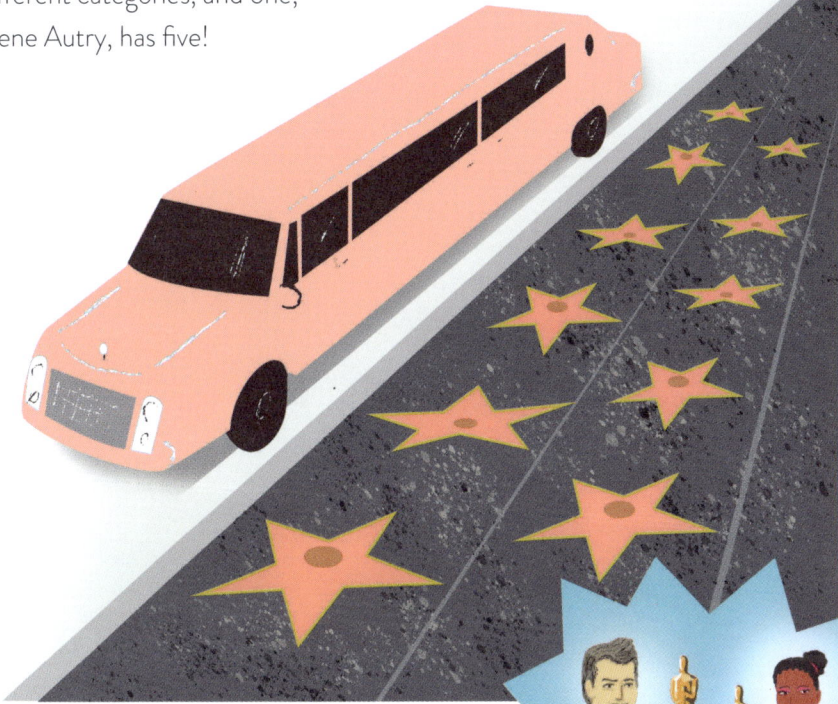

THE OSCARS

Since Hollywood is the hub for film, it's not surprising that it's also the place where the biggest film awards are given out. The Academy Awards is a glamorous, televised awards program that highlight the greatest achievements in film each year. Winners in categories like Best Actress and Best Supporting Actor take home a golden trophy called an Oscar.

The Oscars celebrate more than just film. They also highlight fashion. Celebrities attending the Oscars walk in along a red carpet, where they are interviewed and photographed in beautiful gowns, suits, and other amazing outfits. The carpet itself has become an icon, and an expensive one at that. It costs about $24,000 and takes about 900 hours to install each year.

MONEY

Hollywood's top earning films are also some of the most beloved. Here are the six most profitable movies ever to come out of Tinseltown:

Avatar
$2.92 billion

Avengers: Endgame
$2.79 billion

Avatar: The Way of Water
$2.3 billion

Titanic
$2.2 billion

Star Wars: Episode VII
$2.06 billion

Avengers: Infinity War
$2.05 billion

Making movies isn't cheap. Here are the five most expensive movies ever made:

Pirates of the Caribbean: On Stranger Tides
$379 million

Avengers: Age of Ultron
$365 million

Pirates of the Caribbean: At World's End
$362 million

Avengers: Endgame
$356 million

Avatar: The Way of Water
$350 million

SIERRA NEVADA MOUNTAIN RANGE

Along California's eastern border lies one of the country's most spectacular mountain ranges, the Sierra Nevada. Incredible wildlife, such as mule deer, grizzly bears, and mountain lions, wander its rugged terrain.

Stretching about 400 mi long by 70 mi wide (643 km long by 113 km wide), the Sierra Nevada include Mount Whitney, the highest peak in the lower 48 states. It is 14,494 ft (4,417 m) tall. Yosemite Falls, one of North America's tallest waterfalls, is also found in the range. Its water drops 2,425 ft (739 m). There are four national parks and nine national forests inside the Sierra Nevada.

WHAT'S IN A NAME?

The name *Sierra Nevada* comes from an early Spanish explorer who described the huge mountains in his journal as *una gran sierra nevada*, which means a "great, snow-covered range." The name is appropriate. Areas in the mountains, such as the Sugar Bowl ski resort, get as much as 500 inches (1,270 centimeters) of snow each year.

The Sierra Nevada are sometimes called the "Range of Light." This nickname refers to the light-colored stone of the mountains.

"Of all the mountain ranges I have climbed, I like the Sierra Nevada the best."
– John Muir, conservationist and "father" of American national parks.

LAKE TAHOE

Lake Tahoe is a blue jewel in the Sierra Nevada. At 1,645 ft (501 m) deep, it's one of the deepest lakes in North America. Visitors flock to it each year to swim, boat, and fish. The word *Tahoe* probably comes from a Washoe term, *da ow ga*, which means "the lake."

DONNER PARTY

One of the most famous pieces of Sierra Nevada history is also one of the most gruesome. In 1846, a group of settlers left Illinois to travel west in a wagon train. Poor planning meant that they arrived in the Sierra Nevada range in winter. A blizzard trapped them in an area by Truckee Lake, which is now called Donner Lake. Over the next months, about half of their party would die. The survivors, starving and desperate, ate the bodies of the dead to survive.

GROWING

The Sierra Nevada aren't alive, but that hasn't stopped them from growing. Scientists at NASA are monitoring the mountain range. They found that the range grew nearly an inch between 2011 and 2014.

GENERAL SHERMAN

Sequoia National Park is found in the southern part of the Sierra Nevada range. It highlights and protects some of the world's biggest trees, called giant sequoias, which can naturally grow only in a specific part of the Sierra Nevada range. These towering trees can grow to be 300 ft (90 m) tall or more. Their huge trunks are covered in bark that grows up to 3 ft (1 m) thick, and they have branches that can be 8 ft (2.4 m) in diameter. The trees are old, too. They can live for up to 3,000 years.

The largest living thing on Earth is a giant sequoia named General Sherman. It is 275 ft (84 m) tall. Its trunk is 36 ft (11 m) across at its base. It weighs about 2.7 million lb (1.2 million kg).

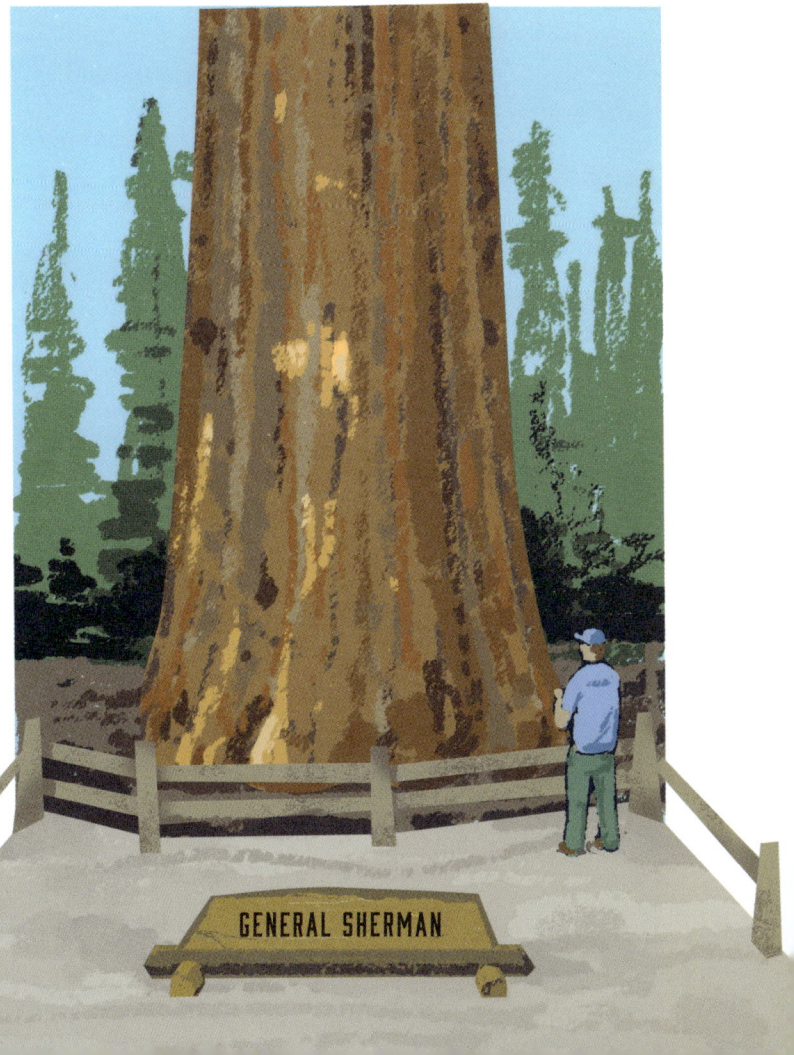

GENERAL SHERMAN

SILICON VALLEY

Silicon Valley is an area in northern California that is home to some of the world's most important technology companies. Apple, Facebook, Netflix, Google, and Yahoo are all based in Silicon Valley. The products, ideas, and services coming out of Silicon Valley have changed the way people around the world live, from how they watch movies to how they buy houses.

WHY SILICON?

Silicon Valley's unique nickname comes from a material used to make computer chips. In 1971, a reporter named Don Hoefler wrote a column about the booming silicon computer chip business in the Santa Clara Valley. He called the region "Silicon Valley, USA." The name stuck.

In the early 1900s, parts of Silicon Valley were called "the Valley of the Heart's Delight" for its rich fruit farms and orchards.

STARTUPS

Startups are brand new companies. They are often led by just one or two people who have an idea or product they think will be successful. Many startups have few or even no employees. The individuals running these businesses must work hard to grow their companies, hire more people, and earn money.

Silicon Valley is practically overflowing with technology startups. These companies go to Silicon Valley for the connections and resources found there. But it's not an easy place to make a profit. Real estate is expensive and competition is fierce. Up to 90 percent of startups fail. That means that only the companies led by the best, and most determined, will survive.

"I'm a Silicon Valley guy. I just think people from Silicon Valley can do anything."
– Elon Musk, founder of PayPal, Tesla, and SpaceX.

GIANTS

The technology companies found in Silicon Valley aren't just hugely important. Some of them are also actually huge. Google's office complex, known as the Googleplex, is a whopping 3 million sq ft (279,000 sq m). That's about the size of 50 football fields. Apple's headquarters are the shape of a huge donut.

STEVE JOBS

Steve Jobs was famous for co-founding The Apple Computer Company with his friend Steve Wozniak in 1976. The pair worked out of Jobs' parents' garage in Los Altos, California, in the heart of Silicon Valley. They began developing personal computers, and within just a few years, Apple was a huge success. Jobs helped create the Macintosh "Mac" computer. After that, he left Apple to help build Pixar into a leading computer animation studio. Eventually, he returned to Apple where he led the company to create personal computers called the iMac, the music program iTunes, and portable music players called iPods. In 2007, Jobs introduced a piece of technology that would forever change the world: the iPhone. Jobs died in 2011 of pancreatic cancer, but the company he founded is still going strong.

WORK PERKS

The work culture in Silicon Valley is intense, driven, and often very stressful. In order to keep their employees from burning out, many Silicon Valley companies offer unique work environments and perks, such as free meals and extra vacation. Others take things up a notch. At Facebook, employees can jog a mile-long path on the roof of their building. At Amazon, some workers are allowed to bring their pets with them to work. Tired Google employees are welcome to relax, work, or even snooze in the company's Nap Pods.

COLORADO

Colorado got its name from Spanish explorers, who noticed a river there that was muddy and red. It was *de color rojo*. Over time, the name applied to the whole area, and was pronounced *Colorado*.

Colorado's nickname, the Centennial State, comes from the year it became a state: 1876. This was 100 years after the United States became a country.

FAST FACTS

Admitted to the Union:
August 1, 1876

State Number: **38**

Population: **5.8 million**

Capital: **Denver**

Nickname: **The Centennial State**

State Animal:
Rocky Mountain bighorn sheep

CLIFF DWELLINGS

Tucked away in Colorado's Mesa Verde National Park are some 600 cliff dwellings. These structures were built by a group of people called the Anasazi, or ancestral Puebloans. Many are small stone dwellings. But others are large, multi-story villages that seem to grow right out of cliffsides. The largest, Cliff Palace, has 150 rooms.

The cliff dwellings were built around the year 1200 CE. Then, only about 100 years later, it seems that the ancestral Puebloans abandoned their cliffside homes. Archaeologists aren't sure why.

CONTINENTAL DIVIDE

A continental divide is a boundary that divides the direction in which water drains on a continent. One of North America's continental divides runs through Colorado. On the eastern side of the divide, water drains toward the Gulf of Mexico and Atlantic and Arctic Oceans. On the western side, water goes toward the Pacific Ocean.

Some of the most adventurous athletes hike the Continental Divide Trail. This is a 3,100-mi (5,000-km) rugged path that follows the continental divide from the border of Mexico to the border of Canada. It takes an average of six months to complete the trail by foot. About 740 mi (1,190 km) of the trail are in Colorado.

ADVENTUROUS LANDSCAPES

Colorado has deserts, valleys, grassy plains, and lots and lots of mountains. Home to much of the Rocky Mountain range, Colorado is a winter sports paradise. Skiers, snowboarders, and snowmobilers all flock to the state in search of fun. Winter hotspot Aspen Snowmass gets about 300 in (762 cm) of snow each year. Breckenridge does even better, with about 350 in (889 cm) annually.

The spring doesn't mean the end of Colorado's outdoor fun. Outdoor adventurers hike, mountain bike, horseback ride, and whitewater raft. For the feeling of whipping down a mountainside on a warm summer day, many turn to alpine slides. These are long, smooth tracks people zip down on special sleds. The state's longest alpine slide is found in Winter Park. It's 3,000 ft (914 m) of winding, zooming fun.

AMERICA THE BEAUTIFUL

In 1893, a poet named Katherine Lee Bates journeyed to the top of Colorado's Pikes Peak. It was a difficult climb. She began in a horse-drawn carriage and then switched to a mule. When she finally arrived at the peak, the view was beautiful. She was so inspired that she wrote a poem called "America." It was published in 1895. Bates made some changes to it in 1904 and 1913, and the poem was shared far and wide. Americans began singing the poem to different tunes, such as "Auld Lang Syne." Eventually, the poem was officially paired with the melody we use today, Samuel Augustus Ward's "Materna." Today, the poem is known by the name "America the Beautiful."

WEATHER

Colorado has four distinct seasons. Its summers are hot and dry and its winters are cold and very snowy. Spring and fall in Colorado are often mild.

ROCKY MOUNTAINS

Stretching from Canada all the way down to New Mexico, the Rocky Mountains include about 100 separate mountain ranges and pass through seven different states. They are usually divided into four major groups: the Southern Rockies, the Colorado Plateau, the Middle Rockies, and the Canadian and Northern Rockies.

The Rockies include some of America's most amazing sights, such as the second highest peak in the lower 48 states, Mount Elbert. It is 14,433 ft (4,399 m) tall. The sprawling mountains are home to nine national parks and dozens of national forests.

SUPERVOLCANO

Yellowstone National Park sits on top of something big, hot, and powerful. Bubbling hot springs on the surface and frequent earthquakes give hints of what it is: a supervolcano. It has had three major eruptions: one 2.1 million years ago, another 1.2 million years ago, and lastly one 640,000 years ago. Each eruption left a huge crater, or caldera, on the Earth's surface. The biggest is the Yellowstone Caldera, which is about 45 mi wide by 30 mi long (72 km wide by 48 km long).

Scientists know that the Yellowstone supervolcano will erupt again, but they don't know when. They use sensitive equipment to monitor the land for earthquakes, changes in volcanic gases, and ground movement.

SAND DUNES

Nestled among the Rocky Mountains are towering mountains of sand. Colorado's Great Sand Dunes National Park features rolling hills of sand as far as the eye can see. The main dune field is like a 30-sq-mi (77-sq-km) sandbox, where visitors can play to their heart's content. One popular activity is sand sledding. Thrill-seekers strap their feet into sandboards, or sit on sand sleds, and then zoom down. Especially brave sledders can even tackle the tallest dune in North America, Star Dune, which is 750 ft (228 m) tall.

MOOSE

The Rocky Mountains provide a habitat for many different types of animals, from bobcats to bighorn sheep. The biggest animals found in the Rockies are moose. Male moose, called bulls, are an average of 7 ft (2.1 m) tall at their shoulder and weigh around 1,500 lb (680 kg). Their antlers can grow up to 6 ft (1.8 m) across.

PIKES PEAK

Pikes Peak is a 14,115-ft (4,302-m) peak near Colorado Springs. Each year, about a half million tourists climb, ride, or drive to the top. There, on especially clear days, they can take the time to enjoy views of five states: Nebraska, Kansas, New Mexico, Oklahoma, and Wyoming.

Some prefer to take in the sights at Pikes Peak at a different pace. Each year, speedy drivers battle it out in the Pikes Peak International Hill Climb. This automobile race takes place on a 12.42-mi (19.9-km) stretch of winding, climbing, and twisting public toll road. In 2018, French racer Romain Dumas earned the course's fastest time ever. He made it to the top in seven minutes and 57 seconds. In comparison, the average, non-racing driver needs about one to three hours to make the trip.

GLACIERS

Some of the Rocky Mountains' most striking landforms were shaped by glaciers millions of years ago. These huge sheets of ice moved slowly over time, grinding down valleys and tearing rocks from mountainsides.

Glacier National Park, located in Montana, features 1,580 sq mi (4,000 sq km) of glacier-carved landscape. It also includes 26 actual glaciers. Scientists and park administrators alike urge people to come see the glaciers soon. They are shrinking because of climate change. They may not be here much longer. Already, the park has lost over 100 glaciers in the last 100 years to warming temperatures.

CONNECTICUT

The name Connecticut comes from the Algonquin word *quinnitukqut*, which means "at the long tidal river." This was the name given to the river there. It was a fitting one. The Connecticut River is the longest river in New England. It is 410 mi (660 km) long. It passes through New Hampshire, Vermont, Massachusetts, and Connecticut. Over time, the name Connecticut became the term used for the land around the river as well.

AN AMERICAN FIRST

Connecticut's nickname, the Constitution State, comes from a document written in 1638–9 called the Fundamental Orders of Connecticut. It gave the Connecticut colony a framework for government, and it is sometimes considered the United States' first written constitution.

FAST FACTS

Admitted to the Union:
January 9, 1788

State Number: **5**

Population: **3.6 million**

Capital: **Hartford**

Nickname:
The Constitution State

State Animal:
Sperm whale

About 60 percent
of Connecticut
is forested.

LANDSCAPE AND WEATHER

Connecticut has a varied landscape. To the west, there are steep hills. The state's highest point, part of Mount Frissell, is in the very northwesternmost corner. In the middle of the state are ridges, valleys, and the Connecticut River. In the east are more hillsides. The state's southern edge is coastline along the Long Island Sound. Though the landscape differs from region to region, you can count on one thing nearly anywhere you go in Connecticut: trees.

Connecticut has warm summers and cold, snowy winters. The northwestern part of the state can get 60 to 75 in (150 to 190 cm) of snow each year. This gives winter sports fans plenty of snow for skiing, snowshoeing, and sledding. Mountain climbers don't have to hang up their gear during the winter season. Instead, they climb ice! Winter in Connecticut is an ice climber's dream, with many frozen waterfalls and icy peaks.

PEOPLE

Connecticut is the fourth most densely populated state. Unlike other states with a few big, crowded cities, Connecticut's population is spread across the state.

While the state has churned out professional athletes, politicians, actors, fashion designers, musicians, and more, it also has a great history of raising children's book authors. Here are some writers who lived in Connecticut:

Suzanne Collins: *The Hunger Games* series.
Maurice Sendak: *Where the Wild Things Are* and many more.
Mark Twain: *The Adventures of Tom Sawyer* amongst many.
Stephenie Meyer: the *Twilight* series.

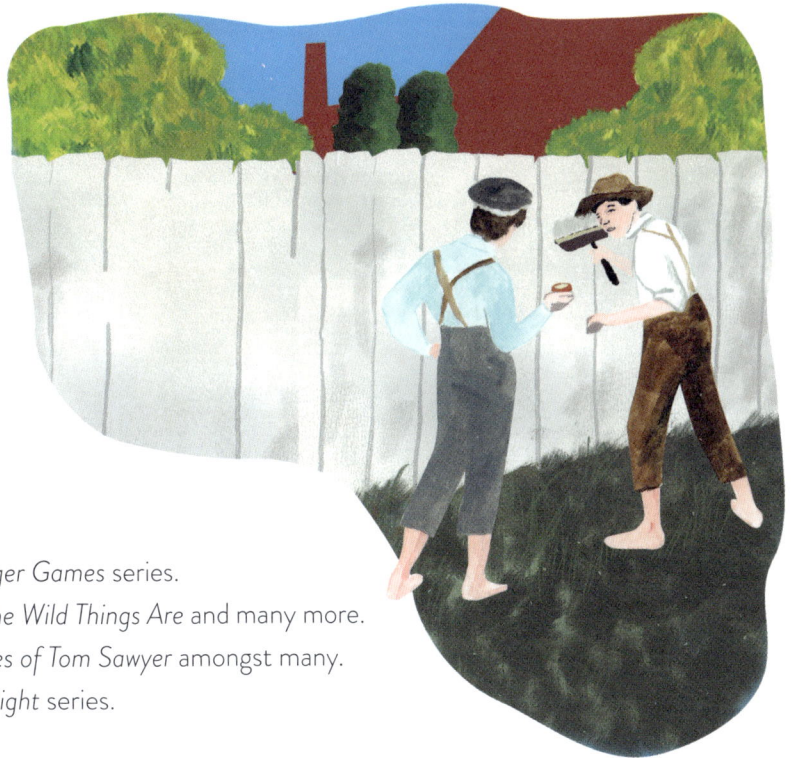

WALK LIKE A DINOSAUR

The Connecticut River Valley is a dinosaur-lover's dream. More dinosaur tracks, or footprints, have been discovered here than any other place in the world. These fossilized remains teach people about the way dinosaurs lived and moved.

In 1966, a Connecticut construction crew found a set of tracks in a slab of sandstone. They investigated the area and found 2,000 tracks. These probably came from a dinosaur such as *Dilophosaurus* that lived 200 million years ago. The area was turned into Dinosaur State Park. A large dome was erected over the tracks. Today, visitors can go to the park, learn about dinosaurs, and even make their own dinosaur footprint cast.

DELAWARE

Delaware was named after Thomas West, Lord De La Warr (Delaware). He was the governor of Virginia in 1610, when an explorer named Samuel Argall visited the area and named it in his honor.

BREAKING FREE FROM PENNSYLVANIA

Delaware used to be part of Pennsylvania. This lasted until June 15, 1776, when the Lower Counties of Pennsylvania voted for freedom from both England and Pennsylvania and became Delaware.

Delaware is the second-smallest state, following Rhode Island. At its narrowest, it is only 9 mi (14.5 km) wide.

SANDCASTLES

Each fall, teams of artists and amateurs alike head to Rehoboth Beach for the Annual Sandcastle Contest. The rules are simple: the sculptures must be handmade, and consist only of natural materials found at the beach. Carvings of castles, animals, people, and more stun onlookers and wow judges.

WEATHER

Delaware has a humid and moderate climate. In the summer, the temperature averages 74 °F (23.3 °C). In the winter, temperatures drop to the 30s °F (0°C). The state's nearness to the ocean impacts the weather there. In the summer, Delaware's coast is cooler than the rest of the state. In the winter, it's warmer near the water.

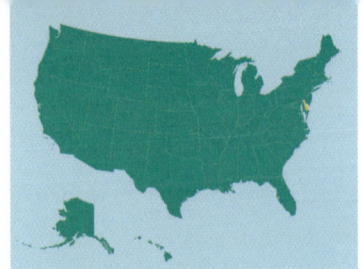

LANDSCAPE

Delaware is on the Delmarva Peninsula, a landform named after the three states occupying it: Delaware, Maryland, and Virginia. It has a 23-mi (37-km) stretch of coastline along the Delaware Bay, and an additional 7 mi (11 km) of Atlantic Ocean beaches.

Running across the state's northern neck is the Chesapeake and Delaware Canal. This waterway was finished in 1829 to shorten the distance from the Atlantic Ocean to Baltimore, Maryland. Rather than sailing all the way around the bottom of the Delmarva Peninsula, ships could cut right through. At first, the canal was privately owned. In 1919, the US government bought it and made it a toll-free waterway. Over the years, the Canal has been deepened and widened to allow for bigger ships to pass through.

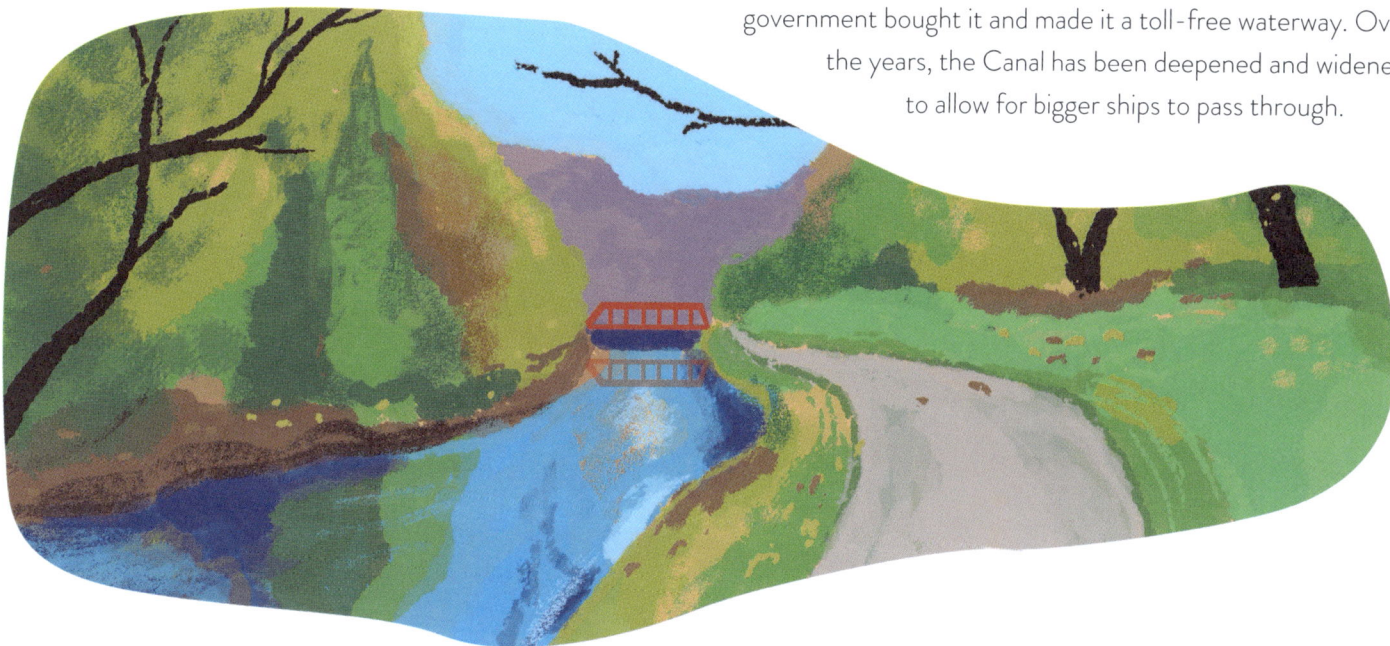

MILES THE MONSTER

NASCAR, Indie Racing League, and United States Auto Club drivers come to the Dover International Speedway to whip around its 1-mi (1.6-km) concrete oval track. But first, they have to get past Miles the Monster, the speedway's giant concrete mascot. Miles is 46 ft (14 m) tall and weighs 20 tons. His glowing eyes can be seen from half a mile away.

Delaware is a very low-lying state. It has an average elevation of just 60 ft (18 m) above sea level. The highest point in the state, an area off of Ebright Road near the Pennsylvania border, is only 448 ft (137 m) high.

BUSINESS ZONE

Delaware might be small in size, but it's big in business. A set of unique tax laws make Delaware an attractive location for companies to incorporate. About 1.5 million companies are currently incorporated in Delaware. That means there are more incorporated businesses than people!

One small building in Wilmington, Delaware is especially important to the business world. Over 300,000 companies are registered there, including Walmart, Apple, and eBay.

MONEY

The story of American money is as unique as the story of the country itself. This collection of currency tells a fantastic tale of invention and creativity.

THE FIRST AMERICAN MONEY

At first, colonists used English, German, and Spanish money in America. Coins called the Spanish dollar were very popular. To make change, colonists simply cut the Spanish dollars into halves, quarters, eighths, or sixteenths. After the Revolutionary War, each of the new American states made their own coins. For a while, American money was a mashup of different state coins, British coins, and cut-up Spanish coins. It was very confusing.

In 1792, the United States Mint was formed. This was a central location that produced all the money for America. The first money produced for the new country was a large copper coin worth one cent. Other coins that followed were copper half cents, silver half dimes, dimes, quarters, half dollars, and dollars. The mint produced gold coins, too, including quarter eagles worth $2.50, half eagles worth $5, and eagles worth $10.

> Foreign coins were accepted as currency in America until 1857.

PAPER OR FABRIC?

Bank notes or bills are often called paper money, but they are not made from paper. American bills are actually made from fabric. They are 75 percent cotton and 25 percent linen, with tiny bits of red and blue fibers woven into it. This fabric is tough and long lasting.

> In 2017, an American one-cent coin minted in 1793 sold at auction for $940,000.

COUNTERFEIT

From its earliest days, American paper money has been designed to be hard to fake, or counterfeit. In colonial times, founding father Benjamin Franklin created complicated designs for bills that included natural elements, such as molds of leaves, because they would be hard to copy. In the 1860s, cameras made it easy for some criminals to take photographs of money and pass the pictures off as the real thing. At the time, cameras could only take black and white images. So, the US Mint printed its dollar bills with green and black ink on one side. Counterfeiters could not reproduce the color.

The nickname "Greenbacks" comes from these early bills.

Time and technology have made counterfeiting harder than ever. Today, American paper money is loaded with clever tricks and subtle elements designed to trick counterfeiters.

For example, the $100 bill has the following protections:

DOLLAR SIGNS

The dollar sign probably developed from an abbreviation for Spanish pesos. In the late 1700s, Spanish pesos were used as a standard unit of value. When Americans noted pesos, they wrote "Ps," often placing the S over the P. As time passed, this symbol evolved into what we now recognize as the modern dollar sign.

BILLIONAIRES

There are 724 billionaires living in America, more than any other country in the world. The three richest Americans are Jeff Bezos, Elon Musk, and Mark Zuckerberg.

POVERTY

About 11 percent of Americans live in poverty. This means that they do not earn enough money to pay for housing, food, and other essential needs.

Serial numbers

Security thread

Security ribbon

Color-shifting ink

Watermark

FLORIDA

A Spanish explorer named Juan Ponce de Leon is credited with naming this state. He first arrived there in 1513 during the Easter season, which is called Pascua Florida in Spanish and means "feast of flowers." This, in combination with the lush flowers he saw there, made Florida the perfect name.

HISTORY

People first arrived in Florida about 12,000 years ago. At the time, the sea level was much lower than it is today. This meant that the land of Florida extended far into the water. In fact, Florida's peninsula today is only half the size it was back then. This vast land wasn't empty. It was bustling with plants, animals, and many now-extinct creatures, such as mastodons, saber-toothed tigers, and giant camels.

The first people who lived in Florida were hunters and gatherers. Over time, they developed ways to farm and formed complicated civilizations. They traveled in canoes, made pottery, and created ceremonial spaces. When Juan Ponce de Leon came to Florida, there were hundreds of thousands of Native people living there. After his arrival, more Europeans came to the area. Over time, Spain, France, and Great Britain would all battle for control of Florida.

LANDSCAPE

Florida is the southernmost of all the 48 mainland states. On the east side of its peninsula is the Atlantic Ocean. The west side is hugged by the Gulf of Mexico. To the south are the Straits of Florida. All this coastline means Florida has some of the country's most incredible beaches.

Though all of Florida is very low—most of the state is just 100 ft (30 m) above sea level—its landscape is still quite varied. In the northern part of the state are hills, including Florida's highest peak, Britton Hill, which is 345 ft (105 m) high. Most of the southern parts of the state are low and swampy.

OVERSEAS HIGHWAY

The Florida Keys are a group of 1,700 islands located off the southern tip of the state. People who want to easily travel between the islands don't have to take a plane or boat. They can simply drive along the Overseas Highway, a 113-mi (182-km) roadway that stretches from Key Largo to Key West, including a jaw-dropping 42 bridges.

WEATHER

Tourists flock to Florida year-round for its beaches, resorts, and beautiful weather. Florida boasts an average high temperature of 79 °F (26.1 °C), with a low of 58 °F (14.4 °C).

DISNEY WORLD

Disney World opened in Florida in 1971. Today, it includes four theme parks, two water parks, and dozens of hotels, spas, golf courses, and other attractions. About 52 million people visit Disney World each year. To handle such large crowds while still keeping the parks magical, Disney designers had to get very creative. Here are some of their most innovative ideas:

- In Disney's Magic Kingdom, employees travel via a system of tunnels called "the utilidors" under the park. This prevents visitors from seeing them outside of their designated stations.

- Guests in Disney World are never more than 30 steps from a garbage can.

- Disney World bathrooms do not include mirrors over the sinks. This keeps traffic moving through the restrooms quickly.

- Gum can stain pathways and ruin other park items. That is why there is no gum sold at Disney World.

- Wait times posted for rides are usually incorrect on purpose. Disney staff overestimate the wait times by five or ten minutes to give riders a feeling of gratitude when the line moves faster than they expected.

GEORGIA

Georgia became the 13th and final British colony in 1733. It was named after King George II, who gave the colony permission to form the year before.

HISTORY

Early people came to Georgia as long as 13,000 years ago. Over time, many Native groups thrived on the land. Evidence of their rich history is found throughout the state. In Fort Mountain State Park, an 855-ft (261-m) rock wall hints at a sophisticated group of people who built it sometime between 500 BCE and 500 CE. Historians aren't sure what its purpose was. It might have been related to defense, or perhaps part of a ceremony. However it was used, one thing is clear: it took a lot of work to construct.

OKEFENOKEE SWAMP

Straddling the border between Florida and Georgia is the Okefenokee Swamp, the largest swamp in North America. Roughly 40 mi (65 km) long and 25 mi (40 km) wide, this vast, wet region includes a variety of features, such as marshes and savannas. There are also islands called hummocks.

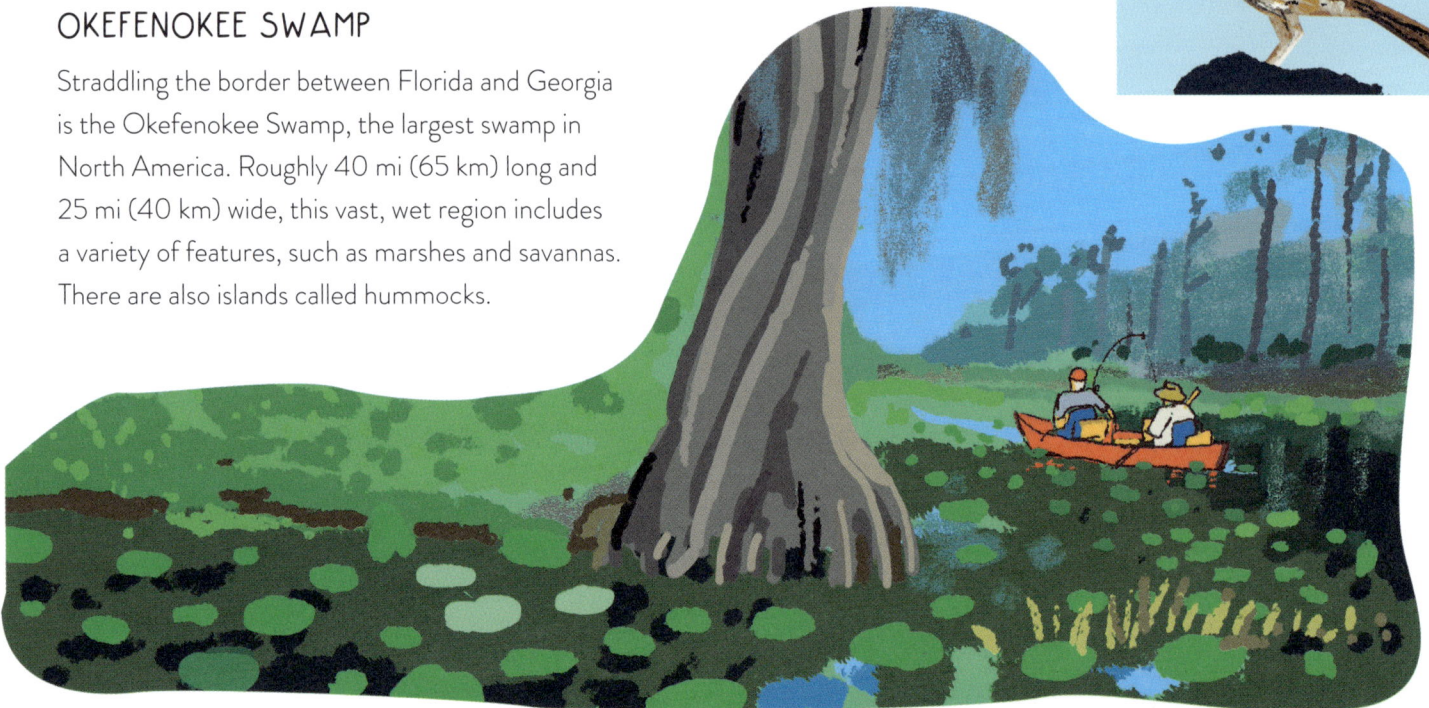

Visitors can explore dry trails on foot or they can see the swamp from canoes, kayaks, or guided boat tours. Amazing animals are found throughout the swamp, including gopher tortoises, beautiful sandhill cranes, and American alligators.

FAST FACTS

Admitted to the Union:
January 2, 1788

State Number: **4**

Population: **10.6 million**

Capital: **Atlanta**

Nickname:
The Peach State

State Bird:
Brown thrasher

Georgia is the nation's largest producer of peanuts, pecans, and poultry. It also grows plenty of peaches, which is how it got its nickname.

GREAT HEIGHTS AND DEEP CAVES

Northern Georgia is home to the Appalachian Plateau and the southern edge of the Blue Ridge Mountains. It is also where the state's highest peak, Brasstown Bald, 4,784 ft (1,458 m), is found.

In addition to its towering peaks, northern Georgia also has some very deep caves. Found in northwestern Georgia is Ellison's Cave, home to the Fantastic Pit. This is the deepest unobstructed underground pit in all of North America, with a depth of 586 ft (178 m). Because of its extreme nature, only experienced cavers can explore the Fantastic Pit.

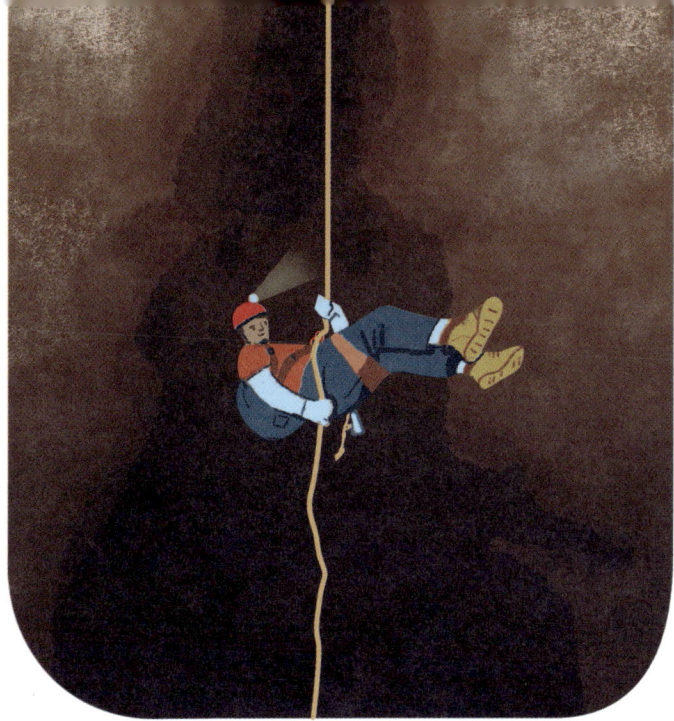

> ## "I have a dream
> *that one day on the red hills of Georgia, the sons of former slaves and the sons of former slave owners will be able to sit down together at the table of brotherhood.* "
>
> *MARTIN LUTHER KING, JR.*

Coca-Cola was invented in Atlanta, Georgia in 1886.

MARTIN LUTHER KING, JR.

In 1929, civil rights leader Martin Luther King, Jr. was born in Atlanta, Georgia. He spent much of his life working to change the way people of color were treated. In 1963, he delivered one of the most famous speeches in American history at the March on Washington for Jobs and Freedom. About 250,000 people listened as he proclaimed, "I have a dream." He spoke about his vision for an equal, fair future. King was assassinated in 1968.

WEATHER

Georgia has hot, humid summers, with temperatures regularly climbing into the 90s °F (32–37 °C). The state has short, mild winters. During January, the state's coldest month, temperatures hover around 50 °F (10 °C).

AMERICAN SPORTS

America is home to some of the world's most beloved professional sports leagues. Players on these teams are paid to compete on an elite stage, and win the hearts of fans at the same time.

PROFESSIONAL LEAGUES

Top performing professional teams and athletes strive to make it into championship events. For football, this means getting to the Superbowl. For baseball, the World Series is the top event. Hockey teams shoot for the Stanley Cup, and golfers aim for the Masters. Some events are open to international competitors. For example, the US Open is the world's top tennis event, and the World Cup is the biggest competition for soccer teams around the globe.

These are some of the main professional leagues and organizations:

- Major League Baseball (MLB)
- National Football League (NFL)
- National Hockey League (NHL)
- National Basketball Association (NBA)
- Women's National Basketball Association (WNBA)
- Women's Tennis Association (WTA)
- Association of Tennis Professionals (ATP)
- Major League Soccer (MLS)
- National Women's Soccer League (NWSL)
- Professional Golf Association (PGA)
- Ladies Professional Golf Association (LPGA)

Football's Superbowl is often the most viewed event in America. In 2023, 113 million people watched the Kansas City Chiefs beat the Philadelphia Eagles, 38–35.

Advertisers pay big for coveted Superbowl air time. In 2023, 30-second Superbowl ads cost more than $6 million.

RIVALRIES

Rivalries often pop up between two teams who are from the same state, who have a long history of competition, or who are fighting for the same prize. Devoted sports fans sometimes take these rivalries personally, feeling that their team *must* beat their opponent. Some of America's most famous rivalries are decades old, including:

- **Army vs. Navy:** This football rivalry dates back to 1890, when Navy beat Army 24–0.

- **Yankees vs. Red Sox:** This baseball rivalry began when star player Babe Ruth was traded from the Red Sox to the Yankees in 1919.

- **Lakers vs. Celtics:** These basketball rivals have faced off 12 times in the NBA finals. Adding to their rivalry is the fact that they're currently tied for the highest number of NBA Championships. Each team has 17.

Collecting baseball cards is a popular American hobby. Some cards are very valuable. In 2021, a Honus Wagner card sold for $6.6 million.

PITTSBURG

SIMONE BILES

Simone Biles has won 37 Olympic and World Championship medals. She is the most decorated American gymnast, and has been called the greatest gymnast of all time.

COLLEGE SPORTS

Most professional athletes get their start playing in college leagues. Some of the country's favorite sporting events are played on the collegiate level, including:

- Basketball's March Madness

- Football's Bowl Games, including the Rose Bowl, Fiesta Bowl, Orange Bowl, Cotton Bowl, and Sugar Bowl

- Baseball's College World Series

- Soccer's College Cup

- Hockey's Frozen Four

MONEY

Top athletes can make huge paychecks in America, especially when they combine their salaries with sponsorship deals. Here are some of the country's top earning athletes:

1. Michael Jordan
This basketball star has netted $2 billion.

2. Tiger Woods
This golf star has earned $1.1 billion.

3. Floyd Mayweather
This boxing star has made $450 million.

4. Serena Williams
This tennis star has earned over $200 million in prizes and sponsorships.

HAWAII

The name Hawaii probably comes from a Native word for "homeland," pronounced *Owhyhee*.

HISTORY

Hawaii was the last state to join the Union, but it has a rich, colorful history that stretches back about 1,500 years. Hawaii was first populated by people who traveled in canoes from the Marquesas Islands. Later, people from Tahiti came as well.

In 1898, Hawaii became a United States territory. Statehood followed 61 years later.

Iolani Palace, in Honolulu, Oahu, is the only royal palace in all of America. It is evidence of Hawaii's monarchy, an institution that began in 1795 and ended in 1893.

FAST FACTS

Admitted to the Union:
August 21, 1959

State Number: **50**

Population: **1.4 million**

Capital: **Honolulu**

Nickname:
The Aloha State

State Mammal:
Hawaiian monk seal

136 ISLANDS

Hawaii is made up of 136 islands, but only seven are inhabited: Oahu, Hawai'i (also called the Big Island), Maui, Kauai, Molokai, Lanai, and Ni'ihau. One island, Ni'ihau, is owned by a private family. They purchased the island from King Kamehameha V in 1864 for $10,000. When the disease polio broke out on the other Hawaiian Islands in the 1950s, travel to Ni'ihau was mostly forbidden. The travel ban worked, and polio did not spread to Ni'ihau. The ban also got Ni'ihau its nickname: the Forbidden Island. Today, tourism there is still very limited and restrictive. This means that Ni'ihau has been beautifully preserved.

Kauai's Mount Waialeale is one of the wettest places on Earth. Each year, it gets around 450 in (11,430 mm) of rain.

VOLCANOES

The Hawaiian Islands were formed when hot magma burst through the Earth's crust as lava then cooled to form rock. At first, this formed layers deep under the ocean. Over time, the layers built up and rose above the water. This process gradually built the islands into their current form.

Today, the Hawaiian Islands are still active volcanic sites. Each is made up of at least one volcano. The Big Island is made up of five, and is home to the biggest active volcano on Earth, Mauna Loa.

SURF'S UP

Hawaii is one of the planet's top surfing destinations. In Hawaiian, surfing is called *he'e nalu*. This means "wave sliding." The islands have plenty of surf spots for beginners, but it's the pros who come to the islands to compete and shine. The Eddie Aikau Big Wave International is an invitation-only surf competition on Oahu's north shore. Organizers only allow the competition to begin when the ocean conditions are absolutely perfect, and the waves are at least 20 ft (6 m) high. This gives pro surfers plenty of wave to show their skills. The contest is named after Eddie Aikau, a legendary surfer and lifeguard who died during a volunteer mission.

ALOHA SPIRIT

Aloha is a Hawaiian word that means many things: hello, goodbye, love, compassion, and peace. In 1986, Hawaiian lawmakers passed the Aloha Spirit law. It says that Hawaiians must act with Aloha. This means that they must show compassion, respect, and affection to all people.

LANGUAGES

Hawaii is the only state with two official languages: English and Hawaiian. The Hawaiian alphabet has 12 letters: A, E, H, I, K, L, M, N, O, P, U, W, and a symbol called an *'okina*. The *'okina* is represented with an apostrophe. It tells the speaker to make a glottal stop, or pause, much as they would when saying "uh oh." Sometimes Hawaiian writers use a marker called a *kahakō* to tell the speaker to elongate a sound, such as the "ah" in *kāne* (male). The letter W often has a V sound. In this way, the word Hawaii is pronounced ha-VAH-ee.

Tourism is Hawaii's biggest industry. Each year, about 10 million visitors come to the islands to swim, golf, and explore.

Pidgin, a language that combines Hawaiian, English, Portuguese, Chinese, and Japanese, is spoken by about 600,000 Hawaiians.

WEATHER

Hawaii is famous for its pleasant, tropical weather. Temperatures typically range between 75 and 90 °F (24–32 °C) during the day. However, with its towering volcanic peaks, there are some spots in Hawaii that experience more extreme weather. The coldest temperature ever recorded there was on Mauna Kea in 1979. It was just 12 °F (-11.1 °C) at the peak.

IDAHO

The word Idaho doesn't mean anything.
A Philadelphia-born man named George Willing made it up.

A NEW HISTORY

Archaeologists used to think that the earliest humans came to North America about 14,000 years ago. A discovery in Idaho turned that theory upside down. At a site in the northwestern part of the state called Cooper's Ferry, archaeologists discovered tools, animal bones, and charcoal. Tests showed that these items were at least 16,000 years old. This discovery changed the way anthropologists think about human history in North America.

40 percent of Idaho is forested.

FAST FACTS

Admitted to the Union:
July 3, 1890

State Number: **43**

Population: **1.9 million**

Capital: **Boise**

Nickname:
The Gem State

State Amphibian:
Idaho giant salamander

LEWIS AND CLARK

While on their epic trek across the country, Meriweather Lewis and William Clark crossed into Idaho in 1805. The explorers traveled through some of Idaho's most rugged terrain, including the Bitterroot Mountains. Their experiences in the mountains were among the most difficult of their entire journey. They were cold, lost, and starving. Fortunately, a village of Nez Perce Indians helped the explorers, enabling them to pass through the state and continue toward the coast.

POTATOES AND MORE

Idaho is the nation's leading potato producer, cranking out one-third of America's spuds. Varieties like Yukon, Russet, and of course, Idaho are always crowd-pleasers.

Potatoes aren't Idaho's only crop. Wheat, barley, sugarbeets, and onions also thrive on the state's rich soil.

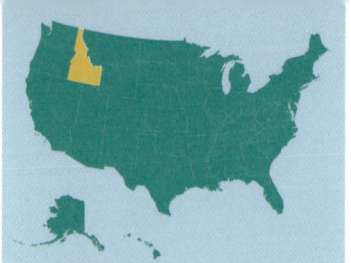

IDAHO
POTATOES

TERRAIN

Idaho's shape is often described as looking like a logger's boot. The Rocky Mountains pass through the upper part of the boot. Idaho's highest point, Borah Peak, is located just south of where the boot might lace. It is 12,662 ft (3,859 m) high.

The Snake River runs from the heel of the boot to its toe. At the state's western border, the river passes through the deepest gorge in North America, Hells Canyon. It is 7,900 ft (2,407 m) deep, nearly 2,000 ft (609 m) deeper than the Grand Canyon.

In southwestern Idaho is the Owyhee Desert. This region of canyons, cliffs, swift rivers, and gorges is sometimes called "the Big Quiet." This is because the region is undeveloped and remote.

WEATHER

Idaho summers are hot, dry, and fairly short. Temperatures often climb into the 90s ° F (32–37 °C) during July and August. In the winters, Idahoans know to expect temperatures in the 20s, 10s, or even lower (-6 to -12 °C), and plenty of snow. The coldest temperature ever recorded in Idaho happened in Island Park Dam in 1943, when thermometers hit -60 °F (-51 °C).

A SKIING PARADISE

Idaho's snowy winters and legendary mountains make it an ideal place to ski. Visitors to the state have 18 ski resorts to choose between, each with unique slopes, lifts, and other attractions.

Idaho skiers made history in 1936, when the Sun Valley ski resort became the first institution to use an alpine chair lift. A ticket to ride the lift cost $0.25. Today, an adult chairlift ticket costs about $160.

ILLINOIS

The name Illinois comes from the Miami-Peoria name *irenweewa*, which means he or she who speaks in the regular way. Over time, French and Ojibwe speakers changed the pronunciation until it sounded like the modern word.

HISTORY

People first came to the land now called Illinois about 12,000 years ago. Much later, an area in southern Illinois became a center for the Middle Mississippian culture. Remains of this busy hub can be found at Cahokia, a complex of raised earthen mounds.

In the 1600s, French explorers came to Illinois. They built forts and missions. In 1717, Illinois became part of the French colony. This history is reflected today in the many cities with French names, such as Des Plaines, Joliet, and Creve Coeur.

WINDY CITY

Illinois' most famous city, Chicago, is often called the Windy City. The source of this nickname isn't very clear. Some people think it has to do with the fierce winds that come off of nearby Lake Michigan. Others point to the city's long-winded politicians, a group said to be "full of hot air."

FAST FACTS

Admitted to the Union:
December 3, 1818

State Number: **21**

Population: **12.7 million**

Capital: **Springfield**

Nickname:
The Prairie State

State Animal:
White-tailed deer

COMEDY

Chicago is famous for producing many popular things: deep dish pizza, the Bulls, and Chicago-style hotdogs. However, perhaps the most important things to come out of the city are its jokes. Chicago has given the world some of its most beloved comedians.

Many of these jokesters got their start at Chicago's famed Second City comedy theater. Such stars as Tina Fey, Amy Poehler, Chris Farley, Stephen Colbert, and Steve Carell worked their way through Second City's ranks before moving on to Hollywood, Saturday Night Live, or other high-profile gigs.

Illinois experiences very cold winters, very hot summers, and everything in between. The state also has its fair share of extreme weather, including blizzards, floods, and tornadoes.

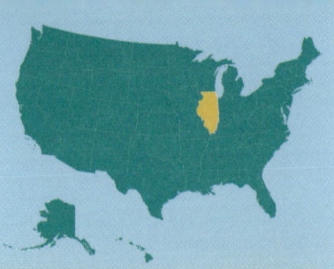

LANDSCAPE

Most of Illinois is made up of plains. In the northwest and southern parts of the states, some hilly areas can be found. Illinois' highest point, Charles Mound, 1,235 ft (376 m), is found in the state's northwestern corner. Shawnee National Forest is found in the southernmost part of the state. Nestled within the forest is an area called Garden of the Gods. Its striking rock formations, wilderness, and beautiful views make it one of Illinois' most photographed natural attractions.

About 75 percent of Illinois is made up of farmland. Most farms there produce crops such as corn and soybeans. Some farms raise cows and pigs.

THE CHICAGO RIVER

The Chicago River system is about 150 mi (241 km) long, flowing north, south, and west of Chicago. Originally, the river emptied into Lake Michigan. As the city grew more populated, debris and sewage began flowing down the river and into the lake. This tainted the city's drinking water. Officials decided to reverse the river's flow. The epic project took eight years and 8,500 workers to complete. In 1900, the river began pulling fresh water from Lake Michigan. This has been called one of the greatest engineering achievements of the millennium.

LAND OF LINCOLN

Though Abraham Lincoln was not born there, he lived in Illinois for 31 years. The city he spent the most time in was Springfield, Illinois. In 2005, the Abraham Lincoln Presidential Library and Museum opened in Springfield. It was the first major experience museum, inviting visitors to learn about history through artifacts, education, and immersive storytelling. Unique theaters and walk-through displays transport learners back through time.

Each year to celebrate St. Patrick's Day, the Chicago River is dyed green. City officials accomplish this by dumping 60 lb (27 kg) of a special dye nicknamed "Leprechaun Dust" into the water.

GREAT LAKES

America's Great Lakes make up the world's largest freshwater system. These massive lakes—Superior, Huron, Michigan, Erie, and Ontario—are found along the border between America and Canada.

LAKE SUPERIOR

LAKE HURON

LAKE ONTARIO

LAKE MICHIGAN

LAKE ERIE

SUPERIOR

Each of the Great Lakes are big, but Lake Superior is the biggest of all. It holds 10 percent of all of the Earth's freshwater, about three quadrillion gallons. If Lake Superior was dumped out, it could cover all of North and South America in one foot of water. Superior's surface area measures an amazing 31,700 sq mi (82,000 sq km), the largest of any freshwater lake on the planet. Superior is deep, too. At its deepest spot, its floor drops 1,333 ft (405 m). That's deep enough to cover four Statues of Liberty stacked on top of one another.

Lake Superior is famous for being clear. In particularly still spots, people can see through 100 ft (30.4 m) of its water.

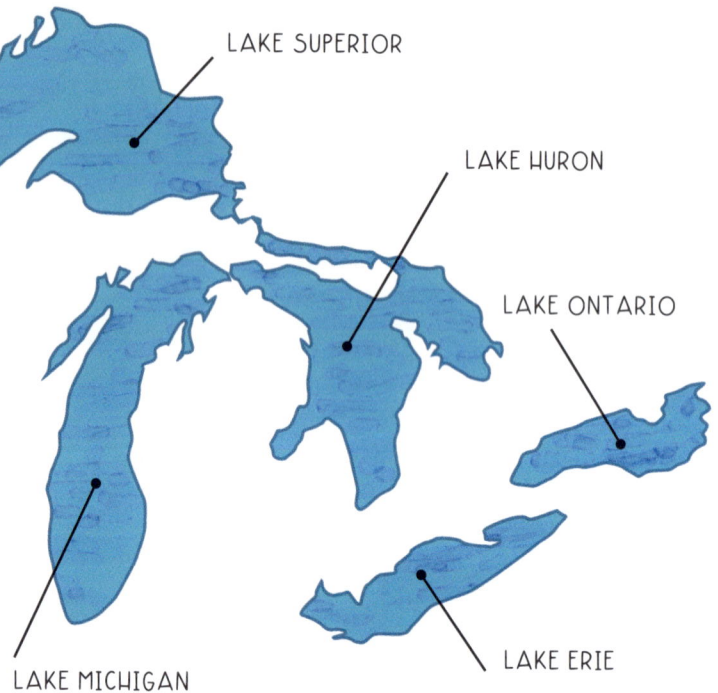

LAKE HURON

Lake Huron is the second biggest Great Lake, with a surface area of 23,000 sq mi (59,569 sq km). It is almost as big as West Virginia. The largest freshwater island in the world, Manitoulin Island, is found on the Canadian side of the lake.

Lake Huron has been the site of some incredible storms. In 1913, a storm called the "Big Blow" hit the lake. It caused 35-ft (10.6-m) waves and sank 10 ships, which led to the deaths of 235 sailors. In 1996, a huge cyclone formed over the lake. At its center was an 18-mi (29-km) eye.

LAKE MICHIGAN

Lake Michigan is the third biggest of the Great Lakes, and the only one that does not cross into Canada. About 12 million people (4 percent of the American population) live along its shoreline. Many of these people live in big cities like Chicago, Illinois, Green Bay and Milwaukee, Wisconsin, and Gary, Indiana. Others live in hundreds of small coastal towns.

Like the other Great Lakes, Lake Michigan can be a dangerous place. Harsh weather and huge waves can make it difficult to cross. However, one part of the lake seems to be especially treacherous. Named after the Bermuda Triangle, the Michigan Triangle is an area between Benton Harbor, Michigan; Luddington, Michigan; and Manitowoc, Wisconsin. Boats, ships, and even an entire airplane are said to have disappeared inside the Michigan Triangle. Other strange incidents have been reported, including blocks of ice falling from the sky and a ship captain mysteriously disappearing from inside his cabin.

LAKE ERIE

Lake Erie is the fourth largest of the Great Lakes. It's also the shallowest. The deepest point in the lake is only 210 ft (64 m). Lake Erie makes up only about 2 percent of all the water in the Great Lakes, but that doesn't seem to bother the wildlife there. About half of all the fish found in the Great Lakes live in Erie.

Like Scotland's Loch Ness, Lake Erie is said to have a sea monster of its own: Bessie. This long-necked beast was first sighted in 1793. People continue to see it today.

Pike

Bass

Trout

Salmon

Walleye

LAKE ONTARIO

The smallest of the Great Lakes, Ontario is still a treasure trove of freshwater, nature, and beautiful sights. About 1,800 islands dot the lake. The largest, Canada's Wolfe Island, has about 1,400 residents.

Many types of fish naturally live in Lake Ontario, including trout, salmon, pike, walleye, and bass. Humans have added other fish to the waters. Wildlife protection and management groups monitor shoals of enormous goldfish in Lake Ontario. These were former pets that were released into the lake. Without the restrictions of fish tanks, they have grown to the size of footballs.

INDIANA

Indiana probably got its name from the many Native, or Indian, tribes who lived on the land. Indiana's state motto is "The Crossroads of America." This references Indianapolis' location at the junction of several important interstate highways that connect the state to many different parts of the country.

HISTORY

In 1988, a construction crew building a road in southwest Indiana cut into a large earthen mound. Silver and copper items poured from the soil. The crew had discovered a sacred place created by the Hopewell people about 2,000 years ago. Archaeologists investigated, unearthing thousands of artifacts, including clay figurines and grizzly bear teeth. They also realized that the many rolling hills nearby were actually earthen mounds, built for burials or ceremonies. The site was named the Mann Site, after the farmer who owned the field. But its archaeological importance earned it a nickname: Indiana's Egypt.

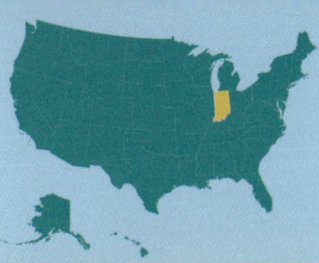

FAST FACTS

Admitted to the Union:
December 11, 1816

State Number: **19**

Population: **6.7 million**

Capital: **Indianapolis**

Nickname:
The Hoosier State

State Bird: **Northern cardinal**

LANDSCAPE

Indiana has a variety of landscapes, including rolling hills, sweeping plains, and winding rivers. At the southern edge of the state are steep hills and limestone formations, including caves. The middle of the state is marked by rolling gentle hills. At the northwestern edge of the state, just along the coast of Lake Michigan, are the Indiana Dunes. These mountains of sand are always shifting with the wind, growing taller or shorter. Visitors come to hike to the top of dunes such as Mount Baldy, which is usually about 125 ft (38 m), or Mount Tom, which is usually about 200 ft (60 m).

Indiana's state capital wasn't always Indianapolis. Up until 1825, it was a city called Corydon.

AGRICULTURE

There are more than 56,000 farms in Indiana. Corn and soybeans are two of the state's major crops. Indiana farmers also produce much of the country's pork, poultry, and eggs. In 2021, more than 10 billion eggs came out of the state.

THE UNDERGROUND RAILROAD'S GRAND CENTRAL STATION

The Underground Railroad was the name for a network of people who helped slaves move north toward freedom from the late 1700s until after the Civil War. A couple in Newport, Indiana (now Fountain City) were especially helpful in this effort. Levi and Catherine Coffin ushered about 1,000 runaway slaves through their home and onto freedom. Today, their home is a museum.

WEATHER

Indiana has four distinct seasons. The winters are cold and snowy, the springs are rainy and cool, the summers are hot and dry, and the falls are cool and wet. In the summer, the state is prone to tornadoes. In 1965, an event called the Palm Sunday Tornado Outbreak rocked the state. In one day, 47 tornadoes swept across several midwestern states, including Indiana.

AMAZING THINGS FROM INDIANA

- Gasoline pumps
- The Jackson 5
- Garfield the Cat
- The Coca-Cola bottle

AGRICULTURE

Farming crops and raising animals for food is a very important industry, and America takes it seriously. The United States is the world's second biggest producer of agricultural goods behind China.

TOP THREE

These are America's top agricultural products:

- Cattle and calves
- Corn
- Soybeans

HOLY COW

In a single day, an American dairy cow's milk can produce the following

4.8 lb (2.2 kg) of butter
OR
10.5 lb (4.8 kg) of cheese
OR
8.7 gal (33 l) of ice cream

BIG AND SMALL

There are about 2 million farms in America. Most are family owned and small, averaging about 435 acres. However, about 2 percent of farms in America are large-scale. These huge operations grow more than half of American farm goods.

The biggest farm in America covers 190,000 acres in California. It is owned by Stewart and Lydia Resnick, and it produces goods such as pistachios, almonds, and mandarin oranges.

On average, each American farm grows enough food to feed 165 people every year.

STATE-BY-STATE

Because the United States has such a wide variety of climates and landscapes, the products grown in each state are often quite different. Alaska produces about 60 per cent of the nation's seafood. North Dakota is America's biggest producer of honey. Idaho grows the most potatoes, Indiana produces the most ducks, and Michigan produces the most sour cherries.

California is America's leading state in agriculture, followed by Iowa, Nebraska, Texas, and Kansas.

ENVIRONMENTAL CONCERNS

Agriculture puts a big drain on the environment. From the water required to irrigate fields to the chemicals used to keep pests away, it is an industry that can be harmful to Earth's living things.

One way agriculture producers can help the environment is to farm organically. Organic farmers do not use synthetic fertilizers or chemical pesticides. Instead, they, use pesticides that come from natural sources and fertilizers made from animal waste. Some organic farmers also use natural methods to keep their crops healthy, such as encouraging predators to hunt pests in their fields, and planting their crops close together to discourage weeds from growing.

Organic goods are often more expensive than nonorganic. This is because organic farming often takes longer, or requires more work for the farmers. This isn't stopping people from buying organic. Sales of organic goods are growing, as is the number of organic farms on American soil. Today, there are over 16,000 organic farms in the United States.

A FARMER'S SCHEDULE

Each farmer's daily schedule will be slightly different, depending on the crop they raise and the season. However, all farmers work long and hard to produce their goods. Here is a schedule a dairy farmer might follow:

3:00 am: Wake up
3:30 am: Begin milking cows
6:15 am: Feed cows and refill water troughs
7:00 am: Eat breakfast
8:00 am: Care for calves; feed them, clean their stalls, change their water
11:00 am: Fill milk truck with the morning's milk
11:30 am: Check out cows and make sure they're all getting enough to eat
12:30 pm: Lunch
12:45 pm: Clean barn and machinery
1:45 pm: Team or family meeting to discuss any issues or tasks that need to be done
3:30 pm: Begin second milking
6:00 pm: Care for calves again; feed them, clean their stalls, change their water
7:15 pm: Dinner
8:00 pm: Bed
9:20 pm: A cow is giving birth! Watch and cheer her on
9:50 pm: Back to bed

IOWA

Like many states, Iowa takes its name from Native languages. The Dakota Indians used to call the Native people in Iowa the *ayuxba* (AH-you-khbah). This meant the "sleepy ones." Neighboring tribes changed the name to *Ayuway*. Over time, this became Ioway, or Iowa.

BETWEEN TWO RIVERS

Iowa is the only state that is bordered by two navigable rivers. On the west side of the state is the Big Sioux River, which joins the Missouri River. On the east side of the state is the Mississippi River.

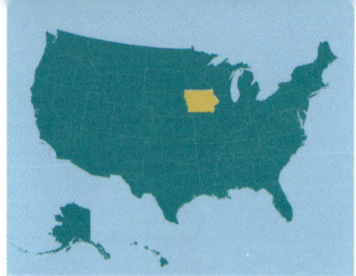

FAST FACTS

Admitted to the Union:
December 28, 1846

State Number: **29**

Population: **3.2 million**

Capital: **Des Moines**

Nickname: **The Hawkeye State**

State Bird:
American goldfinch

FARMING

Iowa is an important state for agriculture. About 90 percent of the land in Iowa is used for farming. Iowa is the country's leading producer of corn. Farmers measure their corn crop in bushels, and one bushel of corn weighs about 56 lb (25 kg). In 2020, farmers harvested almost 2.3 billion bushels of corn from Iowan fields.

Soybeans are another important Iowan crop. These beans can be used to make oil, for animal feed, and for foods humans eat as well. Soy milk, tofu, and miso are all made from soybeans.

Iowa is the nation's top producer of pork. There are about 24 million pigs being raised in the state. That means that pigs outnumber people in Iowa, seven to one!

FIELD OF DREAMS

Iowa's farm fields got the Hollywood treatment in the famous movie, *Field of Dreams*. In the film, the spirit of a baseball player asks, "Hey, is this heaven?" Actor Kevin Costner replies, "No. It's Iowa."

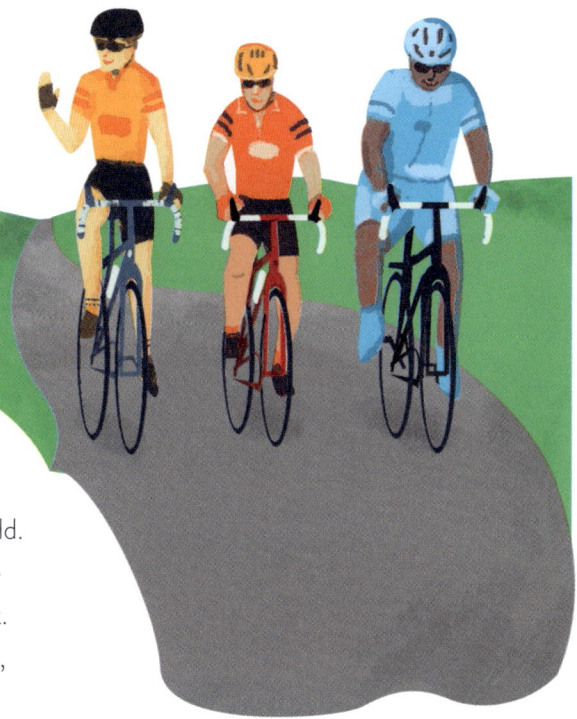

RAGBRAI

Each July, bicyclists gather on Iowa's western edge for an unusual event. It's RAGBRAI, a seven-day-long bike ride across the state. This event is the oldest and biggest recreational bike ride in the world. Though the route varies each year, it's always a long trek. Cyclists average 67 mi (107 km) per day, for a total of about 468 mi (753 km) in the week. Towns along the route make bikers feel welcome. Locals set up food stalls, entertainment, and places to stay overnight.

NOT SO FLAT

Iowa has a reputation for being as flat as a pancake. Because of this, many visitors are surprised to see the state's beautiful, rolling landscape. On the western edge of the state are many Loess (pronounced *luss*) Hills. These were formed over thousands of years when strong winds blew silt and sand from river beds into huge mounds. Over time, the mounds grew. Today, some of the Loess Hills and bluffs are as tall as 250 ft (76 m).

WEATHER EXTREMES

Iowa's weather is never boring. In the summer, the heat can be blistering. Daytime summer temperatures average above 80 °F (26 °C). In the winter, temperatures drop to the teens. Occasional floods and tornadoes keep Iowans on their toes—and glued to their weather apps!

INVENTIONS

Iowans are great inventors. The following items were dreamed up in Iowa:

Sliced bread, by Otto Frederick Rohwedder, 1927

The digital computer, by John Atanasoff and Clifford Berry, 1939-1942

Vending machines, by F.A. Wittern, 1931

Trampolines, by George Nissen and Larry Griswold, 1935

LANGUAGES

Pause on a New York subway or a Chicago El or a Los Angeles market and listen to the voices around you. You're likely to hear English. But you'll probably hear other languages as well: Polish, Spanish, Hebrew, Russian, or many others. The United States is an incredibly diverse country. People have come from all over the world to live there. This is reflected in the way people communicate with one another.

There are over 350 languages spoken in America. After English, the most commonly spoken language is Spanish. After that are Chinese (including Mandarin and Cantonese), Tagalog, and Vietnamese.

BILINGUAL AMERICANS

About 21 percent of Americans can speak more than one language. The most common language combination is English and Spanish. Being bilingual or multilingual is common in the country's biggest cities. In New York City, 49 percent of residents speak more than one language. In Los Angeles, 59 percent do.

While the numbers of bilingual Americans are growing each year, the country is still far behind many other nations that have officially recognized multiple languages. Nations such as Singapore, Switzerland, Moldova, and the Netherlands have four official languages. Serbia has seven. South Africa has 11, Zimbabwe has 16, India has 23, and Bolivia tops the list with 37.

SIGN LANGUAGE

Not all Americans hear. Deaf or hard of hearing Americans use American Sign Language (ASL). This is a visual language. ASL uses hands movements and positions, facial expressions, and body movements to communicate. Users can use signs to represent full words or ideas or they can spell things out using signs for each letter of the alphabet. ASL is used in America and parts of Canada. Other countries have different sign languages.

SAY HELLO!

Here is a handy guide to saying hello in America's 10 most spoken languages:

Spanish: Hola

Chinese (Mandarin and Cantonese): Ni hǎo. 你好

Tagalog: kamusta

Vietnamese: xin chào

French and French Creole: Bonjour or Bonjou

Arabic: 'ahlan أهلا

Korean: annyeong haseyo 안녕하세요

Russian: Privet Привет

German: Hallo

Hindi: Namaste नमस्ते

NATIVE LANGUAGES

There are 169 Native American and Alaskan Indigenous languages. About 370,000 people speak one or more of them. Navajo, which is also called Diné, has the most speakers. About 170,000 people speak Diné. Some languages are spoken by very few people. The languages Eskimo and Tiwa have only about 2,000 speakers each.

FICTIONAL LANGUAGES

As if Americans didn't have enough languages to juggle already, some have decided to learn fictional languages, too! These are languages that come from books, movies, or television shows. For example, in the 2009 blockbuster film, *Avatar*, characters spoke a language called Na'vi. This language was created by a linguist (someone who studies languages). Fans of the movie learned to speak Na'vi, and further developed it themselves. Other fictional languages spoken in America are Dothraki, from *Game of Thrones*, and Klingon from *Star Trek*.

KANSAS

Kansas is named after the Kansa tribe.
Their name means "Wind People," or "People of the South Wind."

HISTORY

People have been living on the land now called Kansas for at least 12,000 years. In the 1500s, Europeans arrived. The first, Francisco Vasquez de Coronado, thought he might find a city of gold there. He traveled from Mexico through New Mexico, Texas, and Oklahoma before arriving in Kansas. He did not find a golden city. However, he did meet a group of Wichita people. Coronado returned to Mexico with no gold, but bearing tales of rich soil that could grow plenty of crops.

French explorers came to the area later. In 1803, the United States bought Kansas from the French in the Louisiana Purchase.

BLEEDING KANSAS

In the years before it became a state, people debated whether Kansas would allow slavery. Its location between the northern and southern states made Kansas an important battleground for pro- and anti-slavery Americans. If Kansas allowed slaves, it would strengthen the south. If it did not, it would add strength to the Union. Between 1854 and 1859, many brutal and bloody clashes took place over the issue on Kansas soil. In 1861, the issue was finally decided. Kansas would be a free state, meaning a state without slavery. However, Kansas hadn't seen the last of the violence. Some of the Civil War's fiercest clashes happened there.

FAST FACTS

Admitted to the Union:
January 29, 1861

State Number: **34**

Population: **2.9 million**

Capital: **Topeka**

Nickname:
The Sunflower State

State Animal:
American buffalo

Kansas' third largest city, Kansas City, sits on the border with Missouri. About 150,000 people live on the Kansas side, while 500,000 more live in the Missouri side.

LANDSCAPE

Kansas has a reputation for being flat, but the state's geography is actually full of variety. The northeast is forested and hilly. In western Kansas, limestone formations jut into the sky. Castle Rock resembles a castle nestled into the scrubby land. Monument Rocks, farther west, is another collection of breathtaking rock outcroppings. Tall red hills, canyons, and buttes are found in Gypsum Hills, in the south-central part of the state.

Across the state's varied landscape, there is one thing that can be found in each of its counties: wild sunflowers. That is why Kansas is called the Sunflower State.

AGRICULTURE

Nearly 90 percent of the land in Kansas is used for farming. Crops like sorghum, corn, and soybeans are grown there. Kansas produces so much wheat that the state is sometimes called the Wheat State. Each year, Kansas farmers grow enough wheat to make every person on the planet six loaves of bread. Kansas has the third largest cattle population. There are 6.5 million cows in Kansas. That's more than twice the number of people.

WEATHER

Kansas is famous for its extreme weather, including hot summers, frigid winters, and fierce tornadoes. It usually gets around 90 tornadoes each year.

This makes it the second most tornado-prone state after Texas.

KENTUCKY

Historian's aren't quite sure where Kentucky got its name. It may have come from the Wyandot word, *kah-ten-tah-teh*, which means "land of tomorrow." It may have come from the Shawnee word, *Kain-tuck-ee*, which means "at the head of the river." Or, it may stem from the Iroquois word, *kenhta-ke*, which means "meadow."

HISTORY

People have lived on Kentucky's land for 14,000 years. In the 1700s, white settlers came to Kentucky. One, a man named Daniel Boone, became a folk hero for his work settling the land. In 1767, Boone traveled through the Cumberland Gap into Kentucky. He returned many times, establishing the settlements Boonsborough and Boone Station.

KENTUCKY DERBY

The Kentucky Derby is the nation's most elite horse race. It takes place each year on the first Saturday in May at Churchill Downs, a racetrack in Louisville. Twenty three-year-old horses and their riders gallop around a 1.25-mi (2-km) track to see who can take first prize. The top five finishers get to split a $3 million payout, with the majority going to the winner.

It is traditional for race audiences to wear elaborate hats to the Derby. The brighter, bigger, and more fantastic, the better!

FAST FACTS

Admitted to the Union:
June 1, 1792

State Number: **15**

Population: **4.5 million**

Capital: **Frankfort**

Nickname:
The Bluegrass State

State Game Animal:
Gray squirrel

FORT KNOX

This heavily guarded complex, located south of Louisville, houses roughly $250 billion worth of gold bars. These gleaming bricks belong to the United States Treasury. Fort Knox was specially constructed to keep the gold and other precious items stored there safe. The steel and concrete building is bomb-proof and burglar-proof and includes a 21-in (53-cm) thick door.

In addition to housing gold, Fort Knox has also kept some other precious items safe over time, including the Magna Carta, the Declaration of Independence, and the Constitution.

WEATHER

Kentucky has mild weather with four distinct seasons. Summer highs average 87 °F (30.6 °C) while winter lows drop to an average of 23 °F (-5 °C). Mild spring weather turns the state's bluegrass fields bright green. In the fall, autumn leaves paint the landscape in reds, oranges, and yellows.

LANDSCAPE

From gentle hills to towering mountains to deep caves, Kentucky's landscape has it all. In the east, the Appalachian Mountain chain crosses the state, and includes Big Black Mountain. At 4,145 ft (1,263 m), this is Kentucky's highest point. In the center of the state is the Knobs Region, a collection of cone-shaped hills. The Knobs surround an area called the Bluegrass region. It contains rolling hills and lush grass—perfect for horse farms. In the west is a rocky area called the Pennyroyal (or Pennyrile). It is named for a type of wild mint that grows there.

MUSIC

Kentucky is known for Bluegrass music. This is a genre of music that highlights banjos, fiddles, double bass, mandolin, and different types of guitars. Bluegrass is usually acoustic, which means it is played without the aid of electricity. Bluegrass groups are often made up of four to seven members, all of whom may take turns as lead musician, and who sing in harmony.

Music fans can hear Bluegrass in many venues throughout the state. A favorite of many locals is the Rosine Barn Jamboree. It offers Bluegrass concerts each Friday night. Visitors who want to learn more about the musical genre can start their evening at the Bill Monroe Museum, dedicated to the "Father of Bluegrass," which is just down the street.

The town Middlesboro is located inside a 300-million-year-old meteorite crater.

These classic products come from Kentucky:

- Corvettes
- Jif Peanut Butter
- Kentucky Fried Chicken
- Dippin' Dots

LOUISIANA

Louisiana was named for the French King, Louis XIV, and is today known for its music, its cultural heritage and its delicious food.

HISTORY

Louisiana has a rich human history, beginning more than 12,000 years ago when people first came to the land. Thousands of years later, Native groups such as the Chocktaw, Atakapa, Chitimacha, Tunica, and Natchez came to live there. They hunted, farmed, and traded on the land.

Beginning in the 1500s, Louisiana experienced many cultural shifts. Spanish explorers arrived there in 1541. Then, in 1682, Louisiana was claimed by the French. Control passed back to the Spanish in 1762, before returning to the French in 1800. Finally, in 1803, the United States bought it in the Louisiana Purchase. Each of these shifts contributed to Louisiana's unique culture.

In 1719, ships carrying captured African slaves began arriving in cities like New Orleans.

FAST FACTS

Admitted to the Union:
April 30, 1812

State Number: **18**

Population: **4.6 million**

Capital: **Baton Rouge**

Nickname:
The Pelican State

State Mammal:
Black bear

Between 150,000 and 200,000 people in Louisiana speak French. Fewer than 10,000 people speak Louisiana Creole, a French-based language.

NEW ORLEANS

New Orleans was established in 1718. Located on a bend in the Mississippi River and close to the Gulf of Mexico, it was an ideal location for a shipping port. Soon, it was populated by people from Europe, the Caribbean, and captured African slaves. In the 1800s, it was home to a large number of free Black people.

Out of this melting pot of cultures came a group of people called New Orleans Creole. These are people who were born in New Orleans, but their heritage reflects their city's dynamic history. Today, New Orleans is known for its Creole culture, French and Spanish architecture, global cuisine, and vibrant music scene.

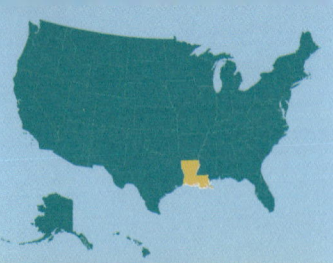

LANDSCAPE

Louisiana's landscape is marked by hills in the northwest and low marshes in the south. There are forests, prairies, and wetlands. The Mississippi River runs along the state's eastern border before passing though Baton Rouge and New Orleans.

Louisiana is the only state that doesn't divide its regions into counties. Instead, it has political subdivisions known as parishes.

WEATHER

Louisiana has long, hot summers, and short, cool, and wet winters. The state is often hit by tropical storms. In 2005, Hurricane Katrina hit the state. More than 1,500 people were killed, and the state suffered more than $100 billion in damage.

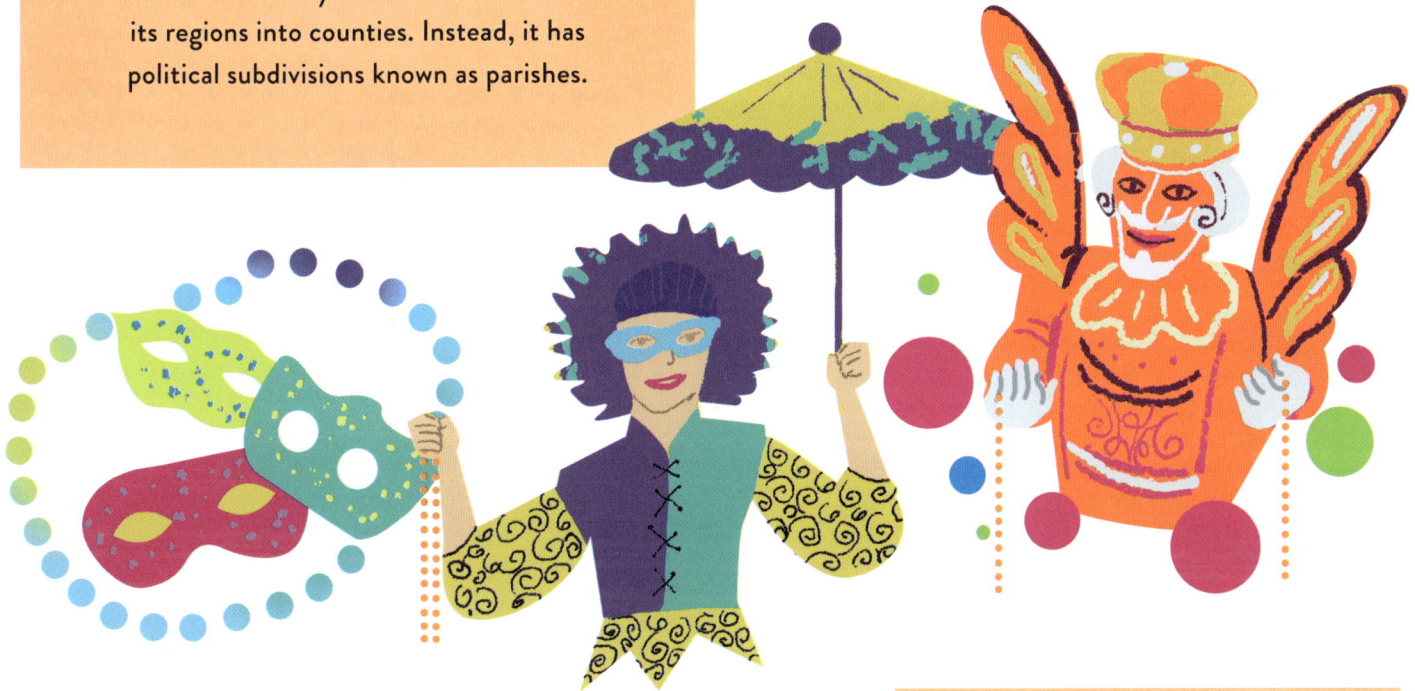

MARDI GRAS

Mardi Gras is French for "Fat Tuesday," which marks the day before Ash Wednesday, the start of the Catholic time of Lent. However, in places like New Orleans, it lasts much longer than just one day. For weeks, the city is home to feasts, parties, and magnificent parades. Celebrants wear vibrant costumes.

Stemming from both southern and French traditions, Louisiana's Cajun food is bold, spicy, and smoky.

CRAWFISH, CRAYFISH, OR CRAWDADS

Are they crawfish, crayfish, or crawdads? Whatever they're called, people in Louisiana love them. These small crustaceans are especially treasured in Breaux Bridge, *la capitale Mondiale de l'ecrevisse*, or the crawfish capital of the world. Residents and visitors alike love a dish called crawfish etouffee, a rich, saucy serving of crawfish over fluffy rice.

MAINE

Maine's name probably comes from the word "mainland."
This distinguished it from the surrounding islands. Over time it was
spelled in different ways, including "Meine" and "Mayne."

HISTORY

When people first came to Maine about 12,000 years ago, they hunted in the dense forests and likely collected seafood such as clams and oysters. A Viking named Leif Erikson came to the land of Maine around the year 1,000. About 600 years later, English settlers came and formed Popham Colony near the present-day town of Phippsburg. Their settlement didn't last and they returned to England after just one year. More small settlements followed, and in 1652, the southwestern part of Maine became part of Massachusetts. This lasted until 1820, when Maine became its own state.

FAST FACTS

Admitted to the Union:
March 15, 1820

State Number: **23**

Population: **1.4 million**

Capital: **Augusta**

Nickname:
The Pine Tree State

State Animal: **Moose**

LIGHTHOUSES

Dotted along Maine's rocky coastline are 65 lighthouses. These tall, often cylinder-shaped structures were built to help sailors navigate their way through the treacherous waters without crushing their ships on rocks or accidentally running ashore in the wrong spot.

Today, the lighthouses are popular destinations for sightseers and history lovers.

- The Portland Head Lighthouse was built in 1790. Alexander Hamilton, the Secretary of Treasury, gave the project a budget of $1,500.

- The West Quoddy Head Light has a slightly confusing name, since the lighthouse is actually found on the easternmost point of the mainland United States. The tower, first built in 1808, is painted in red and white stripes to help sailors spot it through dense fog.

- The Pemaquid Point lighthouse, built in 1827, is on Maine's state quarter.

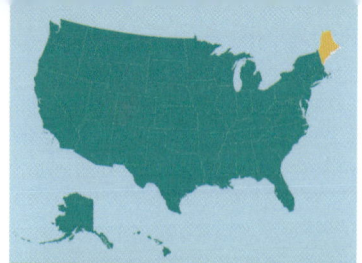

Famous author, Steven King, doesn't just set many of his best-selling novels in Maine. He lives there, too.

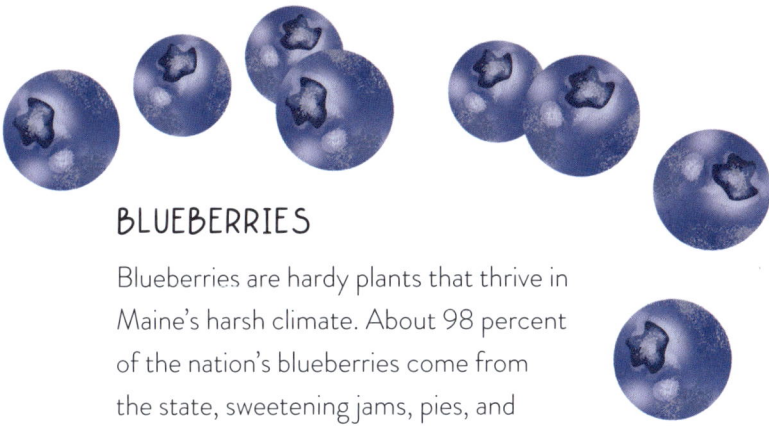

BLUEBERRIES

Blueberries are hardy plants that thrive in Maine's harsh climate. About 98 percent of the nation's blueberries come from the state, sweetening jams, pies, and pancakes all across America.

WEATHER

Maine has mild, warm summers and long, cold, snowy winters. The northern part of the state can get up to 110 in (279 cm) of snow each year. Heavy fog sometimes carpets the coastline.

With 90 percent of this state covered in forest, Maine is a magnet for anyone who loves to hike, camp and fish.

Maine's general coastline is 228 mi (367 km) long. But its tidal coastline, which includes all its inlets and outcroppings, is 3,478 mi (5,597 km) long. That is 51 mi (82 km) longer than California's tidal coastline.

LANDSCAPE

Maine is a land of rugged extremes: mountains, valleys, rivers, and sandy beaches. The Appalachian Mountain range stretches across the state's western border. Mount Katahdin, Maine's highest peak, which towers 5,268 ft (1,606 m) into the air, is in the north-central part of the state. Acadia National Park, located on Mount Desert Island, is home to some of Maine's most incredible wildlife and scenery.

SEAFOOD

Some of the country's most delicious seafood is caught off the coast of Maine. Fishing boats harvest clams, crab, oysters, mussels, and many types of fish. One of the most popular delicacies caught there is lobster. Each year, about 100 million lb (45,359,000 kg) of lobster are caught in Maine's water.

Maine is famous for its lobster rolls. These simple sandwiches are made up of lobster, tossed in either warm butter or cold mayonnaise dressing, served in a griddled hot dog bun.

RELIGIONS

Freedom of religion has been a key issue for the people of the United States since long before it was a country. The ability to practice faith without government interference is what drove some of the first settlers to America in the 1600s. Religious freedom was so fundamental to Americans that it was guaranteed in the First Amendment to the US Constitution.

"*Congress shall make no law respecting an establishment of religion, or prohibiting the free exercise thereof.*"

– First Amendment

PROTESTANTS

Many of the first American settlers were Protestant separatists. They came to America from England, where they felt that the Church of England was too closely tied to Catholicism. They were called separatists because they wanted to separate from the Church of England. This was illegal in England, where the king controlled the church. Living in America meant they had the freedom to practice their faith as they wanted.

These early settlers laid a strong foundation for the Protestant faith in America. Today, nearly half of Americans identify as Protestant.

DIFFERENT FAITHS

There are many different faiths practiced in America. Here is a breakdown of the top groups.

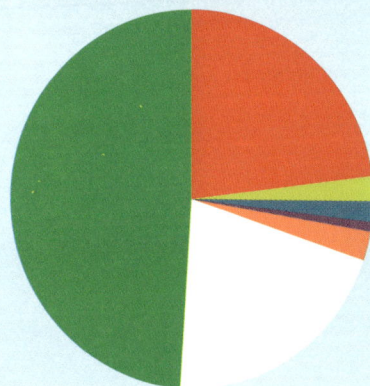

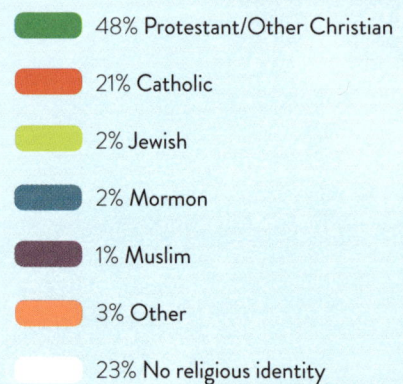

- 48% Protestant/Other Christian
- 21% Catholic
- 2% Jewish
- 2% Mormon
- 1% Muslim
- 3% Other
- 23% No religious identity

HOUSES OF WORSHIP

Religious people often belong to churches, synagogues, temples, or mosques. These are spaces for people to hold ceremonies, worship, and study. In 2020, 47 percent of Americans reported being members in a specific house of worship. This is a decrease from previous years.

OLDEST SYNAGOGUE

Puritans weren't the only settlers coming to America in the 1600s. In 1658, a group of Jewish families came to Newport, Rhode Island. In 1763, the Touro Synagogue was established there. Religious services and special ceremonies, such as weddings and Bar Mitzvahs, are still held at the historic synagogue today.

ISLAMIC CENTER OF AMERICA

Dearborn, Michigan is home to a large population of Arab Americans, which explains why it is also home to the country's largest mosque. The Islamic Center of America is a huge complex that includes a school, library, and meeting place.

MEGACHURCHES

Some churches are big. Others are really, really big. Megachurches are houses of worship that host enormous numbers of Christians each week. America has some of the biggest megachurches ever.

Lakewood Church in Houston, Texas, is the country's biggest megachurch. Each week, about 43,000 people come to its worship services. Lakewood's celebrity preacher, Joel Osteen, also has a television show. More than 10 million American households tune into it each week.

TEMPLE SQUARE

Owned by the Church of Jesus Christ of Latter-day Saints, Temple Square is a complex that includes the world's largest Mormon temple. This is a massive granite structure that was built to last. The walls are 9 ft (2.7 m) thick at the base and 6 ft (1.8 m) thick at the top. Church members encourage tourists to come and learn about their traditions. Each year, 3 to 5 million people visit Temple Square. To make it easy for all people to understand their traditions, Temple Square offers guided tours of the area in more than 40 different languages.

MARYLAND

Maryland was named after England's queen, Henrietta Maria. Her husband, King Charles I, granted Maryland permission to become a colony.

HISTORY

The Chesapeake Bay and its many surrounding rivers and streams made Maryland an attractive place for early people. At least 12,000 years ago, humans began living on the land there. They hunted in the forests and gathered fish and shellfish from the waters. In the 1500s, European explorers came to the area. The following century, more Europeans came, including John Smith. In 1634, English settlers arrived and founded St. Mary's City, Maryland's first permanent settlement.

Maryland played an important role in the Civil War. Though it was a slave state, Maryland did not leave the Union. Some people from the state fought for the Union, while others fought for the Confederacy. Sharpsburgh, Maryland was the site of one of the war's fiercest battles, and the bloodiest single day in American history. The Battle of Antietam lasted just 12 hours and resulted in more than 3,600 deaths.

FAST FACTS

Admitted to the Union:
April 28, 1788

State Number: **7**

Population: **6 million**

Capital: **Annapolis**

Nickname:
The Old Line State

State Bird:
Baltimore oriole

The United States Naval Academy is located in Annapolis.

WEATHER

Maryland has hot and humid summers and cold and snowy winters. The hottest temperature ever recorded there was 109 °F (42.7 °C), and the coldest was -40 °F (4.4 °C).

A REVOLUTIONARY NICKNAME

Maryland's unique nickname, The Old Line State, comes from an important moment in the Revolutionary War. In 1776, 400 Maryland soldiers faced off against 10,000 British soldiers. They were able to hold the British off while George Washington's army fled to safety. These soldiers were called Maryland's Line. George Washington later called Maryland the "Old Line State."

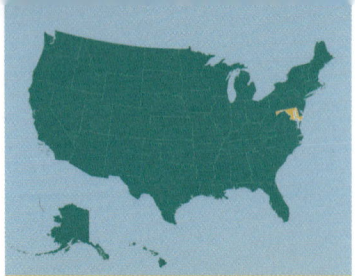

LANDSCAPE

The Appalachian Mountains run through Maryland's western side. The state's highest point, Backbone Mountain, is 3,360 ft (1,024 m) high. It sits on the border with West Virginia. The center of the state is hilly. The eastern part of the state is divided by an estuary called Chesapeake Bay. Estuaries are semi-enclosed bodies of water that connect rivers and streams to an ocean or sea. The Chesapeake Bay opens to the Atlantic Ocean. Fresh water from rivers mixes with salt water from the ocean there, resulting in unique and bountiful fishing. One of the nation's most important ports, Baltimore, is located on Chesapeake Bay. The land around Chesapeake Bay is low and marshy.

BALTIMORE

Maryland's biggest city, Baltimore, is known for many things: crab cakes, historic ships, museums, and art. One of its most popular attractions is the Lexington Market. This historic establishment has been serving delicious foods to customers for over 240 years.

Old Bay Seasoning, an iconic mix of spices often used to flavor seafood, comes from Baltimore. It is named after the Old Bay Line passenger cruise ship that sailed the Chesapeake Bay.

HARRIET TUBMAN

Harriet Tubman was born into slavery in Dorchester County, Maryland in around 1820. In 1849, she escaped to the North to find her freedom. In the following years, she became a "conductor" on the Underground Railroad, a network of anti-slavery activists and homes that helped slaves flee the South. Tubman safely brought around 70 slaves to the North. During the Civil War, Tubman served the Union army as a nurse, spy, and even as the leader of a successful raid.

MASSACHUSETTS

Massachusetts comes from the Algonquin word *massadchu-es-et*,
which means "great hill small place."

HISTORY

Archaeologists have found that the first humans arrived in Massachusetts more than 10,000 years ago. These early people hunted and gathered. Later, they began to farm, make tools, and form complex social groups. In 1497, Europeans began exploring the area. In 1620, English passengers on board the *Mayflower* arrived in Massachusetts. They settled an area they called New Plymouth.

FAST FACTS

Admitted to the Union:
February 6, 1788

State Number: **6**

Population: **6.9 million**

Capital: **Boston**

Nickname:
The Bay State

State Marine Mammal:
Right whale

SALEM WITCH TRIALS

In the late 1600s, colonial Massachusetts was the site of many witch trials. These were legal events in which people suspected of practicing witchcraft were investigated and punished. In Salem, more than 200 people faced accusations of witchcraft. Twenty people were put to death for being witches. Later, the government declared these trials unlawful. In 1957, the General Court of Massachusetts apologized for the witch trials.

WEATHER

Massachusetts has four seasons. Winters are cold and snowy, springs are cool and wet, summers are hot and muggy, and falls are cool and dry. Massachusetts is a popular destination for leaf peepers, people who love to see trees change color in the fall.

LANDSCAPE

The Appalachian Mountains run along Massachusetts' western side, including the state's highest point, Mt. Greylock, which stands at 3,491 ft (1,064 m). Moving toward the state's middle are the Berkshire Hills, a scenic region that is a popular vacation spot. Central Massachusetts features hills and rolling plains.

The eastern edge of the state is made up of coastline, including the hook-shaped Cape Cod. Though Massachusetts is only about 110 mi (177 km) from north to south, its jagged tidal coastline measures about 1,500 mi (2,414 km) long.

Bostonians are famous for their unique accent. They often drop the "r" sounds from words, pronouncing "park" like "pahk." In this way, "Harvard Yard" becomes "Hahvahd Yahd."

BOSTON

Boston is the largest city in New England, with a population of about 680,000. Located on the state's Atlantic coast, Boston is a hub for art, food, sports, and history. The city is often called Beantown. This nickname comes from early residents' fondness for beans baked in molasses.

The Boston Marathon is the oldest and fastest marathon in America. One particularly tough part of the race is Heartbreak Hill, a 91-ft (27.7-m) climb located at the 20th mi (32nd km).

HARVARD

Harvard is one of America's most prestigious and well-known universities. Located in Cambridge, Harvard was founded in 1636. Graduates include some of the world's top thinkers, including eight American presidents:

- Barack Obama
- George W. Bush
- John Adams
- John Quincy Adams
- Rutherford B. Hayes
- Theodore Roosevelt
- Franklin D. Roosevelt
- John F. Kennedy

Getting accepted to Harvard College is no easy feat. In 2022, 61,220 students applied to attend the school. Only 1,954 were accepted. That makes it the country's most selective university. Harvard's yearly tuition is expensive. In 2023, it was about $54,000. Adding in the cost of room, board, books, and other expenses, it can cost about $80,000 per year to attend the university. More than half of Harvard students are eligible for financial aid. This means they can get scholarships to help pay for their education.

MICHIGAN

Michigan comes from an Algonquin word, *mishigamaw*. This means "big lake." There are no wolverines living wild in Michigan. Most people think the nickname, The Wolverine State, came from a dispute between Ohio and Michigan called the Toledo War, when people from Michigan were said to have fought like wolverines.

FAST FACTS

Admitted to the Union:
January 26, 1837

State Number: **26**

Population: **10 million**

Capital: **Lansing**

Nickname:
The Wolverine State

State Game Mammal:
White-tailed deer

HISTORY

Early people first arrived in Michigan about 13,000 years ago, when much of the state was buried deep under a mile-thick (1.6-km) sheet of ice. As time passed and the area warmed, more people came to live there.

In the 1600s, French explorers came to the area. They were followed by more French people, including fur traders and missionaries. Michigan remained under French control until the 1760s, when it was ceded to Great Britain. At the end of the 1700s, Michigan came under the authority of the United States.

CEREAL CITY

In the late 1800s, people looking to improve their health came to the Battle Creek Sanitarium, in Battle Creek, Michigan. There, they exercised, got fresh air, and tried a revolutionary new health food invented by John Harvey and Will Keith Kellogg: cereal. This flaked product was healthy, easy to prepare, and delicious. Kellogg's soon grew to become a leading cereal company. One man who tried the Sanitarium's cereal was C. W. Post. He went on to found his own cereal company in Battle Creek, called Post. In the years that followed, many other cereal companies sprouted up in the small southern Michigan town, earning it its nickname, Cereal City.

People who live in the Upper Peninsula, or the UP, are often called "Yoopers."

LANDSCAPE

Michigan is the only state that is split into two separate areas: the Upper Peninsula, and the Lower Peninsula, which is also called "the mitten," because of its shape. The Upper Peninsula is hilly, with dense forests and crisp, clear streams. The state's highest point, Mount Arvon, is in the Upper Peninsula. It is 1,979 ft (603 m) high. Michigan's Lower Peninsula is generally flat, with some gentle hills in the northern part.

Michigan borders four of the Great Lakes: Huron, Superior, Erie, and Michigan. It has over 3,288 mi (5,291 km) of freshwater coastline, and more than 11,000 inland lakes.

Detroit's Motown Records gave the world some of its favorite musicians, including Marvin Gaye, Diana Ross & The Supremes, and Stevie Wonder.

MOTOR CITY

Detroit, Michigan's largest city, is often called "Motor City." This is because of the important role it played in automotive history. The "Big Three" car companies all got their start there: Ford, General Motors, and Chrysler. Today, Michigan continues to rule the American automotive industry, producing more vehicles than any other state.

About 2 million cars and trucks come out of Michigan's assembly lines each year.

TRAVERSE CITY

Traverse City, in the northern part of the Lower Peninsula, is a popular destination for tourists. In addition to its pristine beaches, visitors enjoy wineries, cherry orchards, and hiking in the Sleeping Bear Dunes National Lakeshore.

Each November, adventurous cyclists race in the Bell's Iceman Cometh Challenge, a 30-mi (48-km) cross-country mountain bike race that stretches from Kalkaska to Traverse City.

WEATHER

Michigan weather has it all: hot summers, breezy and wet springs, vibrant and crisp falls, and Arctic winters. The state often sees blizzards that bring heavy snowfalls. One of the state's most intense blizzards happened in 1978. In just over one day, a storm dropped 8 in (20 cm) of snow in Detroit, 10 in (25 cm) in Flint, and a whopping 30 in (76 cm) in Muskegon. During the storm, about 100,000 cars were abandoned on the undrivable Michigan roads.

STARRY SKIES

Michigan has six dark sky parks. These are areas that are protected from light pollution, which means that they are very dark at night. Their deep, dark skies allow stunning views of the bright stars, planets, and meteors. At spots like the Headlands International Dark Sky Park in Mackinaw City, lucky stargazers can even see the Northern Lights.

MINNESOTA

The name Minnesota comes from the Dakota Sioux words,
Mni Sóta, which mean sky-tinted waters.

"Minnesota Nice" is a phrase people use to describe the state's residents. It refers to their polite and humble nature.

HISTORY

Long ago, Minnesota was buried under thick ice. The ice covering the southern part of the state began to melt around 14,000 years ago. Humans arrived around 2,000 years later.

In the 1600s, French explorers and fur traders came to the area. Part of Minnesota was included in the Louisiana Purchase in 1803. Great Britain ceded more of the territory to Minnesota in 1818, and the next year the first long-term American settlement in Minnesota was established at Fort Snelling.

VIKING CONFUSION

It is often said that Vikings came to Minnesota in the 1300s. Because of this, Viking imagery is found throughout the area, including on the state's NFL team, the Minnesota Vikings. This fondness for Viking culture stems from a hoax. In 1898, a farmer said he found a stone carved with Scandinavian runes that told the story of Viking explorers. Later, experts declared the runestone a fake. This doesn't seem to have bothered Minnesotans, however. They continue to embrace Viking culture today.

LANDSCAPE

Along its border with Canada, the northern part of Minnesota is heavily forested. The state's highest point, Eagle Mountain (2,301 ft, or 701 m), is located at its northeastern tip along Lake Superior. In the southeast are limestone features such as hills, valleys, caves, and bluffs. Western Minnesota is mostly flat and fertile land with some low hills.

FAST FACTS

Admitted to the Union:
May 11, 1858

State Number: **32**

Population: **5.7 million**

Capital: **St. Paul**

Nickname:
The North Star State

State Bird: **Loon**

Minnesota is often called the Land of 10,000 Lakes. This nickname isn't accurate. The state actually has 11,842 lakes.

TWIN CITIES

Minneapolis and St. Paul are Minnesota's two biggest cities. Separated by only seven miles and the Mississippi River, they are often lumped together under the title of the Twin Cities. However, locals maintain that each city has its own distinct identity.

Minneapolis is known for being a hub for art and theater. Residents and visitors alike enjoy the Minneapolis Institute of Art, the Walker Art Center and its famous Sculpture Garden, and the Guthrie Theater.

St. Paul has plenty of cultural attractions, too, including the Science Museum of Minnesota, the Como Park Zoo & Conservatory, and the Minnesota History Center. Standing on the city's highest point is the towering Cathedral of Saint Paul, which dates back to 1915.

FISHING

With more than 5,000 fishable lakes and 18,000 mi (28,900 km) of fishable rivers, it's no surprise that Minnesota is a top location for fishing. About 1.4 million of the state's residents hold fishing licenses. Walleye, northern pike, bass, and trout are the top prizes, but there are 162 different species of fish swimming in Minnesotan waters.

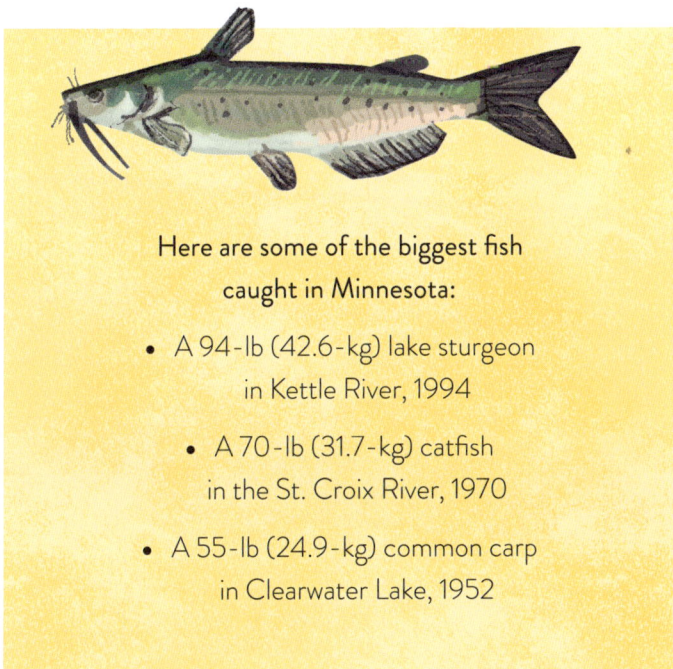

Here are some of the biggest fish caught in Minnesota:

- A 94-lb (42.6-kg) lake sturgeon in Kettle River, 1994
- A 70-lb (31.7-kg) catfish in the St. Croix River, 1970
- A 55-lb (24.9-kg) common carp in Clearwater Lake, 1952

WEATHER

Minnesota has four seasons, with cool and wet springs, hot and muggy summers, crisp and chilly falls, and frigid, snowy winters. In 1885, a journalist visiting St. Paul during the winter called the city "another Siberia, unfit for human habitation." In response, the city put on a massive winter carnival, complete with food, outdoor activities, and palaces carved from ice. This grew into a beloved event that draws more than 250,000 people each year.

HOCKEY

Minnesota is often called the "State of Hockey." An estimated 100,000 people throughout the state play, from rookies to all stars. About 20 percent of NHL players are from Minnesota.

CUISINE

American food is as diverse as its people, with flavors and traditions that trace all across the globe. A look at some of the major food cultures shows just how varied and exciting eating in the United States can be.

TEX MEX

Tex Mex is a cuisine that mixes recipes from northern Mexico with ingredients from Texas. Tex Mex foods often feature beef, flour tortillas, and yellow cheese. Nachos are a popular Tex Mex food item.

SOUL FOOD

Soul food is a type of home cooking cuisine that traces its roots to African American cooks living in the south. It often features items that were inexpensive and accessible to Black Americans, such as beans, greens, pork, and corn.

DINER FOOD

Named after the casual restaurants that typically serve them, these food items are casual, comforting, and always popular with crowds. Hotdogs, hamburgers, and grilled cheese sandwiches are popular examples of diner food. Just don't forget the French fries!

REGIONAL CUISINES

Some regions have developed distinct food items, such as the following:

PLATE LUNCH

A common roadside meal in Hawaii, plate lunches often feature a meat and/or seafood item, rice, macaroni salad, and a dessert.

HOTDISH

A casserole-style dish from Minnesota, hotdish usually includes frozen or canned vegetables, meat, and potatoes.

JOHNNYCAKES

A Rhode Island staple, these cornmeal flatbreads are served at breakfast with syrup and butter, and at lunch and dinner as side dishes.

FOOD BATTLES

In a country as big and diverse as the United States, food rivalries are bound to develop.
Here are some of the most hotly debated food wars:

PIZZA: CHICAGO VS. NEW YORK

Chicago-style pizza usually means deep dish, a high-sided pizza baked in a deep iron dish. This results in a saucy, thick crusted slice that is often eaten with a fork and knife. New York style pizza has a thin, crispy crust. Fans often fold their slice before digging in.

CLAM CHOWDER: NEW ENGLAND VS. MANHATTAN

Both types of chowder feature vegetables, clams, and potatoes. However, Manhattan-style clam chowder has a tomato-based broth, while New England-style clam chowder has a creamy broth. The rivalry between the two chowders got so intense that in 1939, a bill was introduced into Maine's legislature that would make it illegal to put tomatoes in clam chowder.

BARBECUE NORTH CAROLINA VS. KANSAS CITY

Barbecue is all about smoke, fire, and sauce. And while cities across America have their own barbecue claims to fame, the rivalry between North Carolina and Kansas City is one of the biggest. Kansas City barbecue usually features thick, sweet, and sticky sauces, while North Carolina favors thin, vinegary sauces.

GLOBAL CUISINES

Americans eat a lot of different foods from around the world. Here are the five most popular cuisines:

1. Chinese
2. Mexican
3. Italian
4. Thai
5. Indian

Apple pie is one of the most historic and iconic American dishes. In fact, a recipe for it appeared in the first known American cookbook, published in 1796, making the sweet dessert live up to the description, "as American as apple pie."

MISSISSIPPI

Mississippi comes from the Ojibwe word "great river," which referred to the Mississippi River.

Flags from six different nations have flown over coastal Mississippi: France, England, Spain, the Republic of West Florida, the Confederate States of America, and the United States of America.

FAST FACTS

Admitted to the Union:
December 10, 1817

State Number: **20**

Population: **2.9 million**

Capital: **Jackson**

Nickname:
The Magnolia State

State Water Mammal:
Bottlenosed dolphin

HISTORY

There are more than 19,000 archaeological sites in the state of Mississippi. The oldest of these date back to about 12,000 years ago, when people first arrived there. Over the centuries, many Native groups came to live on the land. By the time Europeans arrived in Mississippi in the 1500s, there were about 200,000 people already living there. Over the next two centuries, France, Great Britain, and Spain would all claim ownership of parts of the state. In 1798, Congress created the Mississippi Territory.

RACISM AND CIVIL RIGHTS

In the early 1800s, Mississippi was the country's top producer of cotton, a crop that was grown using slave labor. By the start of the Civil War, there were more than 400,000 slaves living there. Even after slavery was abolished, racism remained a big issue in the state.

In the 1950s and 1960s, Mississippi civil rights leaders fought to gain equality for the state's Black residents. Today, visitors are encouraged to remember their work by following the Mississippi Freedom Trail. It features 25 sites that commemorate important people or events from the civil rights movement.

Today, Mississippi has more elected Black officials than any other state in the country.

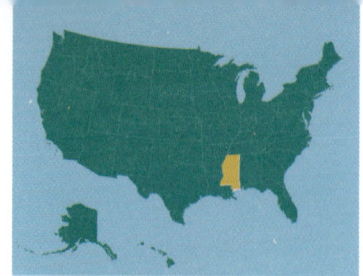

LANDSCAPE

Mississippi is mostly a low-lying state. The Mississippi River forms its western border. In the northwest is a fertile area called the Delta. In the northeast are hills, including the state's highest point, Woodall Mountain. It is 806 ft (246 m) tall. About 60 percent of Mississippi's land is covered in forests. Southern Mississippi features gently rolling hills and sandy soil. The state has 62 mi (99.7 km) of general coastline along the Gulf of Mexico.

SINGERS

Some of the world's favorite singers were born in Mississippi, including the following:

- Britney Spears
- Elvis Presley
- Faith Hill
- Jimmy Buffett
- B.B. King

A style of music known as the Blues originated in the Mississippi Delta.

WEATHER

Mississippi is warm and wet most of the year, with very hot summers and mild winters. During January, its coldest month, the state drops into the 50s °F (10–15 °C). In August, the hottest month, temperatures regularly climb into the 90s °F (32.2–37.2 °C). Mississippi is very rainy. It gets about 50–65 in (127–165 cm) of rain per year. That's much higher than the average rainfall for the other contiguous states, which is just 30 in (76 cm).

Mississippi occasionally gets hurricanes. Some are very violent. In 1969, a Category 5 hurricane named Hurricane Camille hit the state. It included 175 mph (282 kph) winds and a 24-ft (7.3-m) storm surge. There have only been four other Category 5 hurricanes to hit the United States.

CHURCHES AND BIBLES

Mississippi is part of the Bible Belt, a region in the American South that is strongly influenced by Christianity. One of the most religious states in the country, 83 percent of the adults in Mississippi identify as Christian. The country's largest Bible repair company, Norris Bookbinding, is in Greenwood.

Crispy fried chicken is a favorite Mississippi meal, especially when paired with greens and macaroni and cheese.

MISSISSIPPI RIVER

LENGTH: 2,340 mi (3,770 km)   **SOURCE:** Lake Itasca, MN   **MOUTH:** Gulf of Mexico

SIZE

The Mississippi River is the fourth longest in the world. It flows through 10 states and drains water from 32 states and two Canadian provinces. More than 50 cities rely on the Mississippi for drinking water.

Tributaries are rivers or streams that flow into lakes or rivers. The Mississippi has many tributaries, including the Illinois, Arkansas, Ohio, Red, and Missouri Rivers.

POLLUTION

In the past, there was little regulation about dumping waste into the Mississippi. Garbage, chemicals, and sewage could all be tossed into the water. This caused the water to become polluted, which led to people and animals getting sick. Today, rules are in place to reduce the amount of pollution that goes into the water. These help, but there is still much work to do. Scientists have called the Mississippi the most polluted river in America. Because of this, it is not always safe to swim in its waters. People who want to take a dip in the Mississippi should check with local authorities first.

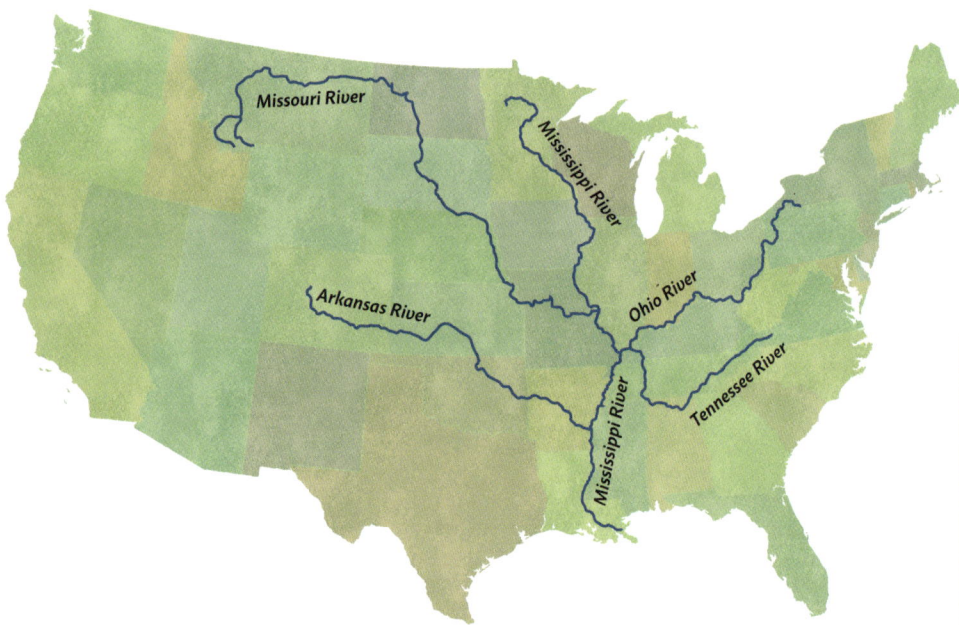

DEPTH

The Mississippi River is only knee-deep near its headwaters, in Lake Itasca. Its deepest point is found near Algiers Point in New Orleans. There, the river is about 200 ft (61 m) deep.

Water speed varies along the river, but it generally takes about three months for water to travel from Lake Itasca to the Gulf of Mexico.

CONTROLLING THE RIVER

Rivers flood naturally. However, because so many people live alongside the Mississippi, many efforts have been made to control its flooding. There are almost 30 locks and dams along its northern route. Farther south, more than 1,000 mi (1,600 km) of levees (embankments designed to stop a river from overflowing) and floodgates have been constructed along the river. Many experts believe these flood control measures are actually making flooding worse. They say that the human-made structures prevent smaller floods that could occur along more of the river's length and instead force water into narrower, faster-moving areas that can flood quickly.

STEAMBOATS

In the 1800s, steamboats were a common sight on the Mississippi. These were steam-powered vessels that used large paddle wheels to move across the water. Compared to other methods of transportation, they were a relatively quick way to move people and goods from place to place.

WILDLIFE

The Mississippi River and the surrounding land is home to a wide variety of wildlife. Over 260 species of fish swim in its water. They make up about a quarter of all the fish species in North America. The high numbers of fish in the water attract hunting birds, such as golden eagles and red-tailed hawks. Mammals like coyotes, gray foxes, badgers, and white-tailed deer can often be found near the river's shores. Amphibians such as blue-spotted salamanders, central newts, and northern leopard frogs live in the river's murky waters. Reptiles such as wood turtles, painted turtles, and timber rattlesnakes may also be found nearby.

MISSOURI

Missouri comes from a word spoken by the Sioux Indians, which means "town of the large canoes." People debate exactly where Missouri's nickname, the Show Me State, came from. Today, it is taken to indicate the spirit of the state's people, who are practical, tough, and want to see proof before making their minds up about something.

HISTORY

Humans have lived in the area now called Missouri for more than 13,000 years. Early people there were hunters and gatherers. Later, they evolved to farm the land and live in settlements.

In 1682, the French claimed the land of Missouri as part of the Louisiana Territory. Later, the land would shift to Spanish control before once again falling under French ownership. Finally, in 1803, the Louisiana Purchase brought Missouri under the control of the United States.

GATEWAY ARCH

St. Louis, one of the state's biggest cities, played an important role in America's westward growth. Settlers looking to move west often traveled through St. Louis, which earned the city the nickname, "Gateway to the West." A monument called the Gateway Arch honors the city's role as an important jumping-off point for pioneers. Part of the National Park system, the stainless steel arch towers 630 ft (192 m) into the air.

FAST FACTS

Admitted to the Union:
August 10, 1821

State Number: **24**

Population: **6.1 million**

Capital: **Jefferson City**

Unofficial Nickname:
The Show Me State

State Animal:
Missouri mule

Samuel Langhorne Clemens was born in Florida, Missouri. He later became famous under his pen name, Mark Twain.

St. Louis is famous for its barbecued spare ribs. They are grilled then dressed in a sweet, tomato-based sauce.

LANDSCAPE

The northern and western parts of Missouri are hilly, with prairies, farms, rivers, and streams. The southern part of the state is dominated by the Ozark Plateau, a rocky area with ridges, caves, and steep hillsides. Taum Sauk Mountain, the state's highest point, is found in this area. It is 1,772 ft (540 m) tall.

Missouri is sometimes called the Cave State. This is because it has somewhere between 6,000 and 7,500 caves. People enjoy exploring these caves in a variety of ways. At the Fantastic Caverns, visitors ride a tram through a huge, beautiful cave. At Cameron Cave, people are invited to carry lanterns and flashlights on a 90-minute walking tour and imagine what cave exploration might have been like in the past. More than 3,000 weddings have taken place in the fittingly-named Bridal Cave.

WEATHER

Missouri winters are cold and snowy, while its summers are hot and muggy. Winter low temperatures plunge down into the 20s °F (-6.6 to -1.6 °C), and sometimes even lower. Summers often top out in the 90s °F (32.2 to 37.2 °C).

BRANSON

Branson is sometimes known as Missouri's entertainment capital. The southwestern city is a popular vacation spot, with a vibrant music scene, dinner shows, aquarium, the Silver Dollar City theme park, and easy access to the natural beauty of the Ozark Mountains.

TALLGRASS PRAIRIES

Tallgrass prairies are grasslands that feature many types of plants, including tall-growing grasses. Missouri used to be covered by about 23,000 sq mi (61,000 sq km) of tallgrass prairie, including some types of grass that grew tall enough to hide both a horse and its rider. Today, less than 1 percent of the prairies remain.

MISSOURI RIVER

LENGTH: 2,315 mi (3,725 km)   SOURCE: Three Forks, MT   MOUTH: the Mississippi River, at St. Louis, MO

SIZE

The Missouri River begins in Three Forks, Montana, where the Gallatin, Jefferson, and Madison Rivers meet. It travels through seven states before joining with the Mississippi River in St. Louis. About one-sixth of the United States' land drains into the Missouri River.

The Missouri River has 95 tributaries, including the Kansas, Yellowstone, James, and the Platte.

A CHANGED RIVER

Today, the Missouri River looks much different than it did 200 years ago. In order to control the river's flow and manage flooding, humans have constructed many dams, levees, and embankments along its course. These shape the river and also provide irrigation to millions of acres of surrounding farmland. Additionally, 36 hydropower units along the river generate electricity for millions of people.

The Missouri River generally flows about 3–5 mph (5–8 kph). That's about the same speed as a person walking.

The Missouri River is often called "Big Muddy" because of the high levels of soil and sand carried in the water.

LEWIS AND CLARK

In 1804, explorers Meriweather Lewis and William Clark traveled up the length of the Missouri. They brought a crew of 43 helpers along with them, and traveled in three boats.

SPORTS

Many people head to the Missouri River each year to paddleboard, fish, hunt, hike, and bike. While these sports are enough for most folks, some extreme athletes look to the river for something more intense: the MR340, world's longest nonstop kayak and canoe race. This three-day event takes athletes from Kansas City, Missouri to St. Charles, Missouri in a heart-pounding aquatic endurance challenge. Competitors must finish the 340-mi (547-km) course in less than 86 hours. The fastest-ever finish happened in 2018, with a team finishing in just 33 hours and 1 minute.

WILDLIFE

The Missouri River is teeming with about 150 species of fish. Common carp, shad, channel catfish, and gizzard shad are all commonly spotted in its waters. One of the river's most unusual fish is the pallid sturgeon. These light-colored fish are typically 30–60 in (76.2–152 cm) long. They can weigh as much as 85 lb (39 kg). Pallid sturgeons live up to 100 years, and are currently an endangered species.

More amazing wildlife can be found on the Missouri's shores. There are at least 50 species of reptiles and amphibians, 60 species of mammals, and 300 species of birds that depend on the river to survive. Bighorn sheep and bison can be seen near the river in Montana. In North Dakota, smooth softshell turtles are a frequent river sight. Along the river's South Dakota shores, bobcats and coyotes can be seen hunting. Along the border of Iowa and Nebraska are vibrant Western Tiger salamanders. Bald eagles can be spotted over the river's route, including in Kansas and Missouri.

MONTANA

Montana comes from the Spanish word for mountain, *montaña*.
The state has more than 100 mountain ranges and sub-ranges.

FAST FACTS

Admitted to the Union:
November 8, 1889

State Number: **41**

Population: **1 million**

Capital: **Helena**

Nickname:
The Treasure State

State Animal:
Grizzly bear

HUNTERS, TRAPPERS, AND EXPLORERS

Humans have been in Montana for at least 12,000 years. They hunted game such as giant bison and mammoths. Much later, many Native groups came to the land.

French fur trappers likely came to the area around the year 1700. Lewis and Clark arrived in 1805. In the following fifty years, more Europeans arrived, including traders, explorers, and missionaries. The discovery of gold encouraged even more settlers to travel to Montana. The state became a US territory in 1864.

BATTLE OF LITTLE BIGHORN

As more and more European people arrived in Montana, they took lands from the Native people already there. They also introduced diseases. In 1876, the Lakota Sioux, Arapaho, and Cheyenne people joined together to fight the US Army in a fight called the Battle of Little Bighorn. They won. However, settlers did not stop coming to Montana. It became an official state just 13 years later.

PREHISTORIC PARADISE

Montana is often called Dinosaur Country. 75 species of dinosaurs have been discovered there, more than any other state, including *Diplodocus*, *Troodon*, and *Stegosaurus*. Dinosaur fans can follow Montana's Dinosaur Trail, a 14-stop statewide exploration of all things prehistoric.

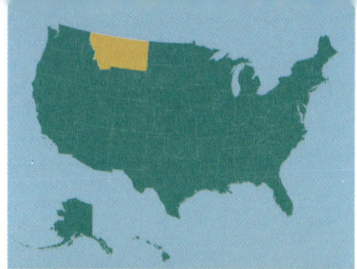

Montana is a T-Rex treasure trove. The first *Tyrannosaurus* fossil was found there in 1903, followed by at least 24 more partial T-Rex skeletons.

LANDSCAPE

Montana is America's fourth-largest state. At 147,000 sq mi (380,000 sq km), it is bigger than Maryland, Virginia, Pennsylvania, Delaware, and New York put together. Across the vast state is a wide variety of landscapes. The eastern part of the state is covered in plains, and includes an area called the Prairie Badlands. Here, amazing rock formations stand out from the barren land. Montana's central region includes more flat land that is occasionally interrupted by islands of mountains. The western edge of Montana is made up of towering mountain ranges and scenic valleys. Yellowstone National Park is found on the border with Idaho and Wyoming. Glacier National Park sits near the border with Canada and is home to the state's highest point, Granite Peak. It is 12,799 ft (3,904 m).

Rich deposits of gold, silver, copper, coal, and oil led to Montana's nickname: the Treasure State.

WEATHER

Summers in Montana are sunny, warm, and dry. They are perfect for hiking, horseback riding, fishing, and mountain climbing. Winters are cold and very snowy, but that doesn't mean the end of outdoor activities. Each winter, people flock to the state to enjoy the powdery snow for skiing, snowmobiling, and snowshoeing. Cooke City, one of the state's snowiest towns, gets about 200 in (508 cm) of snow each year.

Loma, Montana earned a world record on January 14-15, 1972. That day, it experienced the biggest temperature change ever recorded in a 24-hour period. The weather went from -54 °F (-47.7 °C) at 9am to 49 °F (9.4 °C) at 8am the following morning.

NEBRASKA

Nebraska's name comes from the Oto word for "flat water,"
after the Platte River, which runs across the eastern half of the state.
The Platte isn't the state's only major waterway. There are many rivers,
adding more than 79,000 mi (127,000 km) of water in Nebraska.

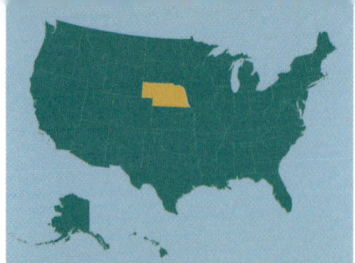

HISTORY

People have lived in Nebraska for at least 13,500 years.

In the 1500s, Spanish and French explorers came to Nebraska. In 1803, it was part of the Louisiana Purchase. Nebraska was an important territory to cross for travelers on the Oregon Trail. One of the most memorable sights for people heading west along the Oregon Trail was Chimney Rock on the state's western edge. Seeing the 500-ft (152-m) rock spire told them they were heading in the right direction. Today it is a national historic site.

FAST FACTS

Admitted to the Union:
March 1, 1867

State Number: **37**

Population: **1.9 million**

Capital: **Lincoln**

Nickname:
The Cornhusker State

State Bird:
Western meadowlark

Kool-Aid was invented in Hastings, Nebraska in 1927.

LANDSCAPE

Nebraska is a mostly flat state, but that doesn't mean its landscape lacks variety. In the east, the state is made up of plains. The central region is dominated by the Sandhills, the largest spread of sand dunes in North America. This region also includes hills, valleys, and small lakes.

In the west are the Badlands, an area marked by amazing sandstone rock formations. Nebraska's highest point is called Panorama Point. It is 5,424 ft (1,653 m) above sea level and sits at the border with Wyoming and Colorado.

INDOOR JUNGLE

Omaha's Henry Doorly Zoo is home to the country's largest indoor rainforest, the Lied Jungle. The 1.5-acre (0.6-hectare) jungle exhibit contains 2,000 different types of plants and 125 animal species.

The Nebraska Cornhuskers' football stadium holds 90,000 people. On game days, locals say that it is the third most populated city in the state.

CARHENGE

One of Nebraska's more unusual attractions is Carhenge, a replica of England's famous monument, Stonehenge. The Nebraska version is made entirely from cars. Completed in 1987, this quirky monument has become a popular tourist attraction.

TRAINS

Union Pacific's Bailey Yard, located in North Platte, is the world's largest rail yard. Every day, about 14,000 railcars pass through it. Visitors who want to take in the massive collection of trains can climb the eight-story Golden Spike Tower which overlooks the yard.

FARMS

Around 92 percent of Nebraska's land is used for farms and ranches. About one in four Nebraskans work in an industry related to agriculture.

The state's top products are:
cattle and calves, corn, soybeans, hogs, dairy

THE GREAT PLAINS

The Great Plains are a huge geographical region that extends in a roughly vertical strip from Texas up into Canada. The Great Plains take up about one-fifth of the lower 48 states' landmass. The Great Plains are mostly covered in grasslands.

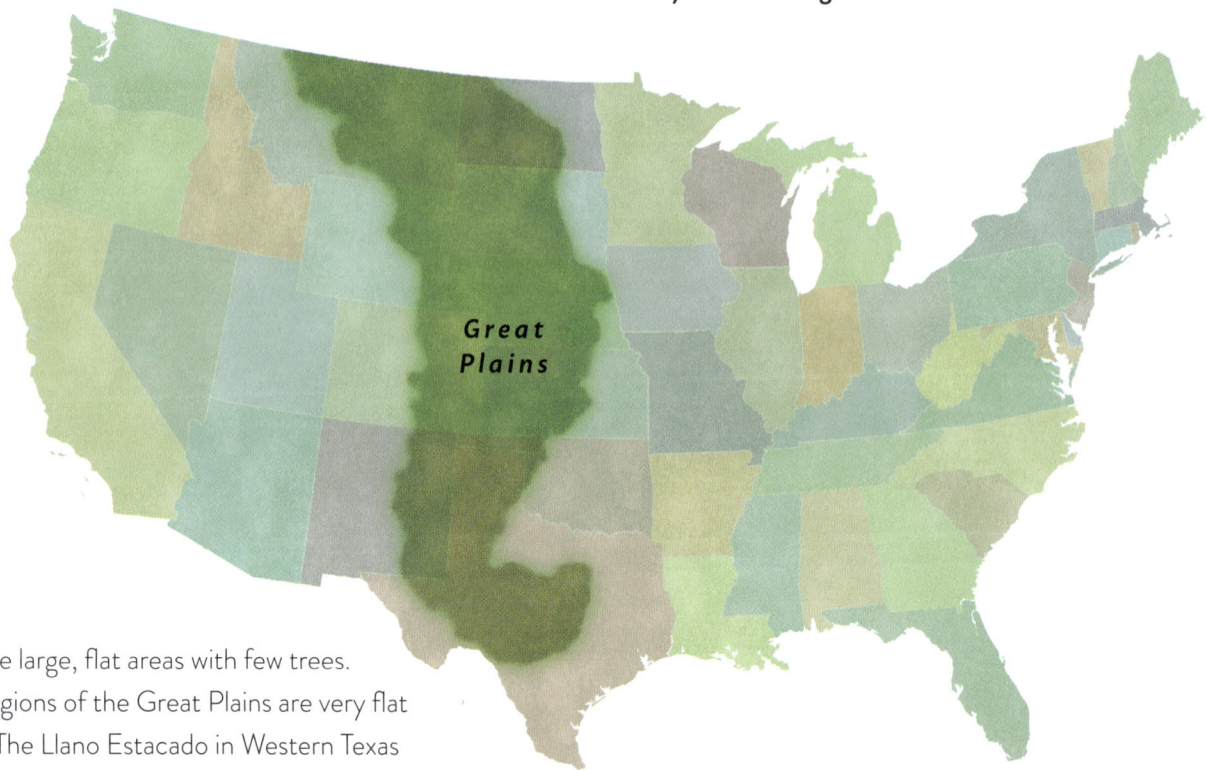

Great Plains

Plains are large, flat areas with few trees. Some regions of the Great Plains are very flat indeed. The Llano Estacado in Western Texas is so flat and featureless that settlers could get lost crossing them. Folklore says that early explorers would lay out stakes behind them to ensure that they traveled in a straight line. This story may be how the area got its popular nickname, the Staked Plains.

Some areas of the Great Plains include tall hills, deep valleys, and even mountains. The Black Hills, as well as the Judith, Bear Paw, and Big Snowy Mountains, are found there.

WIND POWER

Wind whips across the Great Plains. This makes it the perfect place for wind turbines. These are huge windmills that generate electricity when turned by the wind. Most of the country's wind turbines are found in the Great Plains.

The states that produce the most energy from wind power are:
- Texas
- Iowa
- Oklahoma

AMERICA'S BREAD BASKET

The Great Plains are home to much of the country's agriculture. Barley, cotton, corn, canola, soybeans, and sorghum are all grown in the vast region. However, the area's most plentiful crop is wheat. So much wheat is produced from the Great Plains that the area is nicknamed America's Bread Basket.

EXTREME WEATHER

The Great Plains experience some of the country's most extreme weather. From blizzards in the winter to heat waves in the summer, from droughts in the fall to floods in the spring, this region gets it all.

The fastest extreme temperature change ever recorded happened in the Great Plains on January 22, 1943. On that day, Spearfish, South Dakota went from being -4 °F (-20 °C) at 7:30 am to 45 °F (7 °C) just two minutes later. By 9:00 am, the temperature had risen to 54 °F (12 °C). Then, 27 minutes later, the temperatures plunged back to -4 °F (-20 °C). The shift in temperature was so rapid and extreme that some locals reported that the glass in their windows broke.

RODEOS

The Great Plains are home to some of the country's best rodeos. These are popular events in which athletes compete in roping calves, riding broncos, barrel-racing, and more.

One of the most popular rodeo events is bull riding. In this competition, riders fight to stay on bucking bulls. They can hold on with only one hand, and must remain on the bull for eight seconds. Judges award points to both the rider and the bull, and the combined highest score wins.

BUFFALO

Before Europeans came to the American west, the Great Plains were home to more than 30 million buffalo. These huge creatures roamed the land, grazing off the grasses. Native cultures centered around the important animals. Native people used buffalo skin, meat, and bones for food, shelter, clothing, and tools.

When White settlers came to the area, they hunted the buffalo with guns. Their livestock also brought diseases that hurt the buffalo. By the 1890s, there were fewer than 1,000 buffalo left.

Activists worked hard to save buffalo from going extinct. Today, there are about 400,000 buffalo in America.

NEVADA

The Spanish named the state Nevada after the Spanish word for snow, *nieve*, which covered the mountains during the winter. Nevada is nicknamed the Silver State but that's not the only precious metal found there. About 75 percent of all of the gold mined in America comes from Nevada.

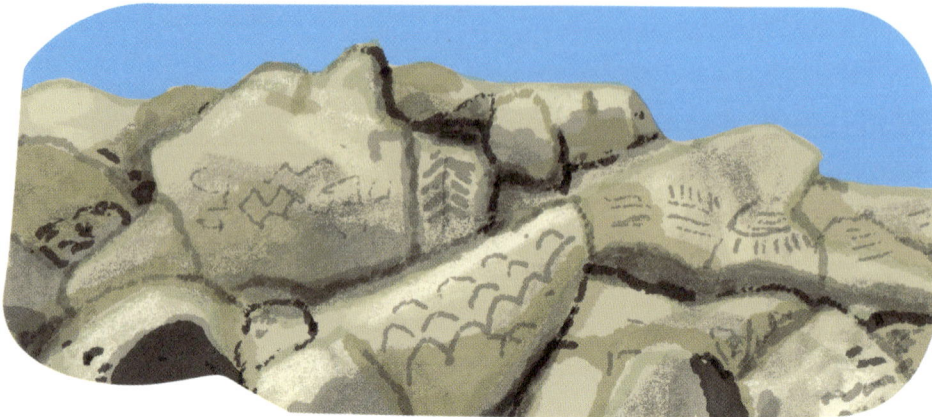

HISTORY

About 14,000 years ago, a group of people carved swirls, diamonds, and trees into large boulders. Those early humans are long gone, but their carvings remain. The Winnemucca petroglyphs are the oldest in the country.

Much later, many Native people came to the area. Spanish settlers claimed the land in 1519. Nevada became part of Mexico in 1821. The United States won the Mexican-American war and took the land in 1848. Eleven years later, silver was discovered at the Comstock Lode. A rush of people came to the area to seek their fortunes.

Nevada is home to more than half of America's wild horses. About 40,000 of these beautiful animals live there.

LANDSCAPE

Nevada has a rugged, varied landscape. The Sierra Nevada mountain range passes through part of the western edge of the state. More than 300 other north-south mountain ranges run across Nevada. The highest point is Boundary Peak, which rises 13,147 ft (4,007 m), and sits on the border with California. Also bordering California is Lake Tahoe, the country's biggest alpine lake. At the southern tip of Nevada is the Mojave Desert.

LAS VEGAS

Nevada's largest city, Las Vegas, gets about 40 million visitors each year. They come to enjoy the city's hotels, food, gambling, and incredible shows. The Las Vegas strip is a stretch of lively hotels, casinos, restaurants, and more. It is so brightly lit that at night, it is one of the brightest spots on Earth.

BY THE NUMBERS:

Las Vegas has:
- **more than 150 casinos**
- **more than 150,000 hotel and motel rooms**
- **the 7th busiest airport in North America**

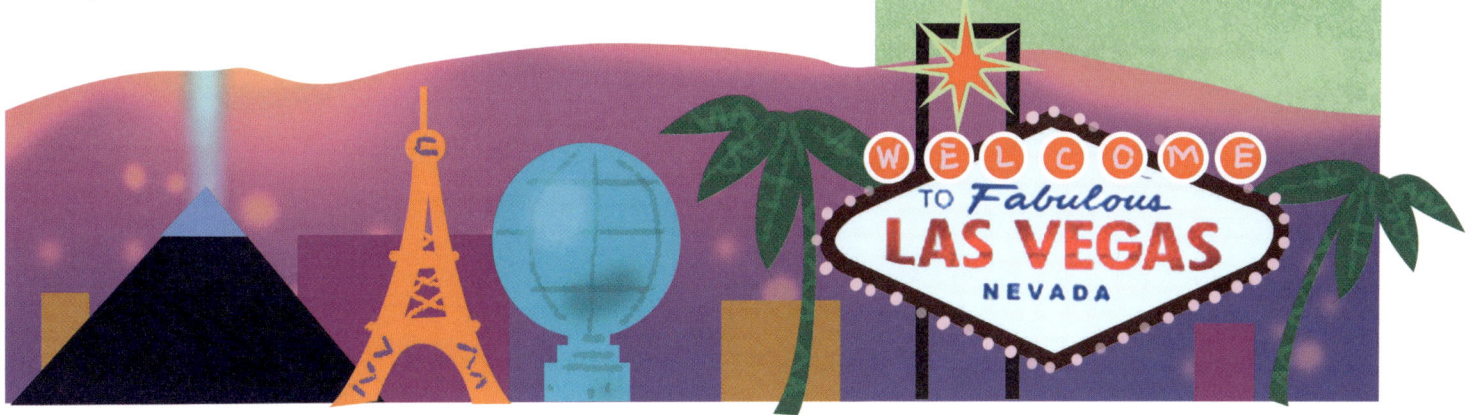

WEATHER

Nevada is the country's driest state. And the driest part of the driest state—the Mojave Desert—is very, very dry. On average, it gets just 2 to 6 in (50 to 150 mm) of rainfall each year. Temperatures in the Mojave range from the 30s °F (-1.1 to 3.8 °C) to above 100 °F (37.7 °C).

In the rest of Nevada, weather is slightly less extreme. Winters are cool and dry, while summers are very, very hot. Some mountain towns get lots of snow, attracting skiers from around the country.

ALIEN COUNTRY

Area 51 is an Air Force installation in southern Nevada. While not much is known about exactly what happens there, many people tell stories that it's a secret facility where scientists study aliens and spaceships. Some people even believe they've spotted UFOs above it. But Area 51 isn't the state's only place famous for its UFOs. A 98-mi (158-km) section of Route 375 is so popular among alien hunters that it's been renamed the Extraterrestrial Highway.

THE GRAND CANYON

The Grand Canyon is a spectacular gorge on the Colorado River in northern Arizona. It formed at least 5 million years ago when the powerful Colorado River eroded through layers of the surrounding rock. This process slowly cut through deeper and deeper layers. It eventually exposed some of the oldest rock surfaces on Earth, including some that are 1.8 billion years old.

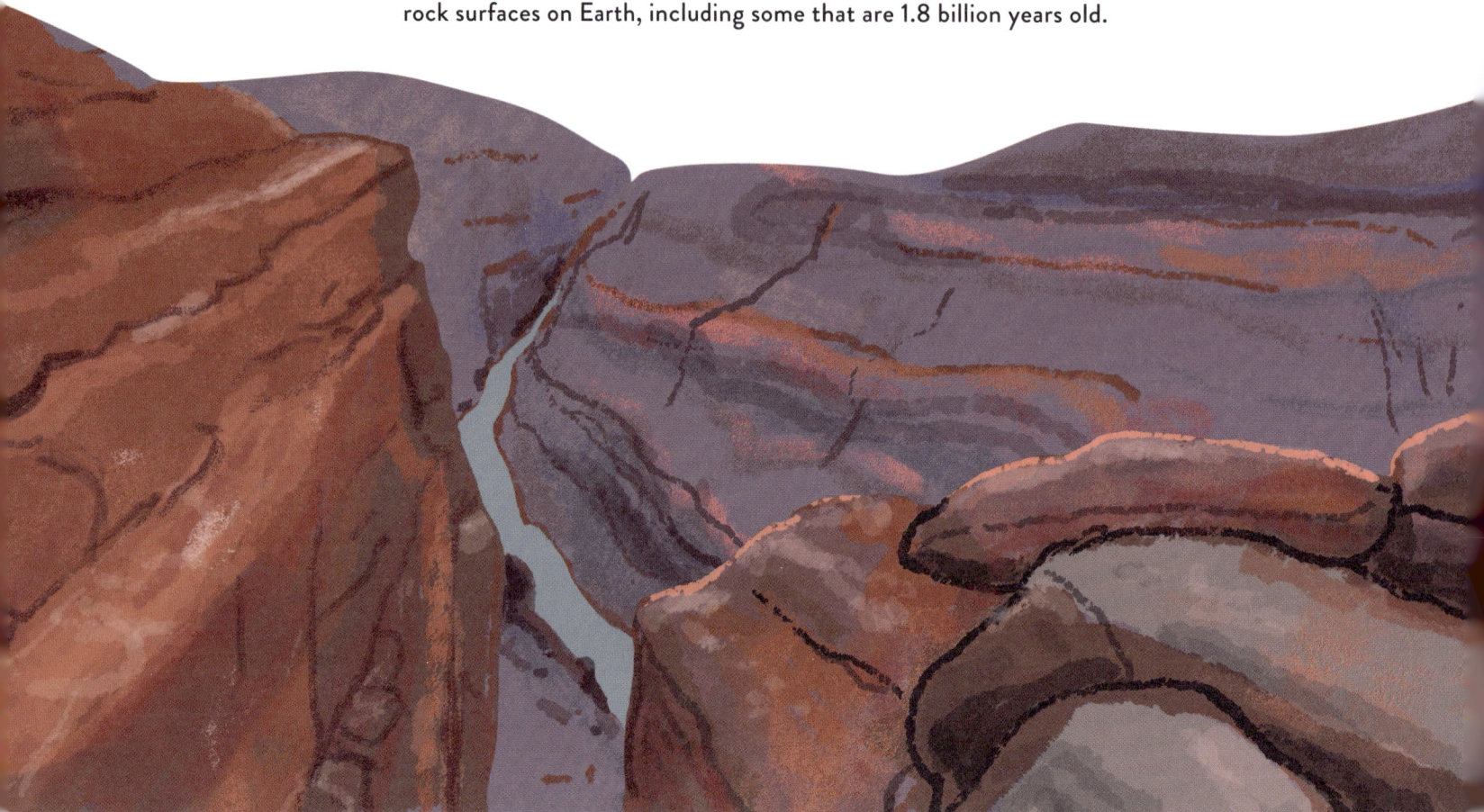

At 1 mi deep, 270 mi (435 km) long, and up to 18 mi (29 km) wide, it is one of the biggest and deepest canyons on Earth. It is so big and deep that different parts of it get different weather conditions. For example, it might be 80 °F (26.7 °C) at the bottom of the canyon and at the same time, 50 or 55 °F (10 or 17.8 °C) at the rim.

In total, the Grand Canyon is 1,904 sq mi (4,930 sq km). That's bigger than the state of Rhode Island!

PRESERVATION

In 1903, President Theodore Roosevelt gave a speech about the importance of protecting the Grand Canyon. He said, "Keep this great wonder of nature as it now is...keep it for your children and your children's children and for all who come after you, as one of the great sights which every American, if he can travel at all, should see." Today, many groups work to uphold that mission. Restrictions on mining, construction, and hunting in the area around the canyon help maintain its natural beauty.

THE COLORADO RIVER

The Colorado River is the powerful waterway that snakes through the Grand Canyon. Within the Grand Canyon, the river has an average depth of 40 ft (12 m) and width of 300 ft (91 m). Flowing downhill, the river drops about 2,000 ft (610 m) as it winds through the canyon. This steep slope makes the deep and wide river water move quickly. It continues to erode the canyon each day, meaning that more and more rock is being exposed.

A popular way to experience both the Grand Canyon and the Colorado River is whitewater rafting. The canyon has more than 80 big water rapids, which challenge rafters to paddle hard and stay on their raft—often soaking them in the process.

The Grand Canyon is one of the seven Wonders of the World.

THE SKYWALK

Visitors wanting a unique look at the Grand Canyon can check out the Skywalk. It is a horseshoe-shaped platform that juts 70 ft (21 m) out over the canyon. The steel-framed structure has glass floors and walls, allowing jaw-dropping views. The Skywalk is located on Hualapai lands, and is managed by the Tribe.

About 6 million people visit the Grand Canyon each year.

STUNTS

The Grand Canyon has long attracted professional stunt people looking for a place to try their death-defying feats. In 1922, a pilot landed his airplane inside the canyon. In 1980, a stunt driver drove off the canyon's edge and then leapt out, floating to safety with a parachute while the car crashed below. In 2006, a skateboarder rode off a huge ramp, slid on a giant rail, and then basejumped into the canyon. Perhaps the most famous canyon stunt ever happened in 1999, when Robbie Knievel jumped a narrow section of the canyon on a motorbike.

Most of these stunts did not take place within the Grand Canyon National Park's boundaries, but in nearby regions of the canyon. Park officials strongly discourage such behavior.

NEW HAMPSHIRE

New Hampshire was named after the English county of Hampshire.
Its nickname comes from the state's many granite quarries.

HISTORY

Humans have lived in New Hampshire for nearly 13,000 years. Europeans
came to the area during the 1500s. In the 1600s, English sailors began fishing
along New England's coast and coming ashore on New Hampshire's Isles of
Shoals. In 1623, the English created their first settlement there. Over time, the
French and English settlers began to argue over the land. They fought and the
Native people supported the French. As more European settlers arrived and
moved westward, many Native people were pushed out of the land.

LANDSCAPE AND WEATHER

The White Mountains cover the northern third
of New Hampshire. Their name probably comes
from their snow-covered caps. This snow makes
for especially good skiing, something many
people come to New Hampshire to do. Olympic
gold medalist, Bode Miller, learned to ski in the
White Mountains. New Hampshire's highest
peak, Mount Washington, is found in the White
Mountains. This 6,288-ft-tall (1,918 m) peak
is one of the windiest places on the planet. In
1934, the wind sweeping across its summit
was clocked at 231 mph (372 kph).

The center of New Hampshire is
marked by hills, valleys, and lakes.
Mount Monadnock, a favorite location
for mountain climbers, is located there
too. About 125,000 people climb
it each year.

FAST FACTS

Admitted to the Union:
June 21, 1788

State Number: **9**

Population: **1.4 million**

Capital: **Concord**

Nickname: **The Granite State**

State Bird: **Purple finch**

At the southeastern corner of the state are 18 mi (29 km) of
general Atlantic coastline. During the warm summers, tourists
and locals flock to the beach to swim, surf, and play.

STATE MOTTO

New Hampshire has an official motto: "Live free or die," which comes from its role in the Revolutionary War. However, it also has an unofficial motto: "As New Hampshire goes, so goes the nation." This references its unique role in politics. Every four years, New Hampshire hosts the first presidential primary, in which voters choose the candidates they want to represent them in the presidential election. This early event often sets the tone for elections.

The first potatoes grown in North America were planted in New Hampshire's Londonderry Common Field in 1719.

In January, 1776, New Hampshire became the first colony to declare itself independent from Great Britain.

New Hampshire has about 1,300 ponds and lakes, as well as 40 rivers.

THE COG

Mount Washington's Cog Railway is the world's second-steepest rack railway. At over 150 years old, it's one of the most historic railways, too. Riders thrill at the 3-hour roundtrip experience that takes them to the top of Mount Washington at grades of up to 38 percent.

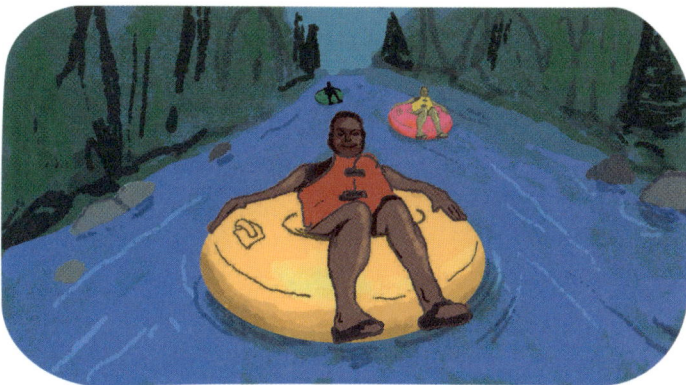

COMEDIANS

New Hampshire has given the country some of its funniest personalities. Adam Sandler, Sarah Silverman, and Seth Meyers are all from the state.

NEW JERSEY

New Jersey is named after the Isle of Jersey in the English Channel. Its nickname is the Garden State because of the amount of food grown there during the 1800s. Today, the nickname still fits. There are more than 10,000 farms in New Jersey, producing over 100 types of fruits and vegetables.

HISTORY

Humans began living in New Jersey at least 10,000 years ago. They likely hunted animals like mastodons and mammoths. In the 1500s, Europeans began arriving in the area. The first was Italy's Giovanni de Verrazano. In 1609, Henry Hudson came and claimed the surrounding land for the Dutch, calling it New Netherland. Later, Dutch, Swedish, and Finnish settlers came to the area. In 1664, the English gained control. New Jersey became one of the 13 English colonies in America.

New Jersey's central location made it an important colony during the Revolutionary War. More than 100 battles were fought there. In 1787, New Jersey was the third state to ratify the Constitution and in 1789, it was the first state to ratify the Bill of Rights.

FAST FACTS

Admitted to the Union:
December 18, 1887

State Number: **3**

Population: **9.3 million**

Capital: **Trenton**

Nickname:
The Garden State

State Animal: **Horse**

New Jersey's coastline is called the Jersey Shore. It is famous for its beach towns, boardwalks, water parks, and amusement parks.

LANDSCAPE

New Jersey has a variety of geographical regions. In the northwest, the state is mountainous. The highest elevation, High Point, is located there, and stands 1,803 ft (550 m) tall. The Delaware Water Gap, along the border with Pennsylvania, is a scenic area where the Delaware River slices through the Appalachian Mountains. In the northeast, the Hudson River runs along the border between New Jersey and New York. Steep cliffs along a portion of the river called the Palisades are striking and beautiful. The southern half of the state is made up of the relatively flat Coastal Plains. The eastern edge of New Jersey is made up of about 130 mi (209 km) of Atlantic coastline.

WEATHER

Summers in New Jersey are hot and humid, and winters are cold and snowy. The spring and fall are usually mild.

POPULATION

New Jersey has the highest population density out of all of the states. Most of its residents live in cities. Here are the most populated:

1. **Newark** (population 312,000)
2. **Jersey City** (population 292,000)
3. **Paterson** (159,000)

PORK ROLL

Nearly every sandwich shop, deli, diner, or bagel shop in New Jersey carries a processed meat called Taylor's Pork Roll. Slices of it are heated on a griddle, and then served in a sandwich with cheese and eggs. It's such a popular dish that the state hosts two pork roll festivals each year.

ATLANTIC CITY

Atlantic City is a popular vacation destination on the Atlantic coast. Known for its casinos, hotels, spas, and restaurants, it hosts about 27 million tourists each year. Visitors enjoy strolling on its famous boardwalk, the oldest and longest in the world.

Saltwater taffy, a popular sweet treat, traces its origins to Atlantic City. It was first served there in 1883.

The streets and properties in the board game, Monopoly, are modeled after Atlantic City.

NEW MEXICO

The name New Mexico dates back to the 1500s. Spanish explorers had discovered great wealth in an area known as Mexico. They hoped to find more treasure to the north, in *Nuevo Mexico*.

HISTORY

The oldest human footprints found in America are in New Mexico. This set of clear prints is at least 21,000 years old. Archaeologists have found many more artifacts tracing human history in the state, including old hunting grounds, tools, and pottery shards.

Thousands of years after those footprints were formed, Native people developed complex settlements on the land. One settlement called Cicuyé was especially impressive. People began building simple homes there around 800 CE. By 1450, the area had developed into a spectacular 5-story fortress. About 2,000 people lived there.

Santa Fe is the oldest capital city in North America. It was founded by the Spanish in 1610.

Spanish explorer Francisco Vasquez de Coronado came to the area in 1540. Following his trip, the Spanish claimed the land. When Mexico declared itself independent of Spain, New Mexico fell under Mexican control. The United States won the Mexican-American War in 1848. This finally made New Mexico a US territory.

WEATHER AND OUTDOOR FUN

New Mexico's summers are hot and dry. The highest temperature ever recorded there was 122 °F (50 °C) in June 1944. The winters are cold and often snowy, depending on the elevation. Some areas of the state average as little as 3 in (7.6 cm) of snow a year, while others get much more. Red River, located in the Sangre de Cristo Mountains, gets about 190 in (483 cm) of snow each year.

GREEN CHILES

Green chiles are a vital part of New Mexico's food scene. These long, thin green peppers are spicier than bell peppers, but milder than jalapeños. They're eaten stewed, in salsas, or plain.

HOT AIR BALLOONS

Each October, hundreds of thousands of people flock to the Albuquerque International Balloon Fiesta to take in the biggest hot air balloon event in the world. More than 500 balloons take to the sky while live musicians and performers entertain people on the ground.

LANDSCAPE

From mountains to flat plains, from dense forests to dry deserts, New Mexico's landscape is incredibly mixed. The eastern side of the state is partly covered by the Great Plains. In north-central New Mexico are the Rocky Mountains, including the state's highest point, Wheeler Peak. It is 13,167 ft (4,011 m) tall. The Rio Grande runs through the middle of the state, snaking past mountains, deserts, and valleys.

The Rio Grande passes through the Rio Grande Gorge, a spectacular 50-mi (80-km) stretch with walls that tower up to 800 ft (244 m).

Carlsbad Caverns National Park is in southeastern New Mexico. It contains 120 caves, including some of the largest in North America. One, the Lechuguilla Cave, is the second deepest cave in America. It is 1,604 ft (489 m) deep. The park's most famous cave is called Carlsbad Cavern. It includes an area called the Big Room, which is North America's largest single cave chamber by volume. When describing the cavern, famed actor Will Rogers said it was "the Grand Canyon with a roof over it."

In south-central New Mexico is an area called White Sands. Here, 275 sq mi (712 sq km) of desert are covered in huge dunes of white sand. Adventurous visitors enjoy sand surfing and sand sledding down the huge dunes.

NEW YORK

New York got its name from England's Duke of York (who later became King James II). He helped capture the land from the Dutch, who had previously called the area New Netherlands. People aren't sure exactly where the nickname the "Empire state" came from. George Washington might have started it by calling New York the "seat of the empire."

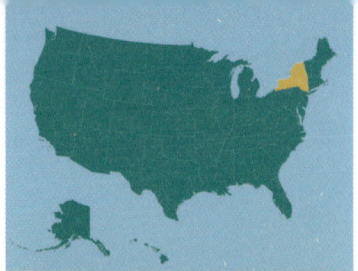

HISTORY

Humans have lived on the land that is now New York for more than 12,000 years. Small groups of early people traveled the land, hunting and gathering. They shared the area with now-extinct animals such as giant beavers and mastodons. Later, many Native groups came to live on the land.

French, Dutch, and English people came to New York in the 1500s and 1600s. The Dutch and English fought over the land, and the English took control in 1664. One of the 13 colonies, New York played an important role in the American Revolution. About one-third of the battles fought in the Revolutionary War took place in New York. Even after the war, the state remained important to the young nation. New York City briefly served as the nation's capital from 1785 until 1790.

The City of New Amsterdam
on the Island of Manhattan 1660

FAST FACTS

Admitted to the Union:
July 26, 1788

State Number: **11**

Population: **19.8 million**

Capital: **Albany**

Nickname:
The Empire State

State Mammal: **Beaver**

The first pizzeria in the country, Lombardi's, opened in New York City in 1905.

LANDSCAPE

Northeastern New York is covered by the rugged Adirondack Mountains, including the state's highest peak, Mount Marcy, which is 5,114 ft (1,559 m) tall. The western part of the state includes the Finger Lakes. These are eleven long, thin lakes that are surrounded by gorges, waterfalls, and beautiful forests. The St. Lawrence River runs between New York and Canada. On the river are a collection of nearly 2,000 small islands called the Thousand Islands. The eastern side of New York meets the Atlantic Ocean. An archipelago, or chain of islands, juts out into the Atlantic. It includes Manhattan Island, Staten Island, and Long Island.

NEW YORK CITY

New York City has many nicknames, including the Big Apple, NYC, and the City that Never Sleeps. Whatever it's called, New York City is a leader in culture, politics, finance, and business. With more than 8.8 million residents, New York City is also the country's biggest city.

New York City is divided into five boroughs, or neighborhoods. They are the Bronx, Brooklyn, Queens, Staten Island, and Manhattan. The iconic skylines often associated with the city are found in Manhattan.

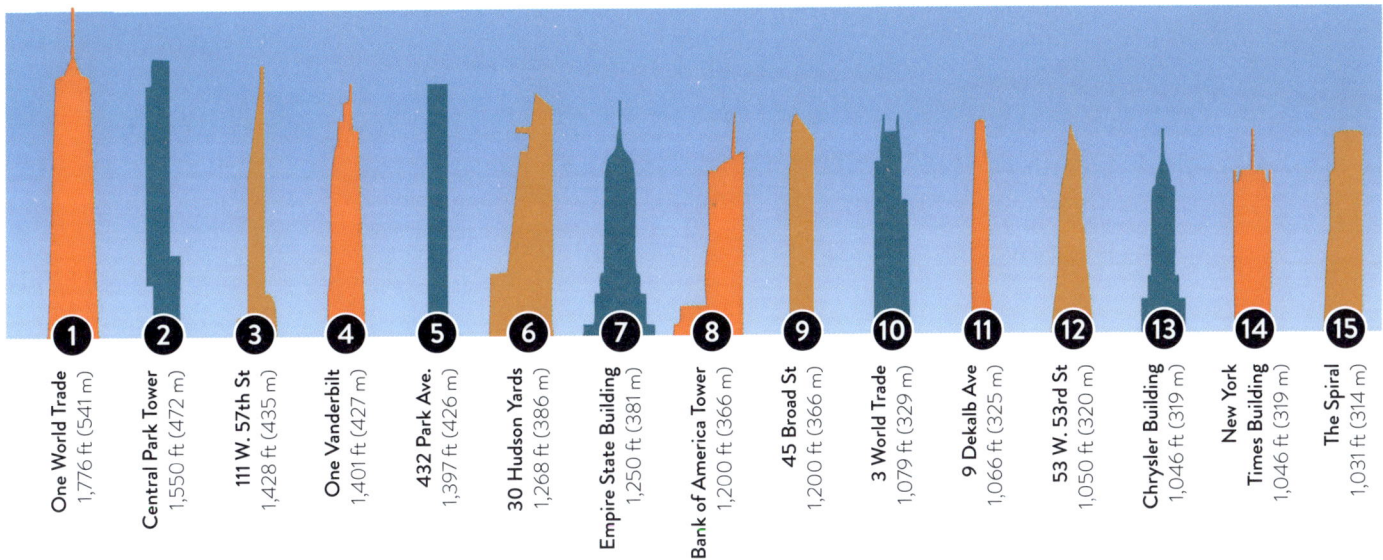

1. One World Trade — 1,776 ft (541 m)
2. Central Park Tower — 1,550 ft (472 m)
3. 111 W. 57th St — 1,428 ft (435 m)
4. One Vanderbilt — 1,401 ft (427 m)
5. 432 Park Ave. — 1,397 ft (426 m)
6. 30 Hudson Yards — 1,268 ft (386 m)
7. Empire State Building — 1,250 ft (381 m)
8. Bank of America Tower — 1,200 ft (366 m)
9. 45 Broad St — 1,200 ft (366 m)
10. 3 World Trade — 1,079 ft (329 m)
11. 9 Dekalb Ave — 1,066 ft (325 m)
12. 53 W. 53rd St — 1,050 ft (320 m)
13. Chrysler Building — 1,046 ft (319 m)
14. New York Times Building — 1,046 ft (319 m)
15. The Spiral — 1,031 ft (314 m)

Central Park is an 840-acre (340-hectare) park located in the center of Manhattan. This giant green space includes walking trails, lakes, playgrounds, fountains, an ice-skating rink, a zoo, and an art museum.

WEATHER

New York experiences four distinct seasons. Springs are wet and cool, summers are hot and warm, falls are cool and crisp, and winters are snowy and cold. The hottest month of the year is July and the coldest is January.

NIAGARA FALLS

Niagara Falls is a series of three waterfalls located on the border between Canada and New York. Two of the falls, Bridal Veil Falls and American Falls, are in New York, while Horseshoe Falls is in Canada.

About 9 million people visit New York's Niagara Falls State Park each year. A popular way to see the falls up close is to ride on board a Maid of the Mist sightseeing boat. Passengers are taken past the base of the American Falls before venturing to the basin of Horseshoe Falls.

BROADWAY

Broadway is New York City's famous theater scene. It is named after Broadway, a wide street that is lined with many theaters. In the late 1800s, Broadway's theaters had electric marquees and signs. Their lights were so bright that the street was nicknamed "the Great White Way."

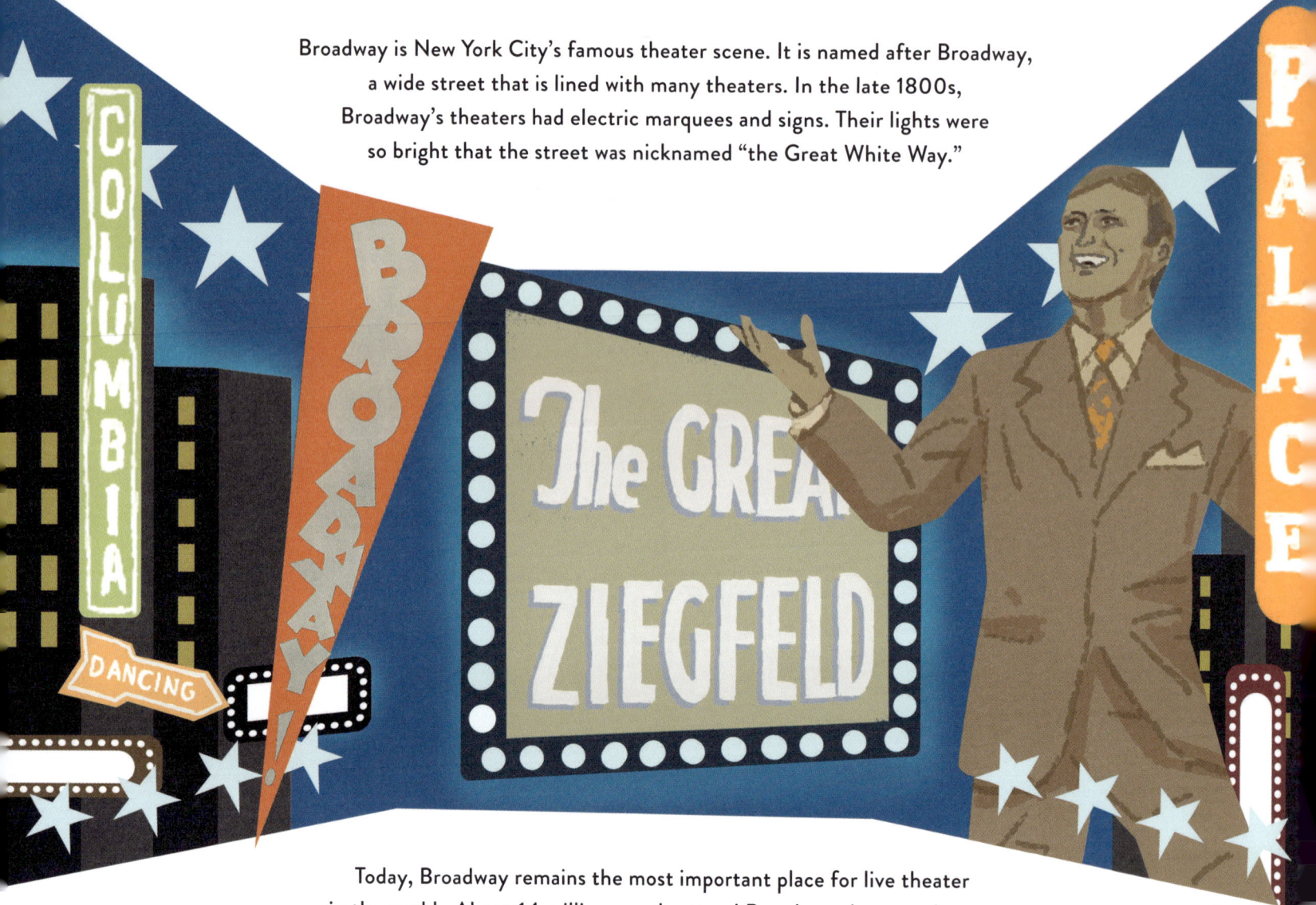

COLUMBIA

DANCING

BROADWAY!

The GREAT ZIEGFELD

PALACE

Today, Broadway remains the most important place for live theater in the world. About 14 million people attend Broadway shows each year.

TIMES SQUARE

Times Square is a bustling area known for its brightly lit billboards, sidewalks crammed with tourists, and iconic New Year's Eve ball drop celebrations. But it is also the heart of Broadway. Each year, some of the most beloved live shows are performed in Times Square theaters.

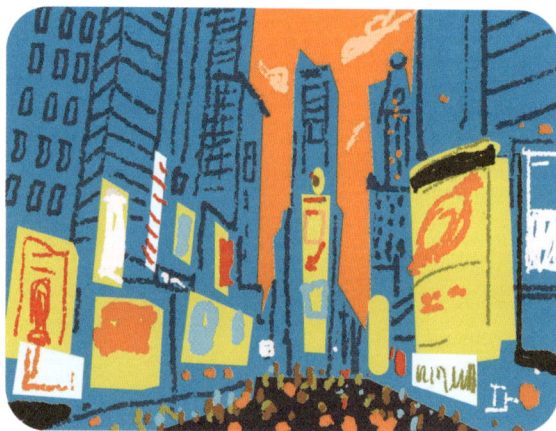

Times Square buildings are legally required to have bright displays. This helps the area maintain its vibrant, showy reputation.

LONGEST RUNNING SHOWS

Some shows come to Broadway for a short time. Others stick around. Here are the longest-running Broadway shows.

Chicago
(running since 1996)

The Lion King
(running since 1997)

MAKING THE CUT

There are 41 Broadway theaters, but only four of them are actually located on Broadway. The rest are in the area known as the theater district. Theaters considered "Broadway" must seat more than 500 people. Smaller theaters that seat between 99 and 499 people are considered "Off Broadway." Theaters that seat fewer than 98 people are called "Off Off Broadway."

Tonys are awards given for achievement in theater. Only shows performing on Broadway are eligible for Tonys.

Tickets to Broadway shows typically range from $20 to nearly $200, depending on the seats and timing. Hopeful *Hamilton* fans can enter a lottery to win tickets for just $10.

TOP EARNERS

The Lion King is a hit Broadway show that uses a mix of puppetry and actors. It is the top-earning Broadway production of all time. Over the course of about 10,000 performances, the show has made more than $1.7 billion.

Broadway performers are paid a minimum of $2,034 per week. Celebrity performers can earn more than $100,000 a week.

ANIMALS ON STAGE

Broadway stages aren't just for humans. Animals have had their share of the spotlight there, too. Small animals, such as dogs, have played lovable sidekicks in plays such as *Annie*. Occasionally, big animals have taken the stage. In 1935, an elephant was a star actor in *Jumbo*.

BROADWAY STARTS

Some of the biggest celebrities got their start on Broadway, including these A-list stars:

- Ariana Grande
- Sarah Jessica Parker
- Nick Jonas
- Kristen Bell
- Anna Kendrick

FLOPS

Not every Broadway show is a smash success with a decades-long run. Some only last a few months. A very few have closed after even shorter runs. One such play, the 1983 *Moose Murders*, lasted one single night on Broadway. Critics called it "titanically bad," "indescribably bad," and "the worst play I have ever seen on a Broadway stage."

NORTH CAROLINA

North Carolina's name comes from the Latin for Charles: *Carolus*.
It is named for England's king, Charles I.

North Carolina used to produce much of the tar used by the English navy.
Workers who went barefoot could get tar on the soles of their feet. At first, calling
someone a "tar heel" was an insult because it meant they worked in a lowly job.
But during the Civil War it became a title North Carolinians were proud of.

HISTORY

About 10,000 years ago, the first people came to North Carolina. They traveled in small family groups, hunting and gathering. Much later, Native people came to live on the land.

In the 1500s, Spanish settlers came to the area. The English soon followed but the people of North Carolina grew tired of British rule. In 1789, it became the 12th state in the Union.

FAST FACTS

Admitted to the Union:
November 21, 1789

State Number: **12**

Population: **10.7 million**

Capital: **Raleigh**

Nickname: **The Tar Heel State**

State Mammal: **Gray squirrel**

INVENTIONS

The following things were invented in North Carolina:
- Pepsi Cola
- Krispy Kreme
- Putt-putt golf
- Vicks VapoRub

WILD HORSES

When early Spanish explorers came to North Carolina, they brought Spanish mustangs with them. Some of these horses were left behind. Over the centuries that followed, herds of Spanish mustangs continued to live, wild, along the Crystal Coast and Outer Banks. Today, hundreds of these horses are still there.

LANDSCAPE

North Carolina's geography can be divided into three sections. To the west are the Blue Ridge Mountains and the Great Smoky Mountains, both part of the Appalachian Mountains. This is where you can find the state's highest peak. Mount Mitchell is 6,684 ft (2,037 m) high. The center of the state is the Piedmont, a region of rolling hills.

In the east, North Carolina's Coastal Plain is low-lying and often swampy. North Carolina has many beautiful beaches along the Atlantic Ocean. It also has a chain of islands called the Outer Banks. Three capes extend from North Carolina into the Atlantic Ocean: Cape Fear, Cape Lookout, and Cape Hatteras.

The area off North Carolina's coastline has been called the "Graveyard of the Atlantic." More than 2,000 ships have sunk there.

In 1903, the Wright brothers achieved the first sustained flight in an aircraft in Kill Devil Hills, North Carolina. The flight lasted 12 seconds and changed history.

BLACKBEARD

One of history's most famous pirates was Edward Teach, commonly called Blackbeard. He often sailed the coast of North Carolina. He even lived in Bath, North Carolina during the summer of 1718.

WEATHER

North Carolina winters are cool and wet, with temperatures occasionally dropping into the 20s °F or lower (-6.7 to -1.7 °C). The coldest temperature ever recorded there was on Mount Mitchell in 1985, when thermometers read -34 °F (-36.7 °C). The summers are very hot and muggy, often into the 90s °F (32.2–37.2 °C). The state's hottest recorded temperature was in 1983, when the Fayetteville airport reached 110 °F (43.3 °C).

NORTH DAKOTA

Dakota comes from the Sioux word for "friend." The state's nickname comes from the International Peace Garden, which is located on the border between North Dakota and Canada. It honors a pledge that Canada and the United States will never go to war against each other.

FAST FACTS

Admitted to the Union:
November 2, 1889

State Number: **39**

Population: **775,000**

Capital: **Bismarck**

Nickname:
The Peace Garden State

State Bird:
Western meadowlark

HISTORY

In the late 1980s, a notch was cut into North Dakota's Lake Ilo Dam in order to lower the lake's water level. Soon after, workers began noticing artifacts, such as tools, stones, and pottery shards, on the lake bed. Archaeologists found 13 prehistoric sites, with a total of 58,000 artifacts. These revealed that humans had been in the area for more than 10,000 years.

In the 1700s, a French Canadian explorer named Pierre Gaultier de Varennes et de La Vérendrye came to the area. Much of the land became part of the French territory called Louisiana. The land passed to the Spanish then back to the French. Finally, the United States bought it in the Louisiana Purchase in 1803. North and South Dakota were not separated until February 22, 1889, when the Dakota territory was split prior to the states' admission to the Union.

The geographical center of North America is found in Rugby, North Dakota.

39TH STATE

The paperwork making North and South Dakota into states landed on President Benjamin Harrison's desk at the same time. He deliberately shuffled the papers so that he wouldn't show favoritism to either state. North Dakota's paperwork came up first, and so it became the 39th state. South Dakota followed as the 40th state.

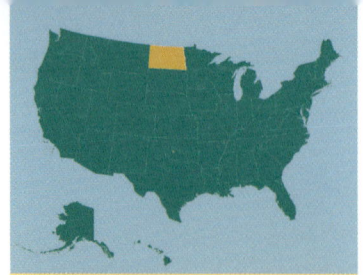

LANDSCAPE

On the eastern edge of North Dakota is the Red River and a surrounding flat river valley. The soil in this region is rich and fertile, making it the perfect place for farms. Crossing the state from the southeast to the northwest is the Drift Prairie. This is an area with low hills, where grain farming is common. The southwestern part of North Dakota is made up of the Missouri Plateau. This is a region of bluffs, cliffs, and steep hills. It also includes an area called the Badlands, a collection of buttes, washouts, and rocky outcroppings. White Butte, the state's highest point, is found in the Badlands. It is 3,506 ft (1,069 m) tall.

FARMS

Over 90 percent of North Dakota's land is covered by farms or ranches. Those farms have an incredible output. North Dakota is the nation's top producer of dry edible beans, spring wheat, canola, flaxseed, and honey.

WEATHER

North Dakota's weather experiences huge swings throughout the year, and sometimes during the course of a single day as well. Winters are frigid, with over 50 days below 0 °F (-17.9 °C). Summers are hot, often exceeding 90 °F (32.2 °C).

POTATO BOWL

The Potato Bowl is a weeklong festival that includes a home game for the University of North Dakota's football team, a parade, and the world's biggest French fry feed. In 2015, over 5,000 lb (2,270 kg) of French fries were served.

North Dakota is home to some of America's most spectacular wildlife, including:
bison
bighorn sheep
elk
moose
pronghorn

OHIO

Ohio's name may come from the Iroquois word for "great river," *oyo*. Ohio is called the Buckeye State after the buckeye tree, which is found throughout the state.

HISTORY

Humans have lived in Ohio for more than 13,000 years. The earliest people hunted large game animals such as ground sloths, and used crude stone tools to butcher the meat. Over the thousands of years that followed, Native people came to live on the land.

French explorers and fur trappers came to the area in the mid-1600s. One hundred years later, the British took control of the land. After the Revolutionary War, Ohio became part of the Northwest Territory. This was an area of land that would later be divided into Michigan, Illinois, part of Minnesota, Wisconsin, Indiana, and Ohio.

A STATE MISTAKE

In 1803, when Congress met to approve Ohio's new statehood, an important step was missed. Congress did not ratify Ohio's constitution. This meant that technically, Ohio was not yet a state. This issue was not resolved until 1953, when Ohio was retroactively granted statehood.

FAST FACTS

Admitted to the Union: **March 1, 1803**

State Number: **17**

Population: **11.8 million**

Capital: **Columbus**

Nickname: **The Buckeye State**

State Mammal: **White-tailed deer**

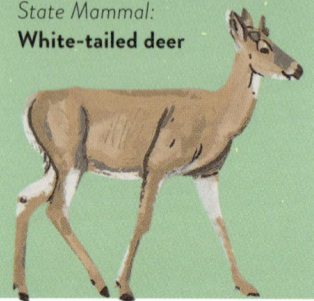

SERPENT MOUND

Southwestern Ohio is home to a 300-million-year-old, 9-mi (14.5-km) wide meteorite crater. In the southwestern part of the crater is a giant earthen mound shaped like a winding snake known as Serpent Mound. Archaeologists think it was created between 900 and 2,000 years ago. Three burial mounds are nearby. This suggests that the area was very important to the people who built it.

Serpent Mound is not the only earthen construction found in the state. Remains of more than 70 mounds have been discovered in southern Ohio alone.

Ohio is the only state with a non-rectangular flag. It is folded in a special way, with 17 folds to represent the fact that Ohio was the 17th state.

WEATHER

Ohio has four different seasons. Summers are hot, winters are cold and snowy, and spring and fall are cool and wet. The state gets its fair share of extreme weather, too, with occasional tornadoes, floods, blizzards, and heatwaves.

BASEBALL HISTORY

Ohio had the first professional baseball team. The Cincinnati Red Stockings were founded in 1867. The team name changed several times over the following years, from the Red Stockings to the Reds to the Redlegs and then back to the Reds.

SPACEFLIGHT

Ohio is the birthplace of 25 American astronauts. These space pioneers have accomplished some amazing feats, including:

- 80 space flights
- Three flights to the moon
- 22,000 hours in space

Neil Armstrong was born in Ohio

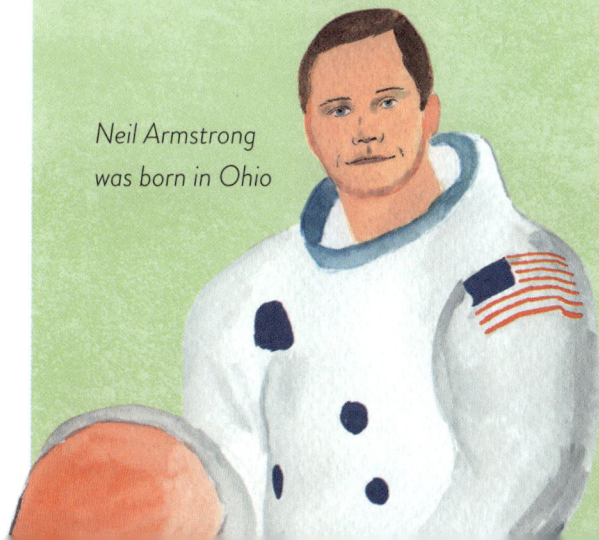

LANDSCAPE

Ohio's eastern half is made up of the Appalachian Plateau, a region of rugged hills and valleys. The western half of the state is mostly low-lying plains, including the Great Lakes Plains and the Till Plains. These areas are very fertile, making them perfect for agriculture, Ohio's largest industry. The Bluegrass Region, a hilly area known for the variety of wildlife found there, is in the southeastern part of the state. Lucky visitors can spot amazing creatures such as the rare green salamander and Allegheny woodrat.

OKLAHOMA

Oklahoma comes from the Choctaw words for "brave nation." The state's nickname comes from an event in April 1889, when people were allowed to rush into Oklahoma and claim land for themselves. While everyone was supposed to wait for the sound of a starting pistol, some people dashed forward early, or too soon. They became known as the "sooners."

DEEP HISTORY

Humans may have lived in Oklahoma for as long as 20,000 or even 30,000 years. The state is home to more than 17,000 historic sites that help archaeologists piece together its rich history.

When Spanish and French explorers came to Oklahoma, beginning in the 1500s, they found a land already occupied by many different Native groups. The Caddo, Wichita, and others farmed some of the land. The Plains Apache, Osage, and Pawnee were among the groups who hunted and gathered there. In the 1700s, many Comanche people came to the area.

In 1803, the Louisiana Purchase made the land of Oklahoma part of the United States. Later, an area of the state was declared Indian Territory. Thousands of Native people from the eastern part of the United States were forced to move there.

ROBBERS CAVE

Robbers Cave is a state park in southeast Oklahoma with huge boulders, dense forests, dark caverns, and deep caves. In the past, outlaws like Jesse James are said to have used it as a hideout. Today, people go to the park to ride horses, hike, fish, and explore its caves.

FAST FACTS

Admitted to the Union:
November 16, 1907

State Number: **46**

Population: **4 million**

Capital: **Oklahoma City**

Nickname: **The Sooner State**

State Mammal:
American bison

Oklahoma is home to 39 tribal nations. Today, about 13 percent of the people living there are Native American.

WEATHER

Spring and fall in Oklahoma are cool, and winters are very cold. Summers are hot and dry. Each year the state experiences an average of 57 tornadoes.

LANDSCAPE

Oklahoma's landscape is extremely varied, with mountains, deserts, valleys, and more. In west-central Oklahoma is the Little Sahara State Park, named for its resemblance to the Sahara Desert in Africa. The Pan Handle is made up of high plains, including the Black Mesa, the state's highest point. It is 4,973 ft (1,516 m) high. Three major mountain systems pass through Oklahoma: the Arbuckles, Wichitas, and Ouachitas. The Red River forms much of the border between Oklahoma and Texas. The surrounding valley is flat and fertile.

> *"Oklahoma,*
> *where the wind comes sweeping down the plain,*
> *And the waving wheat*
> *Can sure smell sweet*
> *When the wind comes right behind the rain."*
>
> —OSCAR HAMMERSTEIN, *from the musical* Oklahoma

Oklahoma is shaped like a pan. Its western region is called the "Pan Handle."

OIL, GAS, AND WIND

Oklahoma is one of the country's top producers of oil and natural gas. The state produces about three times as much energy as it consumes. It is also a leader in wind energy. In 2022, 44 percent of the energy generated in the state came from wind.

ROUTE 66

Route 66 is not America's oldest highway. It is not the longest, the busiest, or the fastest, either. It is, however, an important and beloved part of American culture and history.

HISTORY

In the early 1900s, traveling the country by car was very hard. Most roads were rough and unpaved. Pathways across the country did not often travel in straight lines, and sometimes were called different things in different areas. In the 1910s and 1920s, this began to change. Roads were organized, paved, and given clear signs. In 1926, construction began on a new route between Chicago and Los Angeles called US Highway 66. Some parts were built over existing roadways, while others were new. When finished in 1938, it stretched some 2,448 mi (3,940 km).

Route 66 made traveling from Chicago to the west coast faster and easier than ever before. Its paved surface allowed people to use it in any weather. All along the highway, stores, restaurants, gas stations, and hotels began to pop up to cater to the travelers. Money poured in. Small towns along the route that had been isolated in the past also benefited from the traffic. Route 66 travelers helped support people along the highway even through the Great Depression.

ON FOOT

In 1928, a footrace was organized to raise awareness of Route 66. Racers started in Los Angeles, ran the length of Route 66, and then continued on to New York. The race stretched 3,400 mi (5,472 km). Though 199 runners started the race, only 55 finished. The winner was a 20-year-old Cherokee man named Andy Payne. He finished in 573 hours, and won a prize of $25,000.

Route 66 became the first national highway that was entirely paved in 1938.

DECOMMISSIONED

In the 1950s, newer, faster, and better interstates were constructed across the country. These were more convenient than old roads like Route 66. In 1985, Route 66 was decommissioned, or taken off the official highway system.

In the following decades, many segments of the road have been made into National Scenic Byways, or state routes. Some parts of Route 66 have even been transformed into the US Bicycle Route 66.

Driving Route 66 without stopping takes about 40 hours. However, most travelers dedicate at least two weeks to the trip.

POP CULTURE

Route 66 has inspired movies, television shows, and songs. It appears in novels like *The Grapes of Wrath* and *On the Road*, and in movies like *Rain Man*. From 1960 to 1964, there was even a television show called Route 66.

In 1946, the Nat King Cole Trio recorded "(Get Your Kicks on) Route 66." The song was a hit. Later, artists like Bing Crosby and the Rolling Stones recorded their own Route 66 covers.

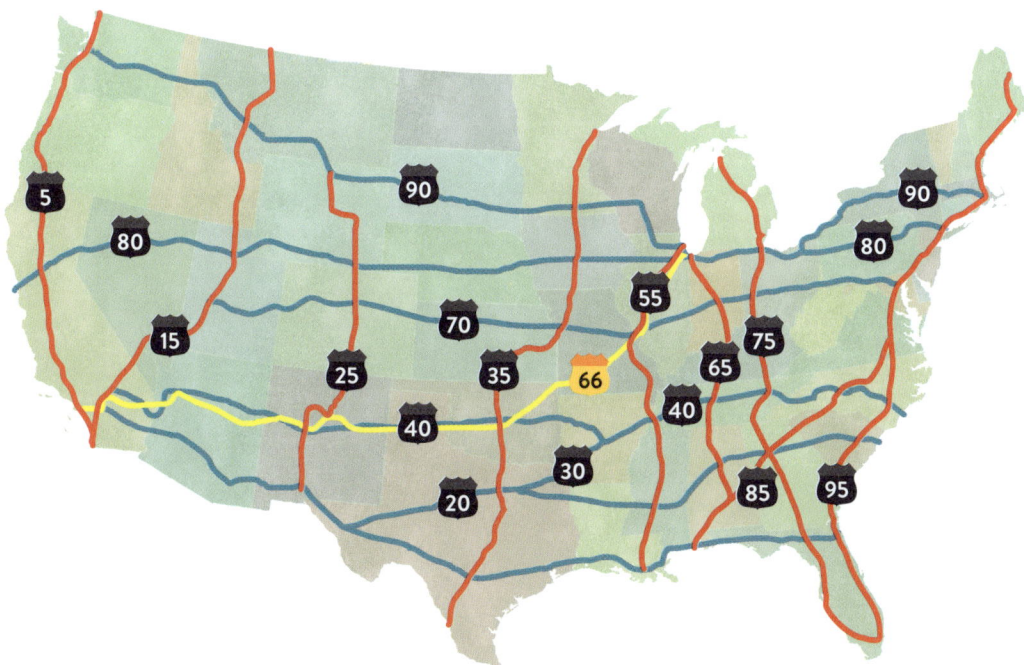

INTERSTATE NUMBERS

To make them easier to use, America's interstate highways are numbered. East-west routes are even numbers. The lowest numbered east-west routes are in the south, and the numbers go higher as they travel north. North-south routes are given odd numbers, with the lowest numbers in the west and the highest in the east.

OREGON

Historians aren't sure how Oregon got its name, though the word probably has Native roots. In 1765, a British soldier wrote about a river there that the Native people called *Ouragon*.

FAST FACTS

Admitted to the Union:
February 14, 1859

State Number: **33**

Population: **4.3 million**

Capital: **Salem**

Nickname: **The Beaver State**

State Animal: **Beaver**

AN ANCIENT KNIFE

Nearly 16,000 years ago, Mount St. Helen erupted. It carpeted the surrounding land in thick ash. In 2012, people dug up the ash to study it. Underneath, they found something amazing: a bright orange cutting tool. This may be one of the oldest tools ever found in America. It tells archaeologists that Oregon might have been one of the earliest places humans lived to the west of the Rockies.

Thousands of years after that early cutting tool was made, Europeans came to the area. When they arrived, they found more than 100 tribes of Native people already living on the land.

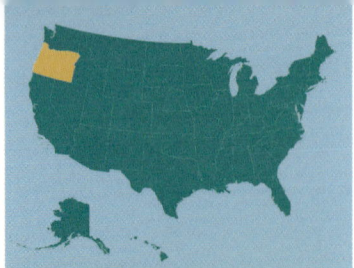

OREGON TRAIL

Settlers who made it across the entire Oregon Trail completed their journey in Oregon City. The ragged travelers were glad to see a community of homes, saloons, blacksmiths, shops, and churches. They filed land claims and prepared for their lives as pioneers in the Pacific Northwest.

Fur trapping was big business in Oregon in the 1800s. Trappers came to the area in search of beavers, whose pelts were used to make hats. Beaver pelts were so valuable that they were called "soft gold."

PORTLAND

Portland, Oregon's biggest city, is known for its coffee, art, and music. It also has a reputation for being a quirky, offbeat place, where people of many different lifestyles come to live. The city's unofficial motto is "Keep Portland Weird."

Portland is famous for being rainy, with an average of 156 days of rain each year. However, it gets plenty of sun, too. There are an average of 144 sunny days in Portland each year.

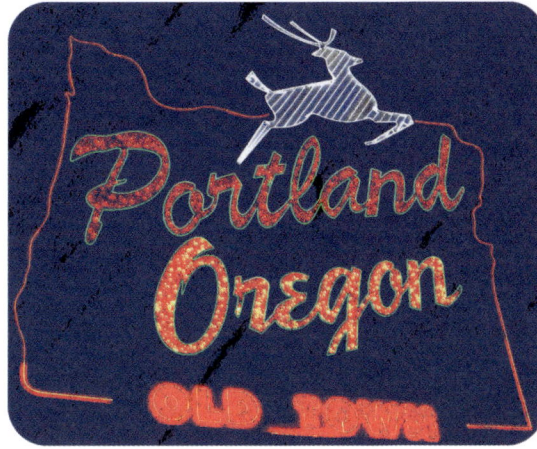

Powell's Bookstore sells a perfume that smells like books.

Portland is:
• the country's most bike-friendly city, with over 350 mi (563 km) of bike lanes on its roads.

• 2020's Number 1 American city for vegans and vegetarians.

• home to the world's largest independently owned bookstore, Powell's.

MOUNTAINS, CANYONS, AND MORE

Along Oregon's Pacific coast are the Coast Range and Klamath Mountains. Moving east is the Willamette Valley. The Cascade Mountains run through the state in a north-south line, and include Oregon's highest peak, Mount Hood. It is 11,249 ft (3,429 m) high. Northeastern Oregon is made up of the Columbia Plateau. This is an area of rolling hills, river canyons, and farmland. It also includes Hells Canyon, America's deepest river gorge.

CRATER LAKE

Nearly 8,000 years ago, a volcanic eruption blasted a huge, deep crater into the earth. Over time, the crater filled with clear, clean water from rain and melted snow. Today, Crater Lake is America's deepest lake. It is 1,943 ft (592 m) deep.

HOOD TO COAST

The Hood to Coast relay road race is often called the "mother of all relays." It is one of the largest and longest relay races in the world. Hood to Coast challenges 8- to 12-member teams to run from Mt. Hood to the Oregon Coast along a 196-mi (315-km) course. The fastest team ever was Nike's Mambu Baddu. They finished in 15 hours, 45 minutes, and 55 seconds, averaging 4 minutes 51 seconds per mile!

RAIN, SNOW, AND SUNSHINE

Oregon's many different geographical regions have different types of weather. On the coast, the weather is often rainy and foggy. The mountains are sunny during summers, with heavy snowfall in the winters. Eastern Oregon is dry, with hot summers and cold winters.

PENNSYLVANIA

Pennsylvania comes from the Latin for "Penn's Woods."
English settler, William Penn, named the area after his father.

MEADOWCROFT ROCKSHELTER

Scholars know that humans have lived in Pennsylvania for more than 19,000 years because of Meadowcroft Rockshelter. This is a rocky overhang that contains the remains of firepits, butchered animal bones, and more than 20,000 artifacts. These items have taught modern humans how their ancesters lived. They also show that this area might be the oldest continually inhabited place in North America.

FAST FACTS

Admitted to the Union:
December 12, 1787

State Number: **2**

Population: **13 million**

Capital: **Harrisburg**

Nickname:
The Keystone State

State Animal:
White-tailed deer

GETTYSBURG

Pennsylvania sided with the Union during the Civil War. The Battle of Gettysburg, in 1863, was fought in southern Pennsylvania. It was one of the most important clashes of the war. It was also the bloodiest. The Union won the battle, but both sides suffered heavy losses. In total, about 7,000 were killed, 27,000 were wounded, and 10,000 went missing.

Four months after the Battle of Gettysburg, President Abraham Lincoln came to the site of the battle and gave his most famous speech, the Gettysburg Address. He began, "Four score and seven years ago our fathers brought forth on this continent a new nation conceived in liberty and dedicated to the proposition that all men are created equal." He concluded his speech, saying "...we here highly resolve that these dead shall not have died in vain—that this nation, under God, shall have a new birth of freedom—and that government of the people, by the people, for the people, shall not perish from the earth."

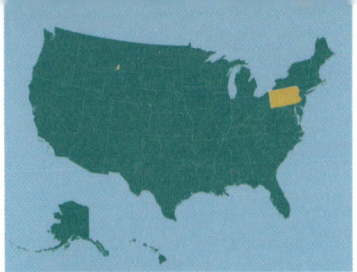

WEATHER

Pennsylvania has four distinct seasons. Summers are humid and hot. Winters are cold and snowy. Springs are cool and wet. In the fall, temperatures drop and trees turn beautiful shades of orange, yellow, and red.

LANDSCAPE

The Appalachian Mountains cross Pennsylvania from the southwest to the northeast. They include the state's highest point, Mt. Davis, which is 3,213 ft (979 m) high. In the southeast, YIKES, the landscape is flat, low, and marshy. The northwestern half of the state is made up of the Allegheny Plateau. It includes dense forests, high hills, and narrow valleys. In the northeast are the Pocono Mountains, an area popular for skiing in the winter and hiking in the summer.

Pine Creek Gorge is often called Pennsylvania's Grand Canyon. It is about 47 mi (76 km) long, and has a maximum depth of 1,450 ft (442 m).

PHILADELPHIA

Philadelphia is Pennsylvania's biggest city, with a population of about 1.6 million people. The bustling city is known for its many historic sites, including the following:

- **Independence Hall**, where the Declaration of Independence was signed.

- **The Liberty Bell**, an important symbol of American freedom. It was rung on many important occasions before getting its big crack, including on July 8, 1776, when the Declaration of Independence was first read to the public.

- **The Mother Bethel African Methodist Episcopal Church**, founded in 1787, is the oldest parcel of land in the US that has been continuously owned by African-Americans.

Philadelphia was the capital of the United States from 1790–1800.

Philly cheesesteaks are made of thinly sliced beefsteak served on a hoagie roll and slathered in cheese. Sauteed onions are usually added on top.

HERSHEY

Hershey, Pennsylvania calls itself the "sweetest place on Earth." This town is home to the famed Hershey's Chocolate Company, the largest producer of chocolates in America. It is also where Hersheypark is found. This chocolate-themed adventure park has more than 70 attractions, including 14 rollercoasters.

NATURAL RESOURCES

Natural resources are materials that occur naturally on Earth, and that have value to humans. Timber, natural gas, coal, and water are examples of natural resources, as are air and sunlight. The United States has a wide variety of natural resources. From its sprawling timber forests to its freshwater lakes to its rich deposits of oil, its land has helped people to survive and thrive for thousands of years.

Many of America's natural resources are considered renewable. This means that they can be used over and over again without running out. Water, sunlight, and wind are renewable. Nonrenewable natural resources cannot be replaced once they have been used up. Fossil fuels are one type of nonrenewable natural resource. They include coal, oil, and natural gas.

MINING AND DRILLING

There are about 12,000 mines in the United States. Workers at these mines dig for nonrenewable natural resources, such as copper, silver, and coal. Arizona is the leading state for mining copper. Alaska mines the most silver. Wyoming is the largest coal-producing state. It produces about 40 percent of the country's coal.

Oil and natural gas are nonrenewable natural resources that provide more than two-thirds of the energy Americans use. People get oil and natural gas by drilling or fracking. Burning oil and natural gas creates pollution. This harms Earth's environment and contributes to climate change.

WATER

Energy produced using water is called hydropower. Most hydropower comes from dams. About half of the nation's hydropower is produced in Washington, Oregon, and California. Hydropower is a renewable resource.

WIND AND SOLAR

Wind and solar power are both renewable resources. Wind turbines harness the power of wind to create electricity. Solar panels convert the Sun's light into electrical energy.

Solar farms are large areas of land covered in solar panels. The largest solar farm in America is Solar Star in California. It has 1.7 million solar panels and can generate enough electricity to power 255,000 homes annually.

Wind farms are fields of wind turbines. The largest wind farm in America is the Alta Wind Energy Center, in Tehachapi, California. It makes enough energy to provide electricity to 275,000 homes each year.

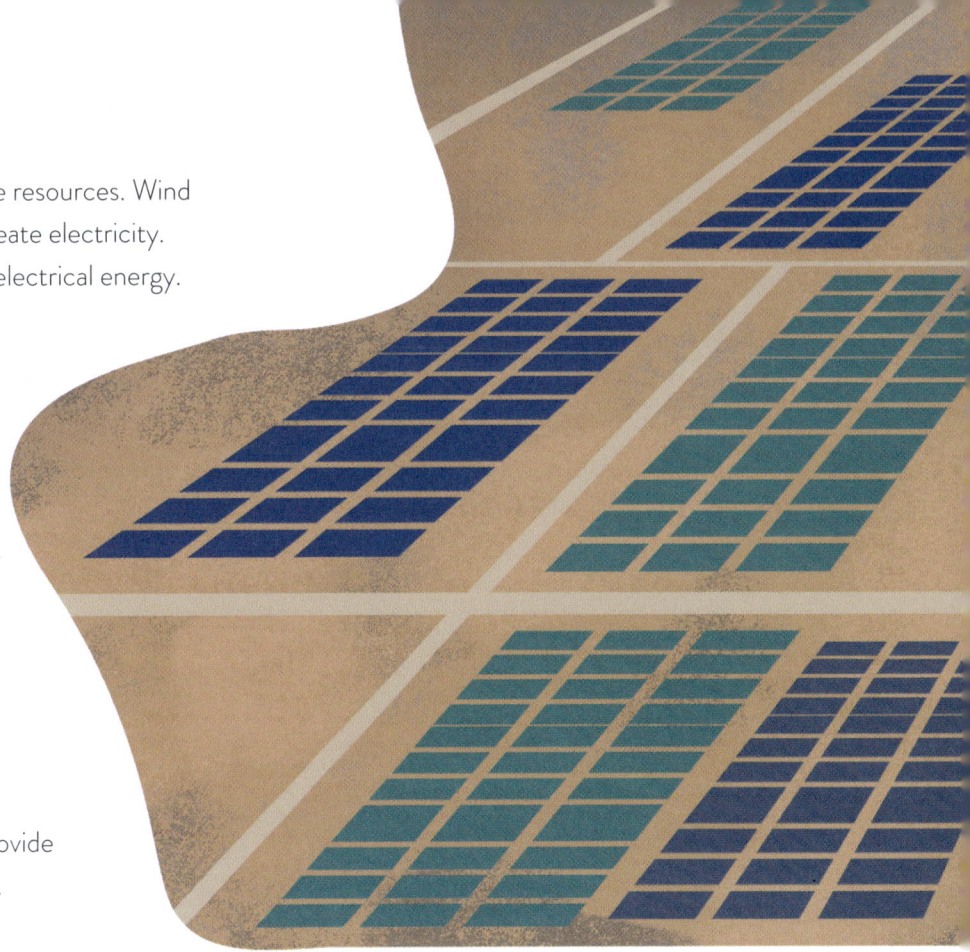

FORESTRY

Forests provide humans with fruit, nuts, wood, paper, and ingredients used in important medicines. They also produce oxygen we need to breathe. They are habitats to many important living things. In America, they are a valued natural resource.

About 50 percent of the timber harvested in America goes to producing paper and pulp. About 20 percent is used for lumber and veneer. The remaining 30 percent is split between wood chips, fuels, and other uses.

NUCLEAR ENERGY

Nuclear power plants churn out an incredible amount of energy. They are efficient and reliable power sources. However, they are not completely renewable because of the fuel they use. Scientists are working hard to turn nuclear energy into a completely sustainable, renewable energy source soon.

The United States is the largest producer of nuclear power in the world. Almost one-fifth of the energy produced in America is nuclear. The biggest nuclear plant in America is Palo Verde, in Arizona. About 4 million people in Texas, Arizona, California, and New Mexico use its power.

RHODE ISLAND

It was a Dutch explorer who named Rhode Island "Roodt Eylandt," which meant "red island." He named it after the red-colored clay along the shore.

Rhode Island is called the Ocean State because it has more than 400 miles (644 kilometers) of coastline. Its small size means that people anywhere within its borders can drive to the ocean in 30 minutes.

NARRAGANSETT

The Narragansett Indians are a group of Native people who live in Rhode Island. Their ancestors came to the land around 30,000 years ago. They hunted, farmed, and thrived on the land. When Italian explorer, Giovanni da Verrazzano, came to the area in 1523, he met a group of Narragansett people. He was impressed by them, and wrote that they were "as beautiful of stature and build as I can possibly describe."

THE SMALLEST

Measuring just 48 mi (77 km) long by 37 mi (60 km) wide, Rhode Island is America's smallest state. Despite its small size, the state includes a variety of geographical regions. The eastern and southern parts of the state are made up of the coastal lowlands. This region is low and flat. It includes Narragansett Bay, which is home to more than 40 islands. Three of the biggest islands are Aquidneck, Conanicut, and Prudence. Block Island is located less than 20 mi (32 km) offshore. The northwestern part of Rhode Island features rolling hills, including Jerimoth Hill, the state's highest point. It is 812 ft (247 m) high.

WEATHER

Rhode Island's warm, pleasant summers make it easy to understand why it is such a popular vacation destination. Sunny beaches and luxurious resorts make it a glamorous place to stay. Winters are cold and snowy.

FAST FACTS

Admitted to the Union:
May 29, 1790

State Number: **13**

Population: **1 million**

Capital: **Providence**

Nickname: **The Ocean State**

State Bird: **Rhode Island red**

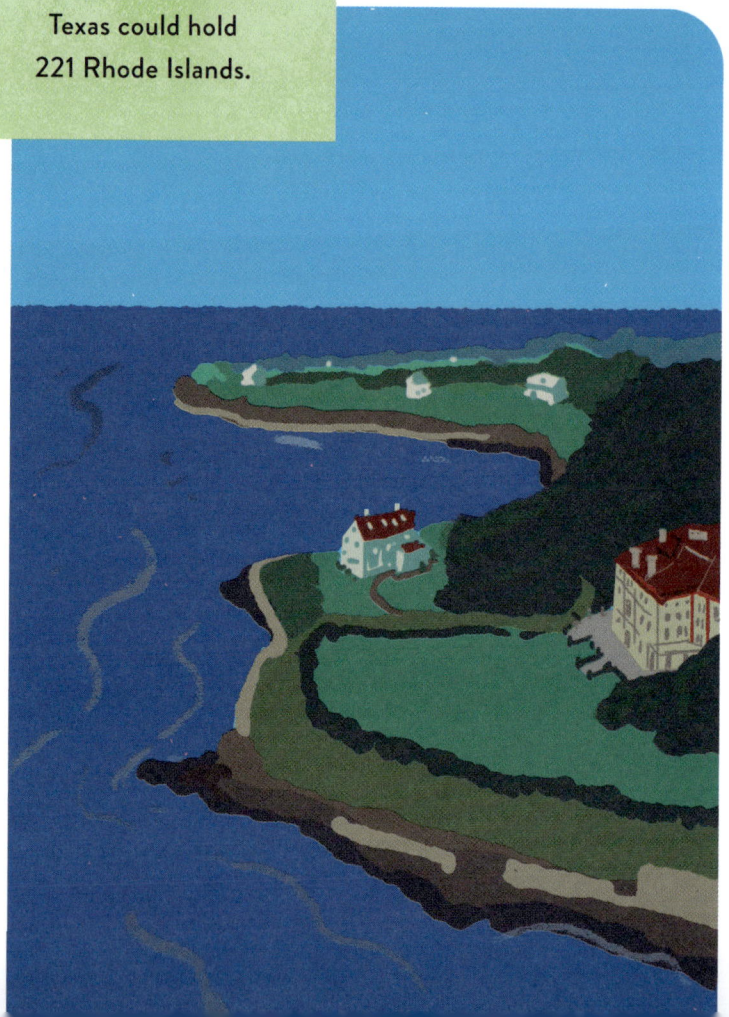

You could fit 425 Rhode Islands into Alaska. Texas could hold 221 Rhode Islands.

NEWPORT

Newport is one of Rhode Island's biggest and oldest towns. Founded in 1639 by a group of settlers seeking religious freedom, it soon grew to become one of colonial America's most important ports.

In the 1800s, wealthy families from places like New York City and Philadelphia built spectacular summer homes in Newport. Some of these homes are still standing. Today, many are open to the public. They allow visitors a chance to imagine what life was like for the country's wealthiest people.

SAILING

The Ocean State is the perfect place for people who love to sail. In fact, Newport is sometimes called "the sailing capital of the world." Many Rhode Island children attend sailing camp during the summers, where they learn to hoist sails, navigate, and gain water confidence. The America's Cup, an elite global sailing contest, has taken place in Narragansett Bay many times.

Participating in the America's Cup is very expensive. Teams must pay an entry fee of about $2 million. In addition, the price of boats, teams, training, and equipment is often well over $100 million.

TENNIS

Another of Newport's nicknames is the Tennis Capital of New England. In 1881, it hosted the first National Lawn Tennis Championship. Later, this would become the US Open. Today, it is the home of the Tennis Hall of Fame.

A BOOK LOVER'S DREAM

The Providence Athenæum is a library and cultural center. Visitors come to explore its 200-year-old history, for weddings and other celebrations, or just to cozy up with the perfect book.

SOUTH CAROLINA

South Carolina was named for English King Charles I.

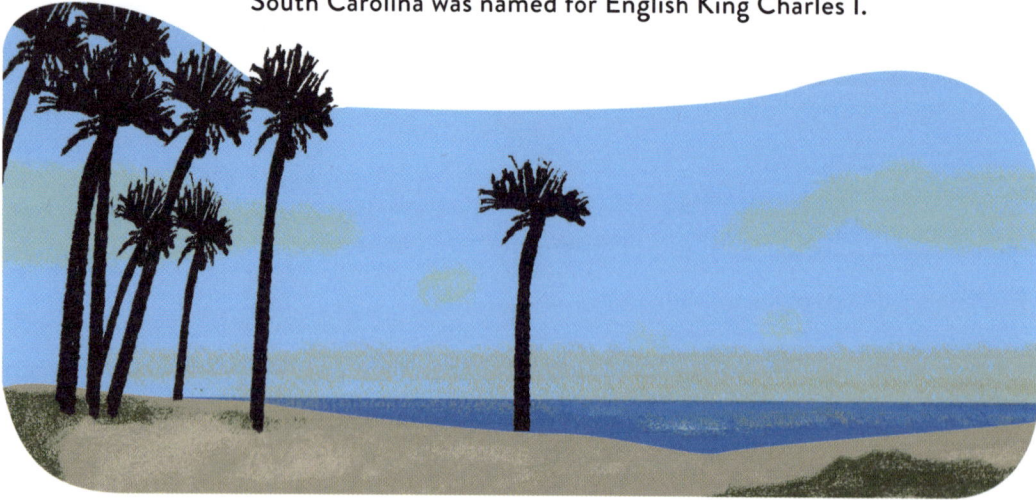

FAST FACTS

Admitted to the Union:
May 23, 1788

State Number: **8**

Population: **5.2 million**

Capital: **Columbia**

Nickname:
The Palmetto State

State Animal:
White-tailed deer

HISTORY

European explorers from France and Spain came to South Carolina in the 1500s. They encountered many groups of Native people who had been living on the land for thousands of years. In 1670, the English made their first permanent settlement there. In 1712, the colony was divided into North and South Carolina.

South Carolina had a thriving economy that relied heavily upon slave labor. In 1861, it was the first state to secede from the Union. About 60,000 men from South Carolina fought in the Civil War. More than 15,000 of them were killed or went missing. South Carolina rejoined the Union in 1868.

Early settlers in South Carolina used many slaves. By 1720, enslaved people made up about 65 percent of the population.

CHARLESTON

Charleston is South Carolina's biggest city. It is often called the Holy City. This has to do with its history of religious freedom, as well as the sheer number of houses of worship there. In 2022, there were more than 400 churches, mosques, and synagogues in Charleston.

Charleston is a popular travel destination for history lovers, foodies, and beach bums. Visitors are encouraged to try the state's official snack: boiled peanuts.

GEOGRAPHY

South Carolina is shaped a little like a triangle. Its elevation is highest in the northwest, where the Blue Ridge Mountains cross the state. Sassafras Mountain, which is 3,560 ft (1,085 m) tall, is South Carolina's highest peak. Moving eastward, the state slopes down. The middle of the state has hills and fertile farmland. On the southeastern side of the triangle is the Atlantic Coastal Plain. This is a low, mostly flat area. South Carolina meets the Atlantic Ocean along its 187-mi (300-km) long coastline. Myrtle Beach, one of the state's most popular destinations, is located on the coast near the border with North Carolina.

WEATHER

South Carolina has hot, muggy summers and mild winters. July is the state's hottest month, with temperatures averaging 91 °F (33 °C). It's the wettest month, too, with an average of 5.5 in (14 cm) of rain.

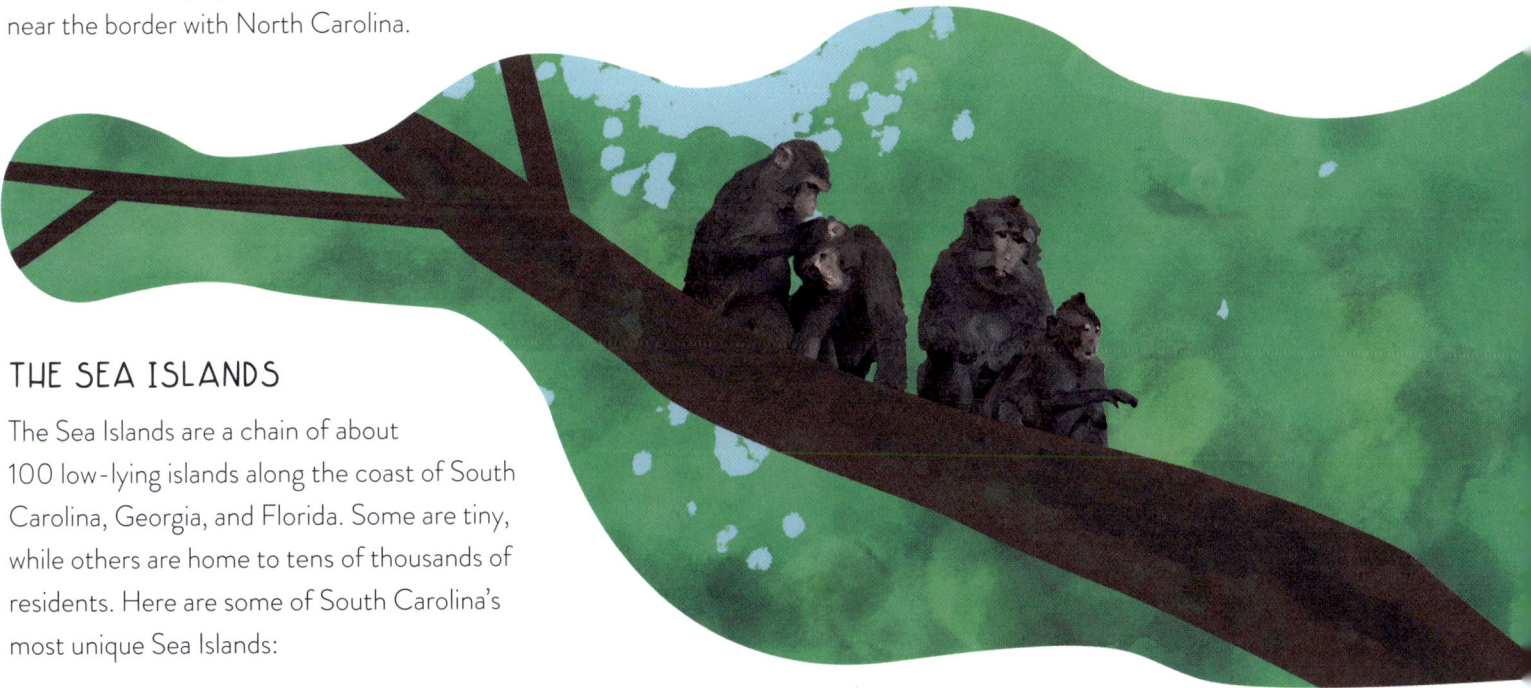

THE SEA ISLANDS

The Sea Islands are a chain of about 100 low-lying islands along the coast of South Carolina, Georgia, and Florida. Some are tiny, while others are home to tens of thousands of residents. Here are some of South Carolina's most unique Sea Islands:

- **Morgan Island** is located off the central coast. Humans are not allowed to live there, but the island is far from empty. About 4,000 Rhesus monkeys live there.

- **Hilton Head** is a boot-shaped island found close to the Georgia border. Its 12 mi (19.2 km) of white sand beaches, resorts, golf courses and restaurants attract 2.5 million tourists each year.

- **St. Helena** is home to the Penn School. Founded in 1862, it was the first Southern school for freed slaves. Over the following decades, the Penn School remained important for Black Americans. Civil rights leaders, including Dr. Martin Luther King, Jr., visited the institution. Today, visitors can tour the historic campus as well as the surrounding grounds.

AMERICA'S CLIMATE

Climate is the word used to describe long-term weather conditions in a particular place. Climate zones are areas with generally consistent climate patterns. There are five major climate zones:
• Tropical • Dry • Temperate • Continental • Polar

An area's climate is impacted by many things, including its physical features, such as mountains and lakes, or its nearness to the equator. Because America is a sweeping nation of mountains, valleys, and deserts that stretches from Florida's southernmost point to Alaska's northernmost reaches, it has a varied selection of climates.

This map shows the climate range in the continental United States:

Hawaii is in a tropical climate zone. But, because of the amazing diversity of its landforms, it is home to many different sub-zones. A visitor hopping from island to island can easily spot lush rainforests, dry deserts, and snow-capped volcanoes, all in a single trip to Hawaii.

Even though Alaska gets very cold weather, only its northern most portion is in a polar zone.

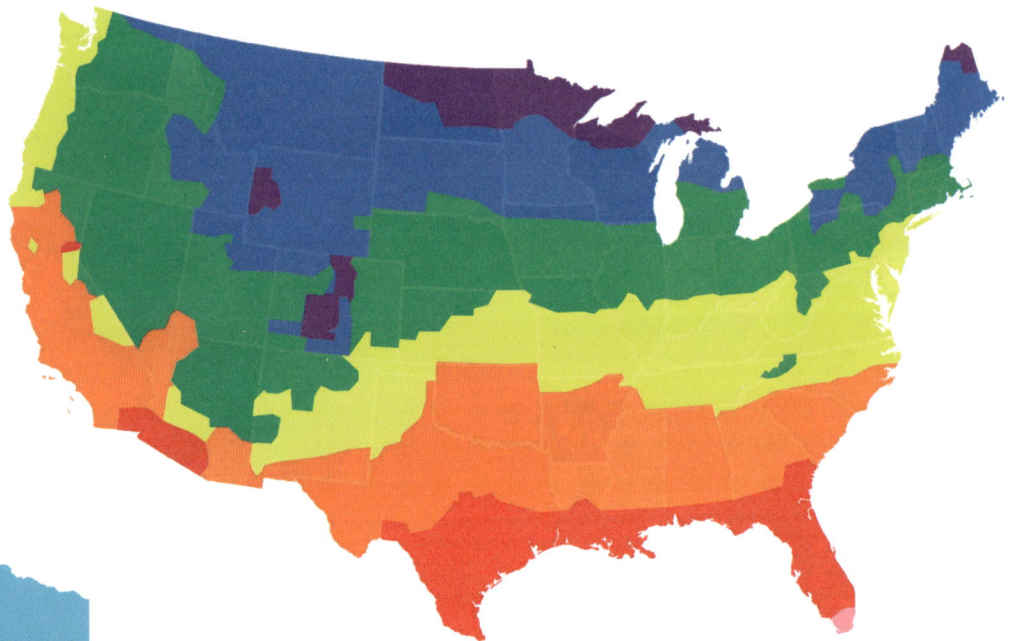

● Very hot humid	● Warm	● Cool	● Very cold
● Hot humid	● Mixed	● Cold	● Subarctic / artic

Weather scientists, called meteorologists, use satellites to monitor America's climate.

WEATHER RECORDS

Weather is the name for short-term conditions, such as temperature, precipitation, and wind. Here are some of America's most historic weather records:

Hottest:
134 °F (56.7 °C)
in Death Valley, California.
July 10, 1913.

Coldest:
-80 °F (-62.2 °C)
in Prospect Creek, Alaska.
January 23, 1971.

Heaviest rainfall in a single day:
49.7 in (126 cm)
in Hanalei, Hawaii, from
April 15 to April 16, 2018.

Heaviest snowfall in a single day:
75 in (191 cm) in Silver Lake,
Colorado from April 14
to April 15, 1921.

CLIMATE CHANGE

America's weather patterns are shifting due to climate change. Since 1901, temperatures in the contiguous United States have risen about 1.8 °F (1 °C). This has led to more droughts and forest fires. It has also contributed to extreme weather events, such as hurricanes. Scientists predict that if humans do not change their behavior, there will be more negative impacts from climate change in the future, including coastal flooding and heat waves.

GOING GREEN

The biggest cause of climate change is human behavior. Burning fossil fuels, cutting down forests, and raising livestock all contribute to this harmful phenomenon. However, there are many human behaviors that can help, too.

- **Bike or walk places, rather than driving.** This helps conserve fuel and reduces pollution.

- **Be an efficient energy user**. Turn your air conditioning up a degree or two, turn off lights when you leave a room, and wear a sweater to stay warm in winter instead of cranking up the heat.

- **Eat less meat.** Raising livestock often takes a toll on the environment.

If all Americans had one meat and dairy-free day a week, it would help the environment as much as if there were 7.6 million fewer cars on the road.

SOUTH DAKOTA

Like North Dakota, South Dakota gets its name from the Sioux word for "friend."

SUE

South Dakota was the birthplace of one of America's most famous residents: a gigantic *Tyrannosaurus rex* called Sue.

Sue was discovered in 1990 by a paleontologist named Susan Hendrickson on the Cheyenne River Sioux reservation. The fossil turned out to be the largest, most complete T-Rex skeleton ever found. It is about 67 million years old.

HUMAN HISTORY

South Dakota became part of the United States in 1803, but its human history stretches back much further. The first people likely came to the area at least 11,000 years ago. They were hunters and gatherers who traveled across the land.

PLAINS, PRAIRIE, AND BADLANDS

South Dakota's geography is split into two by the Missouri River. On the eastern side of the river, the landscape is mostly flat, with prairies, farmland, and rolling hills. On the western side, the Great Plains stretch toward the Black Hills. This is a region of eroded mountains that includes the state's highest point, Elk Peak. It is 7,242 ft (2,207 m) tall. The Black Hills are also home to Mount Rushmore. (To learn more about this famous monument, turn the page.) In the southwest are the Badlands, a maze of striking rock formations including canyons and spires.

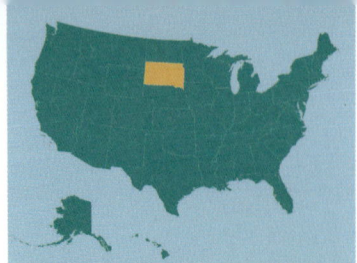

FAST FACTS

Admitted to the Union:
November 2, 1889

State Number: **40**

Population: **895,000**

Capital: **Pierre**

Nickname:
The Mount Rushmore State

State Animal: **Coyote**

South Dakota has more than 9,000 mi (14,400 km) of rivers. Those, plus the state's many lakes, ponds, and streams, give it more miles of shoreline than Florida.

MOTORCYCLES

Each August since 1938, motorcycle fans from across the country gather in South Dakota for the Sturgis Motorcycle Rally. This 10-day event includes races, concerts, and motorcycle day trips around the scenic Black Hills. Crowds at the rally can be very big. In 2015, about 750,000 people attended.

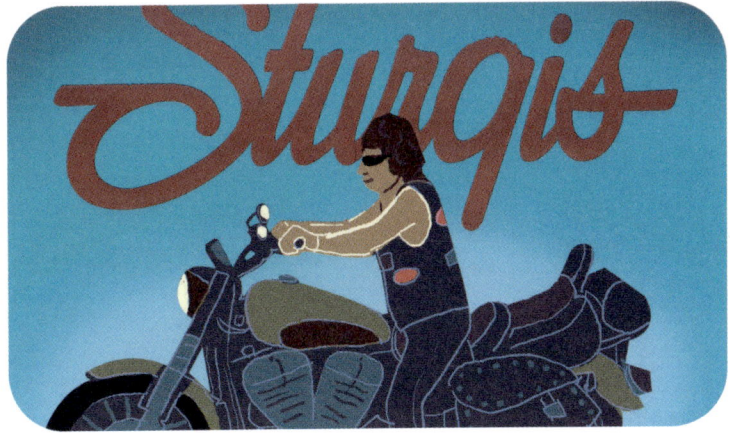

FARMING

Farming is South Dakota's biggest industry. Hay, rye, sunflower, honey, corn, soybeans, cattle, and wheat are among the crops produced there. Nearly 90 percent of the state's land is made up of farms.

South Dakota gets an average of 36 tornadoes a year.

FOUR SEASONS

South Dakota has four very distinct seasons. In the spring, there are mild temperatures and rain showers. Summer is hot and humid, with occasional thunderstorms. Fall brings cool and crisp days. The winter is very cold and snowy.

NATIVE PEOPLE

South Dakota has a population of about 72,000 Native people. It is home to nine tribes:
• Cheyenne River Sioux Tribe
• Crow Creek Sioux Tribe
• Flandreau Santee Sioux Tribe
• Lower Brule Sioux Tribe
• Oglala Sioux Tribe
• Rosebud Sioux Tribe
• Sisseton-Wahpeton Sioux Tribe
• Standing Rock Sioux Tribe
• Yankton Sioux Tribe

WILD WILDLIFE

Custer State Park is in South Dakota's Black Hills. The huge park attracts visitors who want to camp, hike, bike, fish, and ogle the local wildlife. Custer State Park has large populations of animals such as bison, sheep, elk, pronghorn, coyotes, wild turkeys, and burros. Cruising along the 18-mi (29-km) Wildlife Loop Road allows animal lovers to see these wild creatures from the comfort of their vehicles.

MOUNT RUSHMORE

Mount Rushmore National Monument is one of the biggest sculptures in the world, as well as an important symbol of the United States. Carved between 1927 and 1941, it shows the faces of four presidents: George Washington, Thomas Jefferson, Theodore Roosevelt, and Abraham Lincoln. Each man was chosen for specific reasons:

- **George Washington** was the nation's first president. He represents the birth of the United States.

- **Thomas Jefferson**, the third president, was responsible for much of the Declaration of Independence, as well as the Louisiana Purchase. He was chosen to represent the ways the United States grew.

- **Theodore Roosevelt** was the 26th president. He worked hard to help the country's economy grow, including overseeing the construction of the Panama Canal. He represents American development.

- **Abraham Lincoln** was the 16th president. He fought to keep the nation together during the Civil War. He was chosen to represent the preservation of America.

Before

A sculptor named Gutzon Borglum designed Mount Rushmore's epic carvings.

A scale model one-twelfth the size of the finished monument

MOUNT RUSHMORE FACTS

Each face is 60 ft (18.3 m) high, including a 21-ft (6.4-m) nose!

The sculpture is not complete. The original plan was for each president's upper body to be carved as well.

There is a small, secret room located behind Abraham Lincoln's head.

3 million people visit Mount Rushmore each year.

OTHER FACES

The original plan for Mount Rushmore did not include presidential faces. Instead, it featured people who had been important to the development of the American West. Meriweather Lewis, William Clark, Buffalo Bill Cody, and Lakota leader Red Cloud were among the original subjects. However, Gutzon Borglum decided that the sculpture should show presidents. Later, it was suggested that Susan B. Anthony join the presidents. This step was never completed.

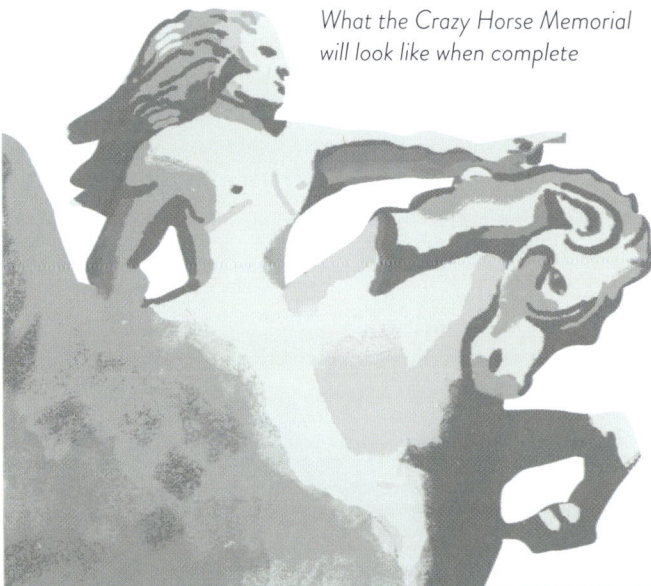

What the Crazy Horse Memorial will look like when complete

CONTROVERSY

Long before four presidents were carved into its side, Mount Rushmore was an important place for Native people. The Lakota called the mountain *Tunkasila Sakpe Paha*, or Six Grandfathers. The Lakota and other Native groups did not want the monument to be carved on their land.

There have been many Native protests at Mount Rushmore. In one of the most famous protests, 23 Native people climbed to the top and camped there for months. They hung a sign that said "Sioux Indian Power."

CRAZY HORSE

Just 17 mi (27.4 km) from Mount Rushmore is another towering Black Hills sculpture. This one is called the Crazy Horse Memorial, and honors an Oglala Lakota chief who defeated American troops at the Battle of Little Bighorn. Construction began on the memorial in 1948 and is still ongoing.

CRAZY HORSE FACTS

When completed, Chief Crazy Horse's arm will be almost as long as a football field.

The Crazy Horse Memorial is on privately owned land. It is being paid for by donations, not federal funding.

Chief Crazy Horse's head is 87 ft (26.5 m) tall.

NATIVE TRIBES TODAY

Today, there are about 9.7 million Native Americans and Alaska Native people living in America. They make up about 3 percent of the country's population. Native people live all across the United States, but have the biggest numbers in the following states:

- California (628,000)
- Oklahoma (392,000)
- Arizona (293,000)

There are 574 federally recognized tribes in the United States. These are Native groups that have a government-to-government relationship with the United States. They also have access to some federal funding. There are more than 200 tribes in America that are not federally recognized.

The three tribal groups with the most people are the Navajo, Cherokee, and Choctaw.

About one-third of Native people live on reservations.

NATIVE LEADERS IN AMERICAN POLITICS

2020 was a historic year for Native politicians. Six Native people won seats in the Senate and House of Representatives. Local elections also saw many Native people elected in leadership positions.

In 2021, Deb Haaland became the first Native American Cabinet Secretary. Haaland, a member of the Laguna Pueblo, was chosen to lead the Interior Department. This is the body that manages public lands, national parks, and wildlife refuges. It is also responsible for upholding the country's relationship with Native tribes.

LANGUAGES

Though there are hundreds of Native American languages, many are in danger of disappearing because the few people who speak them are growing old. Language experts are working to prevent this. Some are teaching the languages in community classes or college courses. Others are using modern tools to solve this problem, developing smartphone apps to teach people Ojibwe, Dakota, Ho Chunk, and more.

MUSIC

Historically, music played an important role in Native American culture. Today, that tradition continues. Some Native people choose to honor their past with traditional instruments and songs. In Rhode Island, an Algonquin Drum Group called the Eastern Medicine Singers perform songs in Massachuset and Wampanoag dialects. Other Native musicians embrace contemporary trends. Sihasin is a band based out of Arizona that blends punk, folk, rock, and Native instrumentals. Frank Waln is a Sicangu Lakota hip-hop artist who highlights Native issues in his music.

Jimi Hendrix, one of the most famous American musicians of all time, has Native ancestry. His grandmother was Cherokee.

MASCOT NAMES

American sports are closely tied to Native American culture, and not just because many elite athletes are of Native descent. Historically, some American sports teams have used names that are now considered offensive and insulting to Native people. Recognizing this, many teams are changing their names, mascots, and branding. In 2021, MLB's Cleveland Indians became the Cleveland Guardians. In 2022, the NFL's Washington Redskins became the Washington Commanders.

NATIVE CUISINE

Today, many Native chefs are changing the American food scene by bringing indigenous recipes and ingredients into the spotlight. In Minneapolis, Minnesota diners at Owamni can enjoy dishes featuring Sioux favorites like wild mushrooms, dandelion greens, turkey, and bison. In Oakland, California Wahpepah Kitchen's Kickapoo chef serves up delicacies made from venison, smoked squash, blue corn, and salmon.

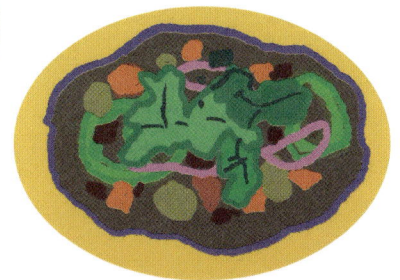

If all the Native-owned land in America were combined, it would equal about 100 million acres. This would make it the fourth-largest state.

TENNESSEE

The word "Tennessee" may come from the name of a Cherokee village, *Tanasi*. The state's nickname comes from the War of 1812, when many Tennesseans volunteered to fight.

Humans have lived in Tennessee for at least 14,000 years.

EUROPEAN ARRIVAL

Long after Native groups made the land of Tennessee their home, Europeans arrived in the area. The first to come was Spanish explorer Hernando de Soto in 1540. Later, English and French people came.

CHANGING NAME AND CAPITALS

After the Revolutionary War, the land of Tennessee was part of North Carolina. Then, some residents tried to make it into a state called Franklin, or Frankland, after Benjamin Franklin. Finally, in 1796, Tennessee became a state on its own.

Tennessee's early leaders couldn't agree on which city should be the state's capital. Over the years, four cities played the part. One city, Kingston, was capital for a single day.

Knoxville 1796–1807
Kingston September 21, 1807
Knoxville 1807–1812
Nashville 1812–1817
Knoxville 1817–1818
Murfreesboro 1818–1826
Nashville 1826–present day

FAST FACTS

Admitted to the Union:
June 1, 1796

State Number: **16**

Population: **6.9 million**

Capital: **Nashville**

Nickname:
The Volunteer State

State Animal: **Raccoon**

Tennessee left the Union in 1861. It returned in 1866, the first Confederate state to do so.

WEATHER

Though Tennessee has four distinct seasons, the weather there is usually mild. Hot and muggy summers give way to cool falls. Winters can be cold, with some snow, and springs are often cool and wet.

LANDSCAPE

Tennessee is home to a wide variety of landscapes. The western part of the state is made up of the mostly flat Gulf Coastal Plain and the fertile Mississippi Delta. Central Tennessee is dominated by the Highland Rim, a ring of hills and valleys. This surrounds the bowl-shaped Central Basin. Farther east are the Cumberland Plateau and Valley and Ridge regions. They rise steeply in elevation. Along the state's eastern edge are the Unaka Mountains, which include the Great Smoky Mountains, and Clingman's Dome, the state's highest point. It is 6,643 ft (2,203 m) high.

GREAT SMOKY MOUNTAINS NATIONAL PARK

The Great Smoky Mountains National Park is America's most-visited national park. In 2021, more than 14 million people came there to camp, hike, climb, swim, and drive though its many scenic areas. Animal lovers delight in exploring the park. Black bears, salamanders, white-tailed deer, coyotes, and elk can all be found in its dense forests. People interested in history enjoy the park, too. Cades Cove is a quiet valley that once housed early settlers. Today, visitors can explore historic cabins, churches, and other structures to learn about what life used to be like in rural Tennessee.

MEMPHIS

With a population of 650,000, Memphis is the second biggest city in Tennessee, after Nashville. The city is known for its barbecue, music, and one of its most iconic residents: Elvis Presley.

The "Jailhouse Rock" singer's mansion, Graceland, is now one of the country's most visited sites. About 600,000 tourists come to Graceland each year to view Elvis's lavish home as well as his private planes, cars, motorcycles, horse stables, and more.

AMERICAN MUSIC

From rap to R&B, polka to pop, and gospel to grunge, the American music scene is as diverse as it is exciting. Artists expressing themselves through rhythm, melody, and words find all sorts of outlets, ranging from street corner performances to huge stadium concerts. Many of America's musical genres are closely tied to the cities where they were born.

COUNTRY CROONERS

Nashville, Tennessee is one of America's most famous hubs for music. It is especially well known for country music. The city is home to the Grand Ole Opry, a live music venue that broadcasts a radio program by the same name—the oldest still-running radio program ever. It also remains a popular destination for musicians hoping to make it big, which is why it is nicknamed the "Songwriting Capital of the World."

The following artists got their big break in Nashville:
- Dolly Parton
- Luke Bryan
- Blake Shelton

THE BIRTHPLACES OF ROCK AND ROLL

Two cities claim to be the birthplace of rock and roll: Cleveland, Ohio and Memphis, Tennessee. Each city has a good reason to make that claim.

Cleveland has long been linked to rock and roll. In the 1950s, a Cleveland-based radio program, hosted by DJ Alan Freed, first began to popularize a new style of music called "Rock and Roll." Later, the city became home to the Rock and Roll Hall of Fame.

Memphis also plays a huge part in American rock and roll culture. It is the location of Sun Studio, a recording studio that helped rock and roll artists like Johnny Cash and Elvis Presley make history. Running through the city is Beale Street, known for its many popular and influential musical clubs.

MUSIC FESTIVALS

Some of the best music festivals in the world take place in the United States. Music lovers flock to these days-long extravaganzas for good tunes, food, and fun. Here are four of the biggest:

SXSW

South by Southwest is a music, film, and comedy festival that draws about 280,000 people to Austin, Texas each year.

Lollapalooza

Close to 400,000 people attend this four-day-long Chicago, Illinois music festival.

Coachella

About 750,000 people attended this two-weekend-long Indio, California festival in 2022.

Summerfest

This Milwaukee, Wisconsin festival draws between 450,000 and 900,000 attendees a year.

One of America's most famous music festivals was 1969's Woodstock Music and Art Fair. About 400,000 people attended this four-day festival in Bethel, New York to watch performers like Jimi Hendrix, The Who, Janice Joplin, and the Grateful Dead.

POP MUSIC

Some of America's biggest pop stars got their start in Orlando, Florida's Walt Disney World. This was where a hit television show called the *All New Mickey Mouse Club* was filmed. Pop artists such as Justin Timberlake, Christina Aguilera, Britney Spears, and JC Chasez used the show to launch their careers.

RAP

Rap music got its start in New York City in the 1970s at neighborhood block parties. As MCs introduced DJs who were going to entertain crowds, they sometimes talked in a rhythmic pattern. This grew into rap. Groups like Run-DMC, Public Enemy, and LL Cool J made rap into the popular genre it is today.

JAZZ

Jazz developed from African and European musical traditions, but it became its own musical style in New Orleans, Louisiana. There, artists like Louis Armstrong pioneered the jazz scene. A combination of instruments such as the trumpet, coronet, saxophone, guitar, and drums, often along with strong vocals, made jazz into an American treasure.

These are the top-selling American albums of all time:

The Eagles
Their Greatest Hits

Michael Jackson
Thriller

The Eagles
Hotel California

TEXAS

The word "Texas" comes from the Caddo word for "friends," *thecas.*

16,000-YEAR-OLD TOOLS

People have lived in Texas for a very long time. In central Texas, archaeologists discovered tools that are more than 16,000 years old.

THE SIX FLAGS OF TEXAS

Over its history, six different flags have flown over Texas. These reflect the different nations that claimed the land.

Spain: 1519–1685
France: 1685–1690
Spain: 1690–1821
Mexico: 1821–1836
Republic of Texas: 1836–1845
United States of America: 1845–1861
Confederate States of America: 1861–1865
United States of America: 1865–today

SPANISH ROOTS

The first Europeans to come to Texas were Spanish. They came to explore the land in the early 1500s. Later, more Spanish people came to the area to spread the Christian religion. The first permanent European settlement in Texas was established in Ysleta in 1681. Today, Ysleta is part of El Paso. The original buildings are gone, but visitors still come to see the historic church and learn about the area's past.

FAST FACTS

Admitted to the Union:
December 29, 1845

State Number: **28**

Population: **29.5 million**

Capital: **Austin**

Nickname:
The Lone Star State

State Large Animal:
Texas longhorn

EVERYTHING'S BIGGER

Texas is the second-biggest state, behind Alaska. It covers an incredible 268,597 sq mi (695,662 sq km). Inside its borders are a wide variety of landforms, from sweeping plains to towering mountains. The Guadalupe Mountains, on the western side of the state, include Texas's highest peak, Guadalupe Peak. It is 8,749 ft (2,667 m) high.

Texas is where the country's largest domed state capitol building is found. Its towering dome stands at 302 ft (92 m) tall. It is also home to the highest speed limit in America. Drivers traveling from Austin to San Antonio can legally cruise at a quick 85 mph (137 kph).

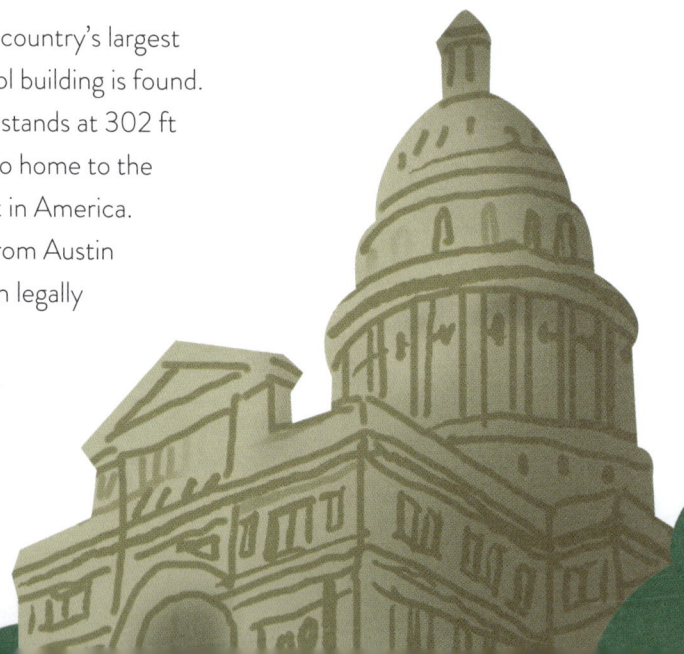

CHICKEN FRIED STEAK

One of Texas's most well-known dishes has an unusual name: chicken fried steak. It is a cut of steak that is battered, fried, and served with white gravy. German immigrants likely brought chicken fried steaks to Texas, preparing them like wiener schnitzel.

Texas' official state dish is chili con carne. It is made from ground beef, chili peppers, and a tomato base.

RANCH LIFE

Texas's sweeping plains are ideal places for cattle ranches. Ranchers manage about 12 million cattle and calves there, the highest number of cows in any state. Beef isn't Texas's only agricultural product. The state also churns out cotton, milk, chickens, corn, and more.

HOUSTON, SAN ANTONIO, DALLAS, AND AUSTIN

Texas isn't just a big state. It's home to some very big cities, too. The biggest is Houston, with a population of more than 2.3 million. Next is San Antonio, with 1.5 million residents. Dallas follows with 1.3 million. Austin, the state's capital, has 966,000 residents.

Cows raised on Texas ranches need to be transported out of state to be sold. In the past, workers called cowboys wrangled herds of cows on long trail drives to market. Today, cowboys are still a symbol of Texas.

WEATHER

Because Texas is such a big state, its weather varies in different regions. However, it generally has hot and humid summers, and mild to cold winters. In 2021, the state experienced a record blizzard that left millions without electricity.

NASA

The National Aeronautics and Space Administration (NASA) is America's government-run space agency. It is responsible for space-related science and technology, including crewed space missions.

HISTORY

NASA was created during the beginning of the Space Race, a contest between the United States and the Soviet Union to become leaders in space. At first, the Soviets were winning. They sent Sputnik, the first human-made satellite, into space. Then they launched the first human, Yuri Gagarin, into space in 1961. NASA soon caught up. American Alan Shepard flew in space one month after Gagarin. John Glenn became the first American to orbit the Earth in 1962. In 1969, America won the Space Race when NASA landed the crew of Apollo 11 on the Moon. No other country has landed humans on the Moon.

Only NASA astronauts have walked on the Moon.

In 2017, more than 18,000 hopefuls applied to become NASA astronauts. Only 12 were chosen. That means 0.066 percent of applicants were selected. To put that in perspective, the hardest university to get into in America is Harvard, with a 3.2 percent acceptance rate.

ASTRONAUTS

The people who crew US space missions are called astronauts. Not anyone can become a NASA astronaut. The selection process is famously difficult, and for good reason. Whoever is selected to fly in space must be extremely smart and cool under pressure. They must also be good at learning foreign languages and getting along with others, since many space missions have international crews.

MANY FACILITIES

NASA has many facilities located all over the United States, including the Jet Propulsion Laboratory in California, the Goddard Space Flight Center in Maryland, the Marshall Space Flight Center in Alabama, and the Johnson Space Center in Texas. Each facility has its own staff and specialties that work together to create a powerful and cutting-edge space agency.

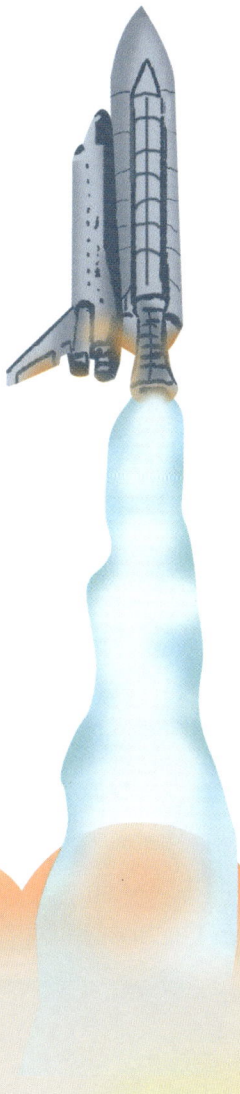

" Houston, we've had a problem. "

When Apollo 13 astronaut, Jim Lovell, said "Houston, we've had a problem," he was speaking to Mission Control in the Manned Spacecraft Center (now Johnson Space Center). His spacecraft had just suffered terrible damage. The crew in Houston worked to help Apollo 13 home.

Most NASA vehicles launch from Cape Canaveral, Florida, and Vandenberg Air Force Base, in California. However, launch sites in Alaska, the Marshall Islands, and Virginia are also used.

ANALOG MISSIONS

NASA scientists and engineers try to test everything for their missions on Earth before asking their astronauts to do it in space. This can require some extreme measures, such as analog missions. These are missions that simulate as much as possible about an upcoming spaceflight, with human crews, tight quarters, and simulated space tasks. Some analog crews are sent to the Arctic. Others are sent to harsh deserts, or even under the sea. These brave people help make spaceflight safe for spacegoing astronauts.

BIG PLANS

NASA's project Artemis will send humans back to the Moon. After that, the agency hopes to explore other destinations in space, such as asteroids. NASA has already sent robots to Mars. The agency plans to send humans there soon.

UTAH

People aren't exactly sure how Utah got its name. One theory is that it comes from the name for a group of Native people, the Utes. Another is that it is from the Apache word, *yuttahih*, which means people who are "higher up."

Utah is called the Beehive State because of its hardworking residents. Like bees in a hive, they work together to support their community.

ANCIENT ART

Humans have lived in Utah for more than 13,000 years. Many of the early people left their mark on the land, literally. Utah is home to many petroglyphs (rock carvings) and rock paintings. Some of these are at least 2,000 years old.

Nine Mile Canyon is often called the "world's longest art gallery." This is because the canyon's steep walls are dotted with more than 10,000 ancient artworks.

FAST FACTS

Admitted to the Union:
January 4, 1896

State Number: **45**

Population: **3.3 million**

Capital: **Salt Lake City**

Nickname:
The Beehive State

State Large Mammal: **Elk**

Utah's southeastern corner meets New Mexico, Colorado, and Arizona. This is the only place in America where four states meet. It is called "Four Corners."

SALT LAKE CITY

Salt Lake City is Utah's biggest city, with a population of about 200,000. It is known for its architecture, beautiful mountain backdrop, food, surrounding ski resorts, and as the center of the Mormon religion.

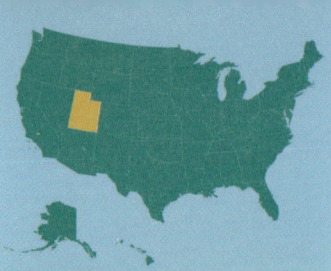

The Sundance Film Festival is held each year in Park City, Utah. It is the biggest independent film festival in America, and one of the most important in the world.

MOUNTAINS, SALT FLATS, VALLEYS, AND MORE

Utah's geography is incredibly varied. The Rocky Mountains pass through the central and northeastern parts of the state and include King's Peak, Utah's highest point. It is 13,528 ft (4,123 m) tall. Monument Valley is in the southeastern part of the state. People go there to take in its stunning red rock formations beneath a wide-open sky. Southwest Utah is home to Zion National Park. This vast park includes red sandstone cliffs, the towering white Checkerboard Mesa, and the incredible Narrows, a very tight section of the Zion Canyon. The Bonneville Salt Flats are in northwestern Utah. This is a 12- by 5-mi (19- by 8-km) area of densely packed salt, left behind when an ancient lake dried up.

THE GREAT SALT LAKE

The Great Salt Lake in northern Utah is the largest saltwater lake in the Western Hemisphere. Its water is salty because the lake has no rivers or streams flowing out of it. Any water that flows into it contains natural minerals and salt. Over time, the water evaporates, but the minerals and salt remain. While tiny brine shrimp, bacteria, and other microscopic creatures live in the Great Salt Lake, there are no fish in its water. It is too salty for them.

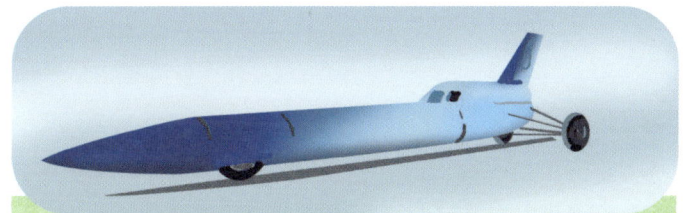

The smooth, level surface of salt flats make them an ideal place for auto racing and record breaking. In 1970, a rocket-powered car zoomed across the Bonneville Salt Flats at the then record-breaking speed of 630 mph (1,013 kph).

Some parts of the Great Salt Lake are 10 times as salty as the ocean.

WEATHER

Utah's varied landscape means that different parts of the state get different weather. The coldest part of the state is Peter Sinks, in the Bear River mountain range. Temperatures there have dropped as low as -69 °F (-56 °C). The hottest place in the state is St. George, on the border with Arizona. This city recorded the state's hottest ever temperature in 1985, when thermometers hit 117 °F (47.2 °C).

VERMONT

Vermont comes from the French words for
green mountain, *vert* and *mont*.

EUROPEAN HISTORY

Vermont was long home to the Abenaki
people. In the 1600s, French explorers came
to the area to claim it as their own. They left
their mark on the state through many place
names, such as Montpelier, Lake Champlain,
and Calais. Later, British settlers came. The
British and French fought over the land until
the British won it in the French and Indian
War (1754–1763).

> Humans first came to Vermont
> around 12,500 years ago.

Vermont sits between New York and New
Hampshire. In the mid-to-late 1700s,
both states began expanding into Vermont.
Vermont residents did not like this. They
pushed back, sometimes violently. The Green
Mountain Boys were a group of soldiers that
formed to fight against New Yorkers who
were claiming land in their state. When the
Revolutionary War broke out, the Green
Mountain Boys joined the fight. In 1777,
Vermont declared itself independent from
Britain. However, it also declared itself
independent from New York. This put it in
a unique situation. It was separate from the
United States. For 14 years, Vermont had its
own money and postal service system. Finally,
in 1791, it joined the Union as the 14th state.

FAST FACTS

Admitted to the Union:
March 4, 1791

State Number: **14**

Population: **646,000**

Capital: **Montpelier**

Nickname:
The Green Mountain State

State Animal: **Morgan horse**

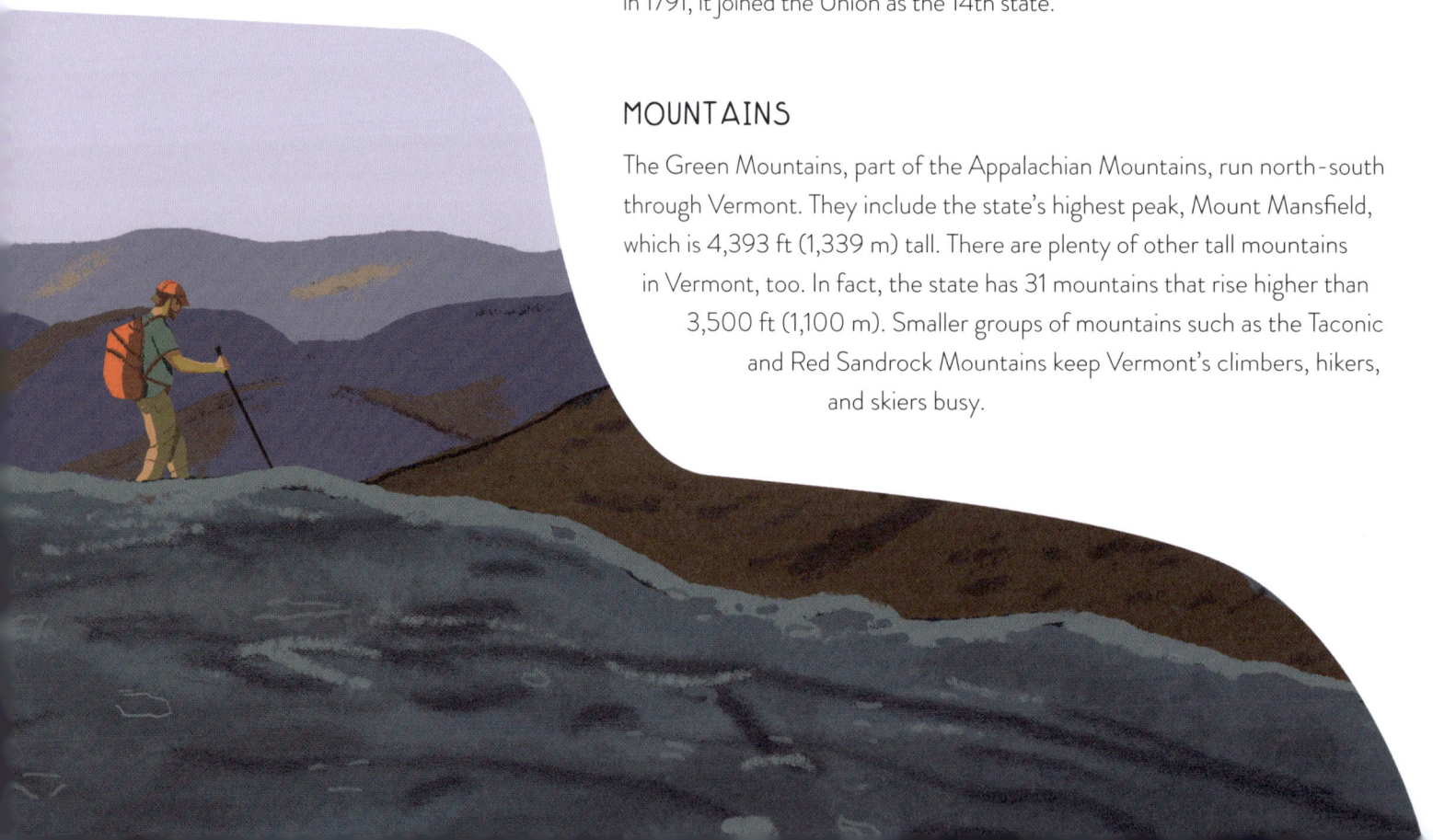

MOUNTAINS

The Green Mountains, part of the Appalachian Mountains, run north-south
through Vermont. They include the state's highest peak, Mount Mansfield,
which is 4,393 ft (1,339 m) tall. There are plenty of other tall mountains
in Vermont, too. In fact, the state has 31 mountains that rise higher than
3,500 ft (1,100 m). Smaller groups of mountains such as the Taconic
and Red Sandrock Mountains keep Vermont's climbers, hikers,
and skiers busy.

LAKE CHAMPLAIN

On the border between New York, Vermont, and Canada is Lake Champlain. This huge lake stretches 120 mi (193 km) long by 12 mi (19.3 km) wide. At its deepest, it plunges to about 400 ft (122 m). Lake Champlain is popular for nature lovers, swimmers, and boaters. It is also said to be home to a mysterious water beast similar to the Loch Ness Monster. This creature is called Champ.

MAPLE SYRUP

Vermont is famous for its sticky, sweet syrup, made from the sap of sugar maple trees. In 2020, the state produced 2.2 million gal (8.3 million l) of the sweet liquid, more than 50 percent of all of America's maple syrup.

WEATHER

Vermont's hot and humid summers are a welcome relief after its biting and cold winters. The springs are mild and wet, while the falls are crisp and cool, the perfect conditions for dazzling autumn leaves. Each year, more than 3 million people visit the state to see its beautiful fall leaves.

Ben & Jerry's ice cream was founded in Burlington, Vermont. In 1983, Ben & Jerry's ice cream was piled into a 27,102-lb (12,293-kg) sundae, a then-world record.

VIRGINIA

Queen Elizabeth I of England was called the Virgin Queen. When she gave permission for English settlers to colonize this region, they named it Virginia in her honor.

The word dominion means territory. Virginia is called the Old Dominion State because it was the first English colony in America.

FAST FACTS

Admitted to the Union:
June 25, 1788

State Number: **10**

Population: **8.7 million**

Capital: **Richmond**

Nickname:
The Old Dominion State

State Dog:
American foxhound

HISTORY

Virginia played a very important role in American history. English settlers first came to the area in 1607, and in 1624, it became the first English colony. Its population grew quickly, and by the time the American Revolution began, it had more than 120,000 residents. Many Virginians fought in the Revolutionary War. The Battle of Yorktown, which led to the British defeat, was fought there.

Slave labor was used in Virginia from 1619. Most slaves were used to farm crops, such as tobacco. By 1860, there were 550,000 slaves in Virginia. That was about one-third of the state's population. During the Civil War, Virginia was part of the Confederacy. A Virginian named General Robert E. Lee led the Confederate troops. About one-half of all the Civil War battles were fought in Virginia.

The first humans likely came to Virginia between 18,000 and 20,000 years ago.

The western part of the state stayed loyal to the Union during the Civil War. This led to its separation, and the formation of West Virginia.

Virginia was the home of such founding fathers as George Washington, Thomas Jefferson, and James Madison.

GEOGRAPHY

Virginia's western landscape includes the Appalachian Plateau, a rocky, forested area. The Valley and Ridge region features rocky ridges, caverns, and the Great Appalachian Valley. The Blue Ridge Mountains run diagonally across the state, and are home to Virginia's tallest point, Mount Rogers. It is 5,729 ft (1,746 m) high. Central Virginia's gently rolling hills reach toward the low-lying eastern coast. This area is wet and swampy. On the border with North Carolina is the Great Dismal Swamp, a 750-sq-mi (1,940-sq-km) stretch of forested wetlands. The Chesapeake Bay separates Virginia's mainland from the Eastern Shore, located on the southern part of the Delmarva Peninsula.

Wallops Island, on the Eastern Shore, is home to one of NASA's launch sites. About 16,000 rockets have launched from Wallops Island.

62 percent of Virginia is forested.

THE PENTAGON

The Pentagon is the headquarters of the United States Department of Defense in Arlington, Virginia. The concrete and steel building is gigantic. One US Capitol building could fit inside each of the Pentagon's five sides. However, the huge structure is also efficient. A person can walk between the two most distant points in the building in about seven minutes.

During the terrorist attack of September 11, 2001, an airplane flew into the Pentagon, killing 189 people.

OYSTERS

Virginia is the third largest seafood-producing state in America, and the first on the East Coast. One of its top-selling products is oysters. There are eight different oyster-harvesting regions in Virginia, each producing oysters with different tastes. This variety appeals to oyster lovers. About 40 million Virginia oysters are sold each year.

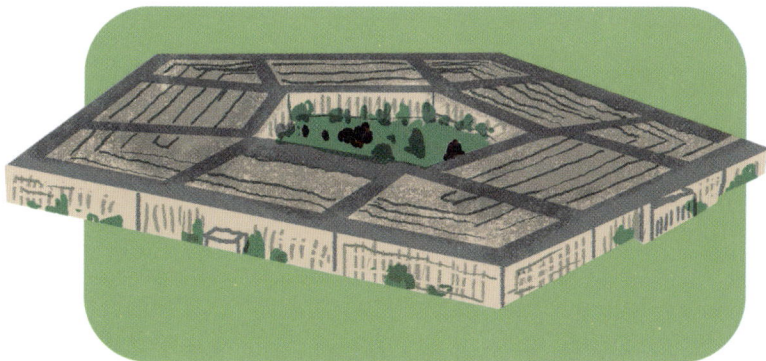

WEATHER

Virginia's summers are hot and humid, usually peaking in temperature in July. The fall and spring are cool and mild, and the winters are very cold and often snowy.

THE APPALACHIAN MOUNTAINS

The Appalachian Mountains stretch from Alabama up into Canada. They pass through 14 US states and reach about 2,190 mi (3,520 km) in length. There are a number of subranges, or smaller ranges, within the Appalachians. These include the Allegheny Mountains, the Blue Ridge Mountains, the Great Smoky Mountains, the Catskills, the Poconos, the Green Mountains, the White Mountains, and more.

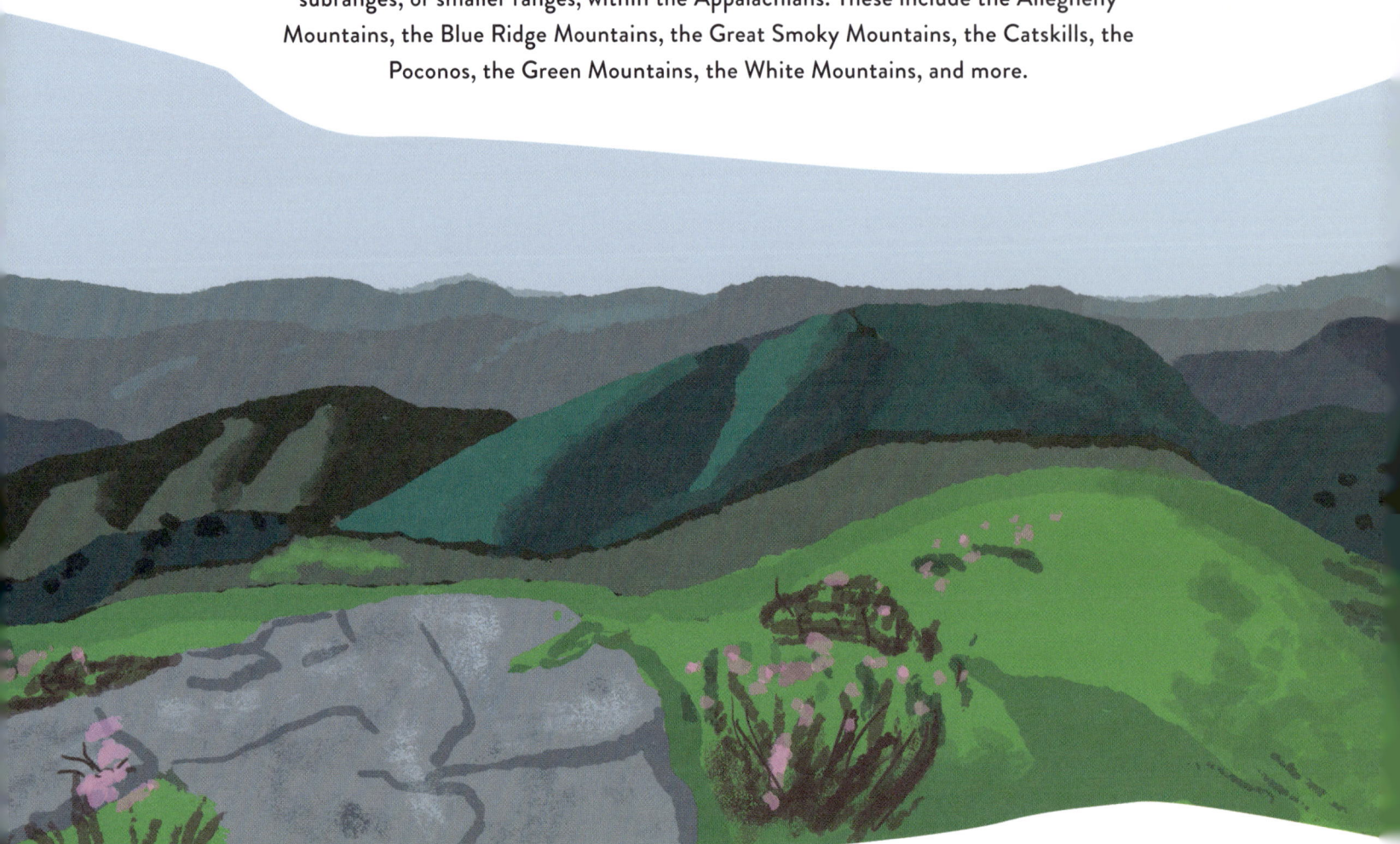

WHAT'S IN A NAME?

The name of the Appalachians likely comes from a Native group called the Apalachee Indians, who lived in northern Florida, nowhere near the mountains. An early mapmaker probably accidentally labeled their territory too far north, which led to the name later being used for the mountain range.

OLD MOUNTAINS

The Appalachian Mountains are among the oldest on Earth. The rock that forms their core is more than a billion years old. The mountains used to be very tall. Scientists believe that some of the peaks in the Appalachians were taller than the Himalayas. In fact, some think that the range included a peak that was taller than Mount Everest!

GREAT HEIGHTS

Here are the Appalachians' tallest peaks:

1. Mount Mitchell (6,684 ft/2,037 m), Black Mountains, North Carolina

2. Clingmans Dome (6,643 ft/2,025 m), Great Smoky Mountains, Tennessee

3. Mount Washington (6,288 ft/1,916 m), White Mountains, New Hampshire

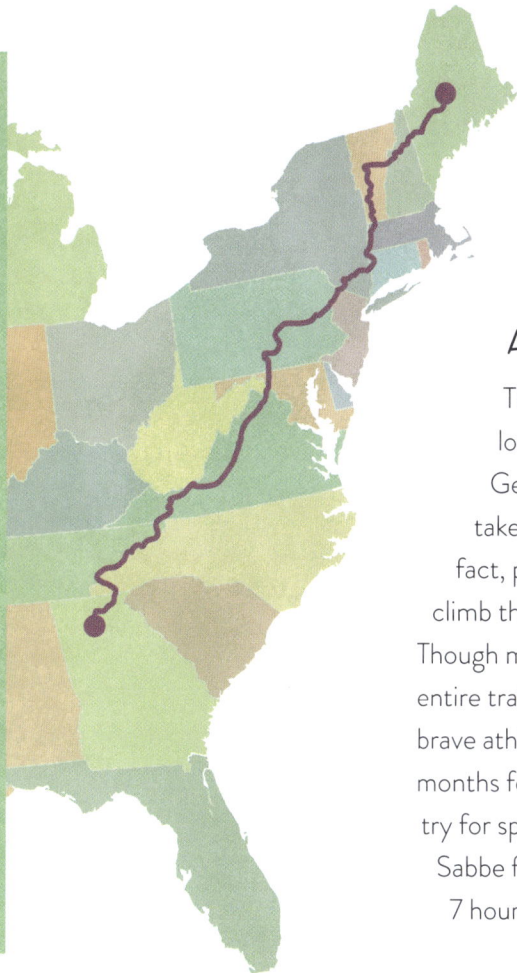

APPALACHIAN TRAIL

The Appalachian Trail is the world's longest foot-hike-only trail. It begins in Georgia and finishes in Maine. The trail takes hikers up and down many peaks. In fact, people who complete the entire trail climb the equivalent of 16 Mount Everests. Though most hikers do not try to finish the entire trail, or do a thru-hike, some do. These brave athletes usually take around five or six months for their foot journey. However, some try for speed. In 2018, a hiker named Karel Sabbe finished his thru-hike in just 41 days, 7 hours, and 39 minutes.

CONTINENTAL DIVIDE

The Appalachian Mountains form the Eastern Continental Divide. Rain that flows down the eastern side of the mountains drains into the Atlantic Ocean. Rain that flows down the western side eventually drains into the Gulf of Mexico.

In 2021, a five-year-old boy named Harvey hiked the entire Appalachian Trail with his parents. It took them 209 days.

COAL

The Appalachian Mountains contain many valuable resources, such as oil, natural gas, and coal. Coal mining is a major industry there. About 27 percent of the coal mined in America comes from the Appalachian region. Many of the Appalachian coal mines use underground mining. This means that people dig holes or tunnels into the Earth to find and extract coal. Some mines use a kind of surface mining known as Mountaintop Removal mining (MTR). This involves blasting away at mountaintops to expose coal. MTR is controversial. While it is safer and easier for miners, environmentalists argue that it is a harmful practice. It changes the landscape, harms wildlife, and pollutes the water. MTR has led to the destruction of about 500 Appalachian mountains.

WASHINGTON

Washington is named after George Washington.
It is the only state named after a president.
The state's nickname comes from its many evergreen forests.

HISTORY

People have lived in Washington for at least 10,000 years. Long after the earliest human visitors, many different Native groups came to the land. In the 1700s, European sailors arrived. In 1848, Congress created the Oregon Territory. This was an area that included modern-day Idaho, Oregon, Washington, and parts of Montana and Wyoming. At first, few Americans lived there. However, travelers on the Oregon trail and others looking to settle the Pacific Northwest changed that. In 1853, the Washington Territory was created from the northwestern part of the Oregon Territory. It became a state 36 years later.

FAST FACTS

Admitted to the Union:
November 11, 1889

State Number: **42**

Population: **7.7 million**

Capital: **Olympia**

Nickname:
The Evergreen State

State Marine Mammal:
Orca

Washington has many square miles of glaciers. It is home to more than 3,000 of these giant, icy slabs.

PUGET SOUND

Puget Sound is a 100-mi (160-km) inlet of the Pacific Ocean. It includes several deep harbors, including Tacoma and Seattle, and is the second-largest estuary in America following the Chesapeake Bay. About two-thirds of Washington's population lives near Puget Sound. Whales, otters, seals, and many other sea creatures live in the Sound.

STARBUCKS

Washington is known for its many coffee shops, coffee-roasting companies, and general coffee appreciation. In 1971, a small coffee shop called Starbucks opened in Seattle's Pike Place Market. Today, it is the biggest coffee chain in the world, with more than 35,000 stores in 80 countries.

MOUNTAINS

Mount Rainier is the highest peak in Washington. It is 14,410 ft (4,392 m) high. Mount Rainier is an active volcano. It has not had a major eruption in more than 500 years. However, scientists warn that its next eruption could send ash and lava into the surrounding areas.

Another famous Washington volcano is Mount St. Helens. This towering peak last erupted in 1980. The explosive eruption blasted away a large part of the volcano's cone, leaving a jagged hole behind.

SEATTLE

Seattle is Washington's biggest city, with a population of 737,000. It is known as a hub for grunge music, art, food, and coffee. Pike Place Market, a large covered farmer's market, draws more than 10 million tourists a year. Fish sellers toss huge fresh fish over the crowds to be weighed and wrapped. Brave shoppers can even try to catch their own.

NOT SO RAINY

Seattle has a reputation for being very rainy. However, it actually gets less rainfall than cities such as New York, Boston, and Miami.

Bill Gates, the founder of Microsoft, investor, and philanthropist, lives in a giant Seattle mansion called Xanadu 2.0. It's 66,000 sq ft (6,131 sq m)—bigger than the White House.

WEST VIRGINIA

West Virginia's name was almost something very different: Kanawha.
This was the name of a Native group in the area, as well as a river.

West Virginia is called the Mountain State because of its rugged landscape.
It is the only state that is entirely within the Appalachian Mountains,
and has the highest elevation of any state east of the Mississippi.

FAST FACTS

Admitted to the Union:
June 20, 1863

State Number: **35**

Population: **1.8 million**

Capital: **Charleston**

Nickname:
The Mountain State

State Animal: **Black bear**

HISTORY

Humans have lived in West Virginia for more
than 10,000 years. In about 1,000 B.C., a
group of people called the Adena came to the
area. They built huge earthen burial mounds.
Grave Creek Mound, in northern West
Virginia, is the largest. Archaeologists think
it was built around 2,100 years ago.

West Virginia has many
cities named after other
places around the world,
including Peru, Cairo,
London, and Athens.

BECOMING A STATE

West Virginia was long home to many Native groups.
In the 1600s, European explorers began to arrive
there, too. West Virginia was part of the British
Virginia Colony until 1776. Then, it was part of the
state of Virginia until 1863. During the Civil War,
West Virginians felt disconnected from their peers
to the east for many reasons. One of these was the

issue of slavery. Many plantation owners in eastern
Virginia used slave labor, and wanted to continue to
do so. In the west, people owned smaller farms and
very few people owned slaves. When Virginia left
the Union for the Confederacy, the people of West
Virginia refused to follow. They remained in the
Union and became their own state.

GEOGRAPHY

There are very few areas of level land in the Mountain State. Instead, there are hills, mountains, ravines, and valleys. West Virginia has two panhandles. One juts north between Pennsylvania and Ohio. The other shoots east between Maryland and Virginia.

The western two-thirds of West Virginia are made up of the Ohio River Valley and the Allegheny Plateau, which includes hills, valleys, and rounded mountains. The eastern side of the state is the Valley and Ridge Province, which includes the Appalachian Mountains and the state's highest peak: Spruce Knob. It is 4,863 ft (1,482 m) high.

The New River flows through southern West Virginia. It is one of the oldest rivers in the world, and has carved deep canyons into the surrounding land. Today, people come to the New River for kayaking, whitewater rafting, and more.

NEW RIVER GORGE BRIDGE

When the New River Gorge Bridge was finished in 1977, it was the longest steel-arch span bridge in the world. It transformed a 40-minute winding drive through the mountains into a one-minute straight shot.

Today, the bridge is known for something different. One day each October, West Virginia hosts Bridge Day. It is a festival during which extreme athletes BASE jump and rappel off the bridge while thousands of festival-goers watch, eat food, and listen to music.

WEATHER

West Virginia has warm, humid summers and cold winters. Spring brings warm and wet weather, while fall is cool and windy. The coldest month of the year is January and the hottest is July.

NEW RIVER GORGE BRIDGE STATS

HEIGHT:
876 ft (267 m)

LENGTH:
3,030 ft (924 m)

WISCONSIN

Wisconsin's name probably comes from the European misspelling of the Miami word *Meskonsing*, which means "river running through a red place." It describes the red color of the cliffs in the Wisconsin Dells.

Early Wisconsin miners dug tunnels to find lead and iron. When the harsh Wisconsin winters came, these miners would crawl into their mines—like badgers crawling into dens—to wait for spring. This led to the state's nickname.

CHANGING HANDS

People have been in Wisconsin for a very long time. An archaeological site in Kenosha shows that humans killed and ate a mammoth there about 14,500 years ago. The land now called Wisconsin was controlled by many different groups of people over time. For thousands of years before European arrival, Native people lived on the land. French explorers came, followed by British. After the Revolutionary War, Wisconsin was part of different territories. From 1788 to 1800, it was part of the Northwest Territory. From 1800 to 1809, it was part of the Indiana Territory. Next, it was part of the Illinois Territory from 1809 to 1818, and the Michigan Territory from 1818 to 1836. Finally, it became the Wisconsin Territory in 1836. Twelve years later it became a state.

LANDSCAPE

Northern Wisconsin is mostly flat. It has about 150 mi (241 km) of shoreline along Lake Superior. Just off shore are the 22 Apostle Islands. Wisconsin's highest point, Timms Hill, is 1,951 ft (595 m) tall.
It is located in a wooded, hilly area called the Northern Highlands. In the middle of the state is a crescent-shaped region called the Central Plain. It is made up of sandy plains and is home to many farms. Southwest Wisconsin is rugged, with many rocky hills, gorges, and caves. Wisconsin's eastern edge meets up with Lake Michigan, with about 400 mi (644 km) of shoreline.

FAST FACTS

Admitted to the Union:
May 29, 1848

State Number: **30**

Population: **5.9 million**

Capital: **Madison**

Nickname:
The Badger State

State Animal: **Badger**

Wisconsin produces 2.8 billion lb (1.3 billion kg) of cheese each year. Because of this, Wisconsinites are often called "cheeseheads."

There are 11 federally recognized tribes in Wisconsin today.

RURAL VS. URBAN

About 97 percent of Wisconsin's land is rural. However, roughly 70 percent of its population lives in urban centers. Here are the state's three biggest cities:

Milwaukee: 587,000
Madison: 265,000
Green Bay: 104,000

BLIZZARDS AND MORE

Wisconsin has hot, humid summers. Spring and fall are often cool and mild, with rain and wind. The state is known for its cold, snowy, and frigid winters. Here are some Wisconsin winter weather extremes:

- In January 1912, Wisconsin experienced seven straight days of subzero (-17.8 °C) temperatures.
- In February 1996, temperatures in Couderay hit a jaw-dropping -55 °F (-48.3 °C).
- During the winter of 1996-1997, Hurley got 277 in (7 m) of snow.

WISCONSIN DELLS

The Wisconsin Dells are a region where the Wisconsin River has cut unusual formations into the surrounding rock. Many people come to view some of these famous formations, such as Chimney Rock, Black Hawk's Head, and Stand Rock. However, there are plenty of other attractions in the Dells that have nothing to do with rocks.

The Wisconsin Dells is also the name of a city that is chock-full of family amusement parks, water parks, and more. This popular vacation destination includes one of the largest indoor water parks in the world, perfect for a state that is famous for its frigid winters.

WYOMING

Historians aren't exactly sure where the name Wyoming came from. It might have come from words in the Delaware, Algonquin, or Munsee languages. Before Wyoming was chosen as the official name, other choices were considered, including Cheyenne, Arapaho, Shoshoni, Platte, Sioux, Big Horn, Sweetwater, and Yellowstone.

Wyoming is called the Equality State because in 1869, it was the first state to grant women the ability to vote. It would be another 51 years before women could vote nationwide.

BIGHORN MEDICINE WHEEL

Humans have lived in Wyoming for more than 12,000 years. At some point during that history, people constructed a huge holy area, or shrine, near Lovell. It is a wheel-shaped ring of stones 82 ft (25 m) across, with spokes and a smaller ring in the middle. At its center is a mound of stones called a cairn. Today, this shrine is called the Bighorn Medicine Wheel. Native groups continue to use it as a spiritual and ceremonial site.

Cheyenne is known as the nation's rodeo and railroad capital.

FAST FACTS

Admitted to the Union:
July 10, 1890

State Number: **44**

Population: **579,000**

Capital: **Cheyenne**

Nickname:
The Equality State

State Mammal: **Bison**

About 150 other medicine wheels have been discovered in Wyoming, Montana, South Dakota, and Canada.

DEVIL'S TOWER

Devil's Tower is a stump-shaped, granite butte in the Black Hills. It juts 1,267 ft (386 m) into the air. Long sacred to more than 20 Native groups, today it is appreciated by tourists and locals alike. About 500,000 people visit Devil's Tower each year. Its many vertical cracks and unique shape make it an ideal place for mountain climbers. Between 5,000 and 6,000 people climb the Tower every year.

GEOGRAPHY

The eastern third of Wyoming is covered by the Great Plains, with the Black Hills sharing the border with South Dakota. The Rocky Mountains run through the middle of the state. In the north is a subrange of the Rockies called the Big Horn Mountains. In the south is another subrange called the Laramie Range. Between the two is a flat area called a basin. Yellowstone National Park is in the state's northwest corner. Grand Teton National Park is just to its south. The state's highest peak, Gannett Peak, is 13,804 ft (4,207 m) high. It is in the Wind River Range.

WEATHER

Wyoming winters are cold and very snowy, especially in the mountains. The summers are hot and muggy. Spring and fall are cooler and milder.

Wyoming's mountains often create unique weather patterns. For example, the mountains near Bighorn Basin keep rainclouds away. This has led to the basin being extremely dry, getting as little as 5 in (13 cm) of rain a year.

ENERGY

Wyoming creates 12 times as much energy as it consumes. This means that much of its energy is used by other states. It is the country's leading coal producer. It also produces oil and natural gas. In addition to these nonrenewable resources, Wyoming also creates large amounts of wind energy.

WASHINGTON, D.C.

Washington, D.C. is the capital of the United States of America.
It is not in a state or a city, but a federal district
called the District of Columbia.

HISTORY

During the United States' first years, several different cities were used as capitals. However, President George Washington knew the country needed a permanent seat. In 1790, he chose a location along the Potomac and Anacostia Rivers. The surrounding states of Maryland and Virginia both had to give up land for the district. This location made sense because it was roughly in the middle of the existing states at the time. In 1791, Washington was given its name to honor the first president.

NEARLY DESTROYED

During the War of 1812, the new capital was nearly destroyed when British troops set fire to important buildings in the city, including the Capitol, the President's House, and the Library of Congress.

In 1847, Washington, D.C. was further changed when Virginia took back the land it had given to the district, shrinking it by about one-third.

THE WHITE HOUSE

The White House is the official residence and workplace of the President of the United States. After the original President's House was destroyed, it was rebuilt in 1817. In the years that followed, many changes and additions were made to it, but the building itself remained intact. Every president since John Adams has lived in the White House. It has 132 rooms, including 16 bedrooms, three kitchens, and 35 bathrooms.

The President's House was nicknamed the White House because of a white colored lime wash that was used to protect it from the weather. In 1901, President Roosevelt made the nickname the building's official name.

US CAPITOL BUILDING

The US Capitol Building is an important place for American government, history, and art. It holds the chambers where the Senate and House of Representatives hold their meetings. It has 540 rooms, which include offices, meeting spaces, and ceremonial areas.

The Capitol Dome is one of the country's most recognized landmarks. It towers 288 ft (88 m) over the building. It is topped with the 15,000-lb (6,804-kg) Statue of Freedom.

WASHINGTON MONUMENT

The Washington Monument is an obelisk that honors President George Washington. When it was completed in 1884, it was the tallest building in the world. Today, it remains a powerful symbol of America. An elevator takes visitors to the observation deck located near the top of the obelisk.

WASHINGTON MONUMENT STATS

HEIGHT:
554 ft, 7 inches (169 m)

BASE AREA:
3,025 sq ft (281 sq m)

ESTIMATED WEIGHT:
91,000 tons (82,500 tonnes)

THE LINCOLN MEMORIAL

The Lincoln Memorial is a monument that honors President Abraham Lincoln. Built in the form of a Greek temple, it features a 19-ft (5.8-m) statue of Lincoln. The monument's 36 columns represent the 36 states that existed in the Union when Lincoln died.

THE MARTIN LUTHER KING, JR. MEMORIAL

The Martin Luther King, Jr. Memorial is located at 1964 Independence Avenue, SW. This address honors the date of the Civil Rights Act of 1964, which King worked hard to bring about. The memorial features a 30-ft (9.1-m) carving of King in the Stone of Hope. Behind it are two large pieces of rock that represent the Mountain of Despair. The monument is meant to represent an important line from King's "I Have a Dream" speech: "Out of the mountain of despair, a stone of hope."

GOVERNMENT AND MILITARY

The American government and armed forces are very powerful and historic.
They represent a diverse and evolving nation.

GOVERNMENT

The American federal government is divided into three
branches: legislative, executive, and judicial. This structure
makes sure that no single branch has too much power.

EXECUTIVE

This branch is made up of the
President, Vice President, Cabinet,
and their supporting agencies and
departments. The executive
branch enforces laws.

LEGISLATIVE

This branch is made up of the House
of Representatives and Senate.
Together, they are the Congress.
The legislative branch makes the laws
that govern the country, assists in
presidential elections, and has the
authority to declare war.

JUDICIAL

This branch is made up of the
Supreme Court and other federal
courts. The judicial branch
interprets and evaluates laws.

MILITARY

The American armed forces are divided into six branches. Each branch has a special purpose, but all work together for a common cause. Today, about 1.3 million Americans are active-duty service members. That's less than 1 percent of the population.

AIR FORCE

The US Air Force (USAF) is the country's aerial military branch. Service members in the Air Force are called airmen.

ARMY

The US Army (USA) is America's oldest and largest military branch. It specializes in ground combat missions. Army service members are called soldiers. US Army Special Forces are known as Green Berets.

COAST GUARD

The US Coast Guard (USCG) is a maritime force that provides national security on American bodies of water. It also performs search-and-rescue missions. Service members are called Coast Guardsmen.

NAVY

The US Navy is a defense force that operates on sea, air, and land. Navy service members are called sailors. SEALs are the Navy's special operations force. Their name stands for sea, air, and land teams.

MARINES

The US Marine Corps (USMC) is part of the Navy. It provides air, sea, and ground-based support, as well as providing protection to American embassies around the world. Service members are called marines. The Marine Corps Special Operations Command (MARSOC) are called Raiders.

SPACE FORCE

The US Space Force (USSF) conducts global operations that support the interests of America and its allies in space. Space Force service members are called Guardians.

MEET THE PRESIDENTS

1789–1797
GEORGE WASHINGTON

Washington had very bad teeth. As they fell out, he wore dentures made from materials such as ivory, metal, and human teeth, but not wood, as is often said!

1797–1801
JOHN ADAMS

Adams was the first president to live in the President's House, later known as the White House.

1801–1809
THOMAS JEFFERSON

Jefferson was an architect. He even designed his own home, Monticello.

1809–1817
JAMES MADISON

Madison was the smallest president at just 5' 4" tall (163 cm), and about 100 lb (45 kg).

1817–1825
JAMES MONROE

James Monroe was one of three presidents who died on July 4. The other two were John Adams and Thomas Jefferson.

1825–1829
JOHN QUINCY ADAMS

Adams went to school in Paris, Amsterdam, Leyden, and the Hague. He graduated from Harvard College in 1787.

1829–1837
ANDREW JACKSON

Jackson was taken prisoner by the British during the Revolutionary War.

1837–1841
MARTIN VAN BUREN

Van Buren was the first president who was born in the United States of America.

1841
WILLIAM HENRY HARRISON

Harrison became ill during his inauguration and died only one month into his presidency.

1841–1845
JOHN TYLER

Tyler was William Henry Harrison's vice president. He became president when Harrison died. Because of this, some called him "His Accidency."

1845–1849
JAMES POLK

Polk was born in a log cabin in North Carolina.

1849–1850
ZACHARY TAYLOR

Taylor was known as "Old Rough and Ready" from his days as a military commander. He became ill and died after 16 months in office.

1850–1853
MILLARD FILLMORE

Fillmore became president when Taylor died. He loved books. In 1851 when the Library of Congress caught fire, he personally tried to put it out.

1853–1857

FRANKLIN PIERCE

Though Pierce was from New Hampshire, a free state, he was pro-slavery.

1857–1861

JAMES BUCHANAN

Buchanan was the only president to be a lifelong bachelor.

1861–1865

ABRAHAM LINCOLN

"Honest Abe" was the tallest president, at 6' 4" (193 cm).

He is known for leading the country through the Civil War.

1865–1869

ANDREW JOHNSON

Johnson was Abraham Lincoln's vice president. He became president after Lincoln's death. The men who planned Lincoln's death intended to kill Johnson, too, but his assigned killer did not follow through.

1869–1877

ULYSSES S. GRANT

Grant's first name wasn't Ulysses. It was Hiram.

1877–1881

RUTHERFORD B. HAYES

Hayes had many firsts as president. He was the first to visit the West Coast while in office, the first to host an Easter Egg Roll on the White House lawn, and the first to have a telephone in the White House.

1881

JAMES GARFIELD

In 1880, Garfield wrote, "Assassination can be no more guarded against than death by lightning and it is best not to worry about either." One year later he was assassinated.

1881–1885

CHESTER ARTHUR

Before becoming a lawyer, Arthur was a school teacher.

1885–1889

GROVER CLEVELAND

Cleveland's first name was Stephen. Grover was his middle name.

1889–1893

BENJAMIN HARRISON

Harrison served in the Union Army as a Brigadier General during the Civil War.

1893–1897

GROVER CLEVELAND

Cleveland is the only president who served two non-consecutive terms.

1897–1901

WILLIAM MCKINLEY

McKinley's face appeared on the $500 bill, which is no longer printed. He was assassinated.

1901–1909

THEODORE ROOSEVELT

Roosevelt, McKinley's vice president, became President after his assassination. At age 42, Roosevelt was the youngest president ever.

1909–1913

WILLIAM H. TAFT

After leaving the White House, Taft became a Supreme Court Justice.

1913–1921

WOODROW WILSON

Wilson was a child during the Civil War, and president during World War I.

1921–1923

WARREN HARDING

Harding was a newspaper publisher before going into politics. He died of a heart attack while in office.

1923–1929

CALVIN COOLIDGE

Coolidge, Harding's vice president, came into office after his death. He is the only president who was born on the 4th of July.

1929–1933

HERBERT HOOVER

Herbert Hoover was nominated for the Nobel Peace Prize five times for his humanitarian work.

1933–1945

FRANKLIN D. ROOSEVELT

The fifth cousin of Theodore Roosevelt, FDR was the longest-serving president. In 1947, Congress passed the 22nd Amendment, which limited a president to two terms in office.

1945–1953

HARRY S. TRUMAN

The "S" in Truman's name isn't an initial. His middle name was just the letter S.

1953–1961

DWIGHT EISENHOWER

Known as "Ike," Eisenhower was an important figure in the Army during World War II. In 1946 he was made a five-star general, the highest US military rank.

1961–1963
JOHN F. KENNEDY
Kennedy's family was very rich and gave him a lot of money. Because of this, he donated his presidential salary to charity. He was assassinated in 1963.

1963–1969
LYNDON JOHNSON
Johnson was JFK's vice president. During his presidency, he declared a War on Poverty, and established programs to help feed, educate, and support the poor.

1969–1974
RICHARD NIXON
Nixon resigned from the presidency after an election scandal. He famously said, "I'm not a crook."

1974–1977
GERALD FORD
Before going into politics, Ford was a star football player. He had offers to play for both the Detroit Lions and the Green Bay Packers.

1977–1981
JIMMY CARTER
Before becoming president, Carter was a peanut farmer.

1981–1989
RONALD REAGAN
Before becoming a politician, Reagan spent 30 years as a successful Hollywood actor.

1989–1993
GEORGE H. W. BUSH
Bush went to Yale University, where he was a member of a secret society called the Skull and Bones.

1993–2001
WILLIAM CLINTON
Clinton was impeached for having an inappropriate relationship with a White House intern. His wife, Hillary, went on to become the US Secretary of State and presidential candidate.

2001–2009
GEORGE W. BUSH
Before going into politics, Bush owned and managed a baseball team.

2009–2017
BARACK OBAMA
The first African American president, Obama won two Grammys for the audio recordings of his books.

2017–2021
DONALD J. TRUMP
Before becoming president, Trump made his name as a real estate mogul and television star.

2021–2025
JOSEPH BIDEN
As a child, Biden struggled with a stutter. He overcame it by reading Irish poetry in front of a mirror.

COMMONWEALTHS

COMMONWEALTH STATES

Kentucky, Virginia, Pennsylvania, and Massachusetts are all commonwealths. This label does not impact their state status, or the way they are governed. It simply reflects the language used when their state constitutions were written in the 1700s and 1800s. At the time, "commonwealth" was a way to refer to an organized political community.

PUERTO RICO

Population: **3.3 million**
Capital: **San Juan**
Year it became a commonwealth: **1952**

The Commonwealth of Puerto Rico is located in the Northeast Caribbean Sea. It includes the large island called Puerto Rico, along with more than 140 others. The largest of the remaining islands are Culebra and Vieques.

Christopher Columbus first came to Puerto Rico in 1493. He made it into a Spanish colony. The United States took Puerto Rico from Spain in 1898. In 1917, Puerto Rico became a US territory. The official language was declared to be English. During World War II, many Puerto Ricans fought in the American armed forces. Puerto Rico also played an important role as a military base.

Today, Puerto Rico is a popular tourist destination because of its tropical climate, amazing wildlife, and beautiful beaches.

COMMONWEALTH TERRITORIES

The United States has five permanently inhabited territories: the Northern Mariana Islands, Puerto Rico, Guam, American Samoa, and the US Virgin Islands. Two of these, the Northern Marianas Islands and Puerto Rico, are commonwealths.

American commonwealth territories are led by their own elected governments. However, their official head of state is the US president. Commonwealth residents are US citizens, but cannot vote in presidential elections. Commonwealth territories use US currency. They also use the US Postal System.

NORTHERN MARIANA ISLANDS

Population: **58,000**
Capital: **Saipan**
Year it became a commonwealth: **1978**

The Commonwealth of the Northern Mariana Islands (CNMI) is located in the western Pacific Ocean. It is a 300-mi (483-km) archipelago made up of 14 islands. The islands in the northern part of the CNMI are volcanic. The southern CNMI islands are made of raised limestone.

Saipan is the CNMI's biggest island. It is 46 sq mi (119 sq km), or about the same size as San Francisco. Next in size are Tinian (39 sq mi/101 sq km) and Rota (33 sq mi/85 sq km). Most of the islands are tropical, with warm temperatures and lots of rain.

People have lived on the CMNI for thousands of years. In the 1500s, the Spanish claimed the islands. In 1899, Spain sold the islands to Germany. Japan took over in 1914 and kept the islands until 1944, when America gained control during World War II. Three years later, the islands became trustees of the United States.

Five species of endangered whales live in the waters near the Northern Mariana Islands.

TERRITORIES

Guam, the US Virgin Islands, and American Samoa are territories of the United States. Much like the commonwealth territories, they use American money and the United States Postal System. They govern themselves and call the US president their head of state. The residents of Guam and the US Virgin Islands are US citizens, while the people who live in American Samoa are American nationals. This status gives them slightly fewer rights than citizens.

GUAM

Population: **169,000**
Capital: **Hagåtña**
Year it became a territory: **1898**

Guam is an island in the western Pacific Ocean, just south of the Commonwealth of the Northern Mariana Islands. Guam's first residents were the Chamorro people. They came to Guam about 3,500 years ago. In the 1500s, the Spanish came and claimed the land. The US captured Guam during the Spanish American War in 1898, and the Japanese later took it in 1941. After fierce fighting, Americans retook Guam from the Japanese in 1944.

Today, Guam is a popular vacation spot for tourists. Over a million people travel to Guam to snorkel along its colorful coral reefs, relax on its pristine beaches, and explore its bustling markets.

Guam is home to Earth's tallest mountain, Lamlam. Unlike other famous peaks, like Mount Everest, Lamlam's bulk is hidden beneath the ocean. Though it rises 37,820 ft (11,527 m) from its base at the bottom of the Mariana Trench, only 1,332 ft (406 m) of the mountain are above sea level.

Guam is the westernmost part of the United States.

US VIRGIN ISLANDS

Population: **106,000**

Capital: **Charlotte Amalie**

Year it became a territory: **1917**

The US Virgin Islands are a collection of about 50 islands located where the Atlantic Ocean and the Caribbean Sea meet. They are just south of the British Virgin Islands. The three largest US Virgin Islands are St. Thomas, St. Croix, and St. John.

Humans have lived on the Virgin Islands for thousands of years. Beginning with Christopher Columbus in 1493, many Europeans began to arrive on the tropical islands. The French, Spanish, Dutch, and British all fought for the land. Many slaves were brought from Africa to the islands in order to work in the sugar cane fields. Thousands more passed through the islands as part of the slave trade. In 1848, a historic slave uprising occurred on St. Croix that caused slavery to be abolished on the islands. In 1917, the United States bought the US Virgin Islands from Denmark.

The US Virgin Islands are a vacation hotspot. About 2 million tourists travel there each year to enjoy the sandy beaches, clear harbors, and beautiful swimming.

AMERICAN SAMOA

Population: **44,000**

Capital: **Pago Pago**

Year it became a territory: **1900**

The National Park of American Samoa is spread across three islands. It is the only National Park Service site that is located south of the Equator.

American Samoa is located in the South Pacific Ocean, about halfway between Hawaii and New Zealand. It is made up of five volcanic islands: Tutuila, Aunu'u, Ofu, Olosega, and Ta'u, as well as two atolls called Rose Atoll and Swains Island. Including the surrounding waters, American Samoa is about the same size as Oregon. About 90 percent of American Samoa is covered in tropical rainforests.

People have lived in American Samoa for thousands of years. Europeans arrived there in the 1700s. In the 1800s, the United States, Britain, and Germany fought for control over the area. In 1899, nine islands on the western side became part of Germany (and later became the independent nation of Samoa). The remaining islands to the east soon became an American territory.

AMERICA'S NEIGHBOR:
CANADA

Canada is the United States' neighbor to the north.
Known for its sweeping landscapes, frigid winters, maple syrup, and hockey
teams, Canada has long been a trusted ally to the United States.

Date of Independence: **July 1, 1867**
Population: **38 million**
Capital: **Ottawa**
National Animal: **Beaver**

NORTHERN GIANT

At 3.8 million square miles (9.9 million sq km), Canada is the second-largest country on Earth, behind Russia. The Pacific Ocean, Atlantic Ocean, and Arctic Ocean all border Canada, adding up to a stunning 151,000 mi (243,000 km) of coastline. Stretching from west to east, Canada has six different time zones. Its massive land is divided into ten provinces and three territories.

Canada is a constitutional monarchy. This means that the British monarch is the head of state. An elected official called the prime minister is the head of government.

LONG BORDER

Canada and America share a 5,525-mi (8,891-km) border. This is the longest international border in the world. People interested in crossing between the countries have many opportunities to do so. There are more than 100 land border crossings, and people can also cross by ferry or aircraft. A passport is required to cross the international border.

Canada is more than 40 times
the size of the United Kingdom.

WILDERNESS

Canada's vast lands are home to some spectacular wildlife. White-tailed deer are common sights. Elk and moose can be spotted drinking from lakes or rivers, or wandering through the woods. Predators like black bears, grizzly bears, and polar bears find plenty to eat in Canada's rivers, streams, coastlines, and forests. The water surrounding Canada is teeming with life, too, including blue whales, beluga whales, and orcas.

BUSTLING CITIES

Canada's bustling cities are hotspots for art, culture, food, architecture, and more. The country's three biggest cities are Toronto (2.8 million people), Montreal (1.7 million), and Calgary (1.3 million).

Ottawa, Canada's capital city, is home to about 1 million people. It is located in southeastern Ontario, on the Ottawa River. Its name comes from the Algonquin word, *adawe*, which means "to trade." It is a fitting name, since Ottawa is an important hub for business

WILD WEATHER

Canada experiences a wide range of weather. Cities like Windsor, Ontario, and Kelowna, British Columbia often enjoy warm summer temperatures that can climb above 80 °F (26.9 °C). In 2021, Lytton, British Columbia reached a scorching 116 °F (46.7 °C). Canada's western coast can get very rainy. Moresby Island gets an average of 20 ft (6.3 mm) of rain each year.

Canada is best known for its frigid and long winters. Fluffy snow, driving sleet, and icy winds transform Canada each winter. The country's coldest area is in Eureka, Nunavut, where the average daily temperature is just -3 °F (-19.7 °C). Mount Fidelity, in Glacier National Park, is the country's snowiest spot. It gets about 45 ft (13.7 cm) of snow each year.

AMERICA'S NEIGHBOR:
THE UNITED MEXICAN STATES

The United Mexican States is America's neighbor to the south. Mexico, as it is often called, is known for many things, including its distinctive cuisine, fascinating history, beautiful landscapes, and vibrant culture.

Independence Day: **September 16, 1810**
Population: **132 million**
Capital: **Mexico City**
National Animal: **Golden eagle**

GOVERNMENT

Mexico is made up of 31 states and one federal district. It is a federal republic, led by a government of elected leaders. The head of the country is the president. They are limited to a single six-year term in office.

In addition to Spanish, there are more than 63 indigenous languages spoken in Mexico. The most common is Nahuatl, which comes from the Aztecan language.

HISTORY

The first humans may have arrived in Mexico as long as 30,000 years ago. The Olmec people formed the earliest complex civilization there. The Maya and Aztec followed, along with other groups. These people left amazing ruins behind.

Chichen Itza: this former Mayan metropolis is now one of the New Seven Wonders of the World.

Tulum Ruins: these coastal ruins are perched on cliffs overlooking the sea.

Calakmul: this site used to be an important Mayan city. Today, people can climb its 150-ft (46-m) high pyramid.

MEXICO CITY

Mexico's capital, Mexico City, is located in the south-central part of the country. It is home to more than 9 million people. It is a hub for food, music, art, dance, and architecture. Some of its most famous buildings draw millions of tourists each year, including:

- **The Metropolitan Cathedral.** Built between 1573 and 1813, this stunning building is filled with precious artworks.
- **The Museo Soumaya.** This modern museum houses about 66,000 pieces of art. It is the most-visited art museum in Mexico.
- **Palacio Postal.** This working post office features a bold mix of architectural styles.

MEXICAN-AMERICAN BORDER

America's border with Mexico is 1,954 mi (3,145 km) long. There are 48 places for land border crossings, including 28 in Texas alone. Each year, about 350 million people pass through these border crossings. People can also cross the border on aircraft or boats.

Some areas of the US-Mexico border are fenced or walled. These structures are intended to stop people from illegally crossing from Mexico into the United States. However, there are also many stretches of the border with no fence or wall. Each year, about 2 million people illegally cross the border.

Mexican food is so beloved that some people are trying to make sure that it is protected. In 2010, it was recognized by UNESCO as a "Masterpiece" that should be protected.

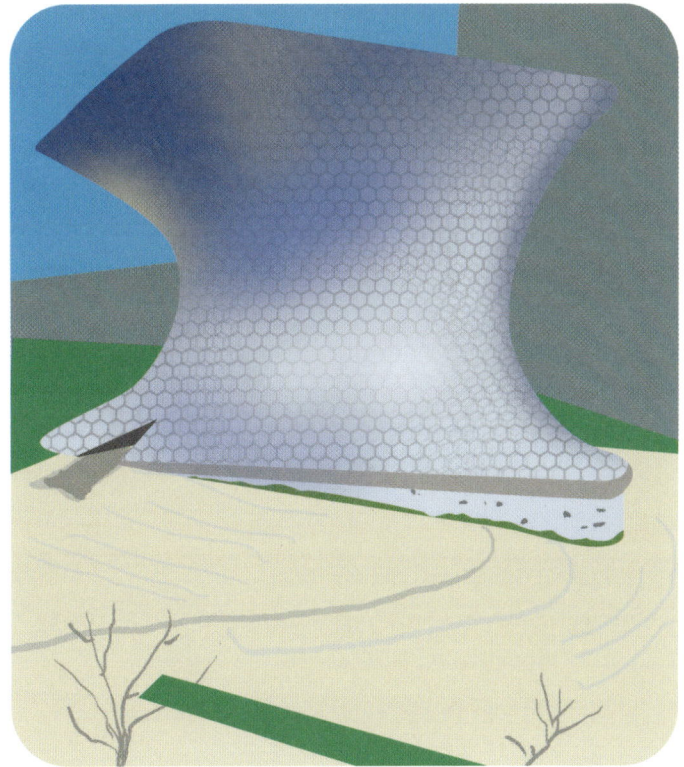

LANDSCAPE

Mexico is a roughly triangular country that covers about 762,000 sq mi (2 million sq km). It is about one-fifth the size of the USA. At its widest point, Mexico is 1,850 mi (3,000 km) across. At its narrowest, it is just 135 mi (217 km) from the Pacific Ocean to the Atlantic Ocean.

Mexico has about 6,000 mi (9,656 km) of coastline. The Baja Peninsula lies alongside Mexico's western coast, creating the Gulf of California. Mexico's eastern coast curves around the Gulf of Mexico. The Yucatan Peninsula extends northward from Mexico's southeastern point, separating the Gulf of Mexico from the Caribbean Sea.

Mexico is home to a wide variety of landscapes, from lush rainforests in the south to blistering deserts in the north. Mountains run through much of the country.

FANTASTIC FACTS

The United States is the third most populated country on Earth, behind China and India.

Washington, D.C.'s Library of Congress houses the largest library collection in the world, with about 170 million items. Its smallest book, *Old King Cole*, measures just 1/25 by 1/25 in (1 x 1 mm).
The biggest book is *Bhutan: A Visual Odyssey Across the Kingdom*. It measures 5 ft by 7 ft (1.5 x 2.1 m).

17 percent of American presidents have died on the job. Four were assassinated, or killed, and four died of natural causes.

The United States is the world's most generous nation. Americans donate money and volunteer to help others more than citizens of any other country.

American female astronauts are a record-breaking bunch. Peggy Whitson holds the record for most time spent in space by a female: 666 days. Christina Koch has the record for the longest space mission for a woman: 328 days.

The Hoover Dam is made from enough concrete to build a two-lane highway from New York City to San Francisco.

S'mores were invented in America in 1927.

The US gets more tornadoes than any other country. Each year, about 1,200 of these powerful storms touch down on American soil.

The longest location place name in the United States is Massachusetts' Lake Chargoggagoggmanchauggagoggchaubunagungamaugg. Locals often call it Webster Lake.

BIGGEST AND SMALLEST

The smallest town in America is Monowi, Nebraska. It has a population of one, a woman named Elsie Eiler.

New York City is America's biggest city. It has a higher population than 39 of the 50 states.

QUIRKY NAMES

America is home to some cities and towns with interesting names. Here are a few:

Big Foot
Texas

Booger Hole
West Virginia

Boring
Oregon

Good Grief
Idaho

Random Lake
Wisconsin

Last Chance
Iowa

Ding Dong
Texas

Why
Arizona

Whynot
North Carolina

OLYMPIC CHAMPIONS

America is an Olympic leader. The United States has won more Olympic medals than any other country, with 1,174 gold, 952 silver, and 833 bronze medals.

Michael Phelps, an American swimmer, has more Olympic medals than any other athlete in history. During his career, he earned 23 gold, three silver, and two bronze medals.

INDEX